A CHRONICLE OF CRANBORNE AND THE CRANBORNE CHASE

A CHRONICLE OF CRANBORNE AND THE CRANBORNE CHASE

T.W. WAKE SMART

INTRODUCTION BY
DESMOND HAWKINS

THE DOVECOTE PRESS LTD

First published in 1841
This second edition first published in 1983 by
The Dovecote Press Ltd
Stanbridge, Wimborne, Dorset
ISBN 0 946159 08 4

Designed by Humphrey Stone

Printed in an edition of 500 copies by
Biddles Ltd, Guildford, Surrey
and bound by The Newdigate Press Ltd,
Dorking, Surrey

CONTENTS

INTRODUCTION

An author who cannot point to a book bearing his name might be judged a failure. *A Chronicle of Cranborne* was published anonymously and is – so far as I know – the only volume from the pen of Thomas William Wake Smart; but he is certainly not without honour in his own country. When he died, in 1894, he was described by J.C. Mansel-Pleydell, president of the Dorset Natural History and Archaeological Society, as 'the last of the little band of men who, in the early part of this century, combined to develop the archaeological and antiquarian history of the county'. Certainly the name of Wake Smart has gained lustre with the passing of time and copies of his book have been increasingly prized by those lucky enough to come upon a survivor from what cannot have been a large edition when it first appeared in 1841 (it lists 210 copies for subscribers). The decision to reissue the book acknowledges the esteem in which this pioneer of local history is held today.

Though Dorset was his county, the range of his interests extended into neighbouring Wiltshire and Hampshire. The urban settlements of the Avon Valley – Ringwood, Fordingbridge and of course Salisbury – have played as prominent a part in Cranborne's history as Wimborne or Blandford. And the history of Cranborne is much more than the history of a large village or small town. In more ways than one the place has a unique character. In Wake Smart's lifetime Cranborne was the largest parish in Dorset, including among its constituent parts, Alderholt and Verwood – until in 1894 they were detached as separate new parishes. For many centuries it was the administrative centre of the hunting-ground or 'Chase' which took its name: King John came here to hunt the deer, and so did James I. It was with a well-founded confidence that Dr. Smart made the claim that Cranborne 'assuredly will be deemed to possess a strong claim on the Antiquary's notice'.

There is not a great deal to be gleaned about the man himself. His father, Robert Smart, surgeon, had started to practise at Cranborne in 1976 and Wake Smart was born there in 1806. He studied medicine at Bart's and in Paris. On the death of his father in 1840 he took over the Cranborne practice; and in 1842 he collaborated with a Blandford surgeon, E.D. Spooner, in the publication of 'A Retrospect of Medicine and Surgery'. He is also credited with being the first to propose intravenous saline injections for Asiatic Cholera.

His interest in medical matters was not sustained, however. In 1845 he sold his practice in Cranborne and went to Torquay for the winter. In 1851 he was elected to the honorary post of physician at the Salisbury Infirmary but resigned within a couple of years. He appears to have spent a substantial period as private physician to the Earl of Warwick – an appointment which suggests a degree of leisure in which to pursue the antiquarian interests that increasingly engaged his energies. In his later years it was as an archaeologist that he won the respect of his contemporaries. Cranborne Chase provided rich opportunities for field-work, on the basis of which he gave lectures to learned societies and contributed papers to their proceedings.

Bearing in mind the demands a medical training makes on a young man it is surprising that Wake Smart was able to complete the voluminous research embodied in *A Chronicle of Cranborne* while he was still in his mid-thirties. What spurred him on must have been the locally engrossing controversy which surrounded the disfranchisement of Cranborne Chase and the consequent abolition of the preservation of deer for hunting. Throughout his boyhood the autocratic rights of the Lord of the Chase, under the ancient laws of the forest, must have been a constant topic of conversation among his elders. He was in his early twenties when the last Lord of the Chase, Baron Rivers, assented to the extinction of his rights by a special Act of Parliament. Feelings had run high on both sides of the argument for years before the matter was resolved: a decade later Wake Smart judged that the passions of the most partisan had subsided enough to accept the 'cool and dispassionate survey' that he presented in his book.

The readers for whom he wrote had an intimate familiarity with the matter which modern readers are unlikely to match: it may therefore be helpful to interject here a brief account of the historical background and the concluding events. By ancient custom all wild beasts belonged to the monarch, who devolved the right or franchise to preserve and hunt them in a defined territory – usually to a member of the royal family or a suitably 'noble' connection. The definition of the territory was by means of a 'perambulation' certified by a jury.

The earliest perambulation of Cranborne Chase was ordered by King John, confirmed in the reign of Henry III, and confirmed again by Edward I in 1279/80. The Lordship of the Chase was held by, or close to, the monarch until James I gave it to his chief minister, Robert Cecil, whom he ennobled as Viscount Cranborne and subsequently Earl of Salisbury. The Lordship of the Chase thus became a franchise which could be bought and sold by local landowners: it passed through several hands before it was acquired by the Pitt family, who were in due course raised to the peerage as the Barons Rivers.

The enormous extent of the Chase within what came to be known as the Outer Bounds of the original perambulation was a source of discontent, not merely from a dislike of the mediaeval law of vert and venison in its restraint on free hunting but more specifically for the frustrations it imposed on normal farming practices. Wake Smart's research revealed a persistent friction between the Chase keepers and the farmers and poachers who transgressed the law. Accompanying these disputes and prosecutions was a groundswell of opinion that the franchise should be limited to the so-called Inner Bounds, and more particularly that any part of Wiltshire should be regarded as outside the jurisdiction of the Chase court. The eventual abolition of the franchise was increasingly advocated.

It was along these lines that partisan elements took shape in the last quarter of the eighteenth century. Some of the principal landowners held the view that the sport of hunting the deer and the pleasure of tasting venison exacted too high a price, socially and economically. Lord Temple, a kinsman of the Pitts who owned Eastbury, the great Vanbrugh mansion at Tarrant Gunville, broached the matter informally with Lord Rivers; and in 1787 a meeting of interested landowners was held at the Woodyates Inn. As the franchise had proved to be legally unassailable it was the question of compensation for its surrender that dominated the proceedings.

A committee was empowered to negotiate with Lord Rivers: this tortuous process, extending over forty years, is summarised by Wake Smart in pages 240 – 242. The meeting of the landowners in 1803, at *The Thatched House* in London's St. James's Street, coincided with the death of Lord Rivers at the age of 83. His successor found a more yielding mood in the committee but the renewal of negotiations was inconclusive. As year followed year with no evidence of progress, individual attitudes began to harden, and the controversy came into the open with the publication of the two books described in Wake Smart's preface (pp vi & vii). William West, whose *History of the Forest or Chace known by the name of Cranborn Chace* was published in 1816, was a Quaker living in Shaftesbury. By his own account he began writing in 1813 a survey 'with a view only to agricultural purposes' but he was 'indulged with the inspection of a number of authenticated papers' which prompted him to undertake 'a work of much difficulty, for the information of the public, on the still contested question of the bounds of the Chace.'

What these papers were, and how they came to him, are matters on which the book throws no light. However, in a subsequent letter to one of the committee of landowners – John Eliot of Ashmore – West indicated that the papers in question 'were kindly lent to me by King and Johns, who are eminent solicitors at Blandford, which papers contained some extracts from a cursory survey of the lands within the Chace or affected by it, made or commenced by the late – Davis, Steward to the Marquis of Bath, and perhaps finished by the present – Davis. It appeared that the lands subject to feed and damage by the deer amounted nearly to 32,000 acres.'

The name of 'King', the Blandford solicitor, takes on a particular significance in view of the events of 12 January 1814, described by Wake Smart on page 235 and involving Mr. Thomas King of Alvediston. The Kings were a long-established family, farming in the Wiltshire villages near Shaftesbury and having therefore a vested interest in the contention that Wiltshire land was exempt from the restrictions of Chase law. King had had an earlier brush with the Chase keepers and was evidently interested in provoking a test case over the damage caused by deer to arable crops. In so doing he probably had an 'understanding' with Mr. Wyndham, the owner of Norrington Farm which King rented. Wyndham was one of the committee of landowners opposed to the preservation of deer, as was his friend and neighbour Thomas Grove of Ferne who had extensive estates in the Donheads, Berwick St. John and Tollard Royal. It is interesting to note, in passing, that when Grove bought Ashcombe in 1815 the catalogue of the sale contained a reference to Lord Rivers's 'claims to have some rights and privileges' of the Chase: the sale was therefore subject to these 'if any such rights or privileges exist.' The unpublished diary of Grove's daughter, Charlotte, reveals Wyndham's involvement in Thomas King's action.

William West's book did not go unchallenged. William Chafin's *Anecdotes and History of Cranborne Chase* is a staunchly conservative presentation of traditional hunting practices and customs. Contemplating the argument that the vice of deer-stealing could be extirpated only by destroying all the deer, he enquired if the farming interests wished sheep-stealing to be eliminated by the same method. It is not, however, as a polemicist or a systematic historian that Chafin repays reading but as a 'character' and a gossip whose family had for several generations been intimately engaged in the social and administrative life of the Chase. His father, George Chafin, had been Head Ranger of Cranborne Chase and one of Dorset's two members of Parliament – the other then being George Pitt, the first Baron Rivers. It was George Chafin who in 1710 initiated the building of the splendid mansion at Chettle which became the family seat where William eventually died. William's grandfather, Thomas, had held the post of Ranger in his day and William himself was honorary keeper of Bursey Stool Walk when it became the practice to farm out individual walks to local dignitaries: the keeper of Cobley Walk was for a period the Prince of Wales. It is therefore his personal observations and his inherited family traditions that are William Chafin's most valuable testimony.

The publication of the two books, by West and Chafin, coincided with the momentous action of Thomas King and the presentation which followed at the Lent Assize in Salisbury in 1816, summarised by Wake Smart on pages 235 – 239. Additional light on these events comes from the following entries in Charlotte Grove's diary, which suggest that King was a 'front man' for more powerful interests:

1816
Feb 22. Mr. Wyndham called. He is very earnest about his Chace cause against Lord Rivers.
March 2. Mr. King breakfasted with us. The Chace cause is put off.
July 10. My father and brothers rode into the Chace to meet Mr. Wyndham. The latter is very anxious about his Chace cause.
July 31. Charles (her brother) went to Salisbury to hear Mr. Wyndham's Chace cause.
Aug. 1. Charles returned from Salisbury. The Chace cause not finished. He gave us a very good account of it.
Aug. 2. Mr. Wyndham has gained his Chace cause against Lord Rivers. I am *delighted* about it.
Aug. 4. We went to Berwick church. Mr. Boys (the rector) did not *rejoice so much* as he *ought* upon the Chace cause being gained.

According to the report in *The Salisbury Journal* the jury did not bring in its verdict until two in the morning. Rivers's counsel sought to limit the argument to the legal validity of the historic boundaries of the Chase, but his opponent Mr. Serjeant Best made a powerful attack on the restrictiveness of mediaeval claims as being incompatible with modern circumstances. It was apparently this view of the matter, rather than the strict letter of the law, which finally gained the verdict. Its wider implications were not lost on Lord Rivers and the committee of landowners engaged in desultory negotiations with him. Together they had to dispose of the long wrangle over compensation and promote an Act of Parliament to disfranchise the Chase.

The text of the Act is included by Wake Smart in his Appendix (pp 291 – 293). The criteria used to assess the annual payment from each landowner are not described, nor are they immediately intelligible when one examines a list of payments in relation to the acreages involved. Fortunately John Eliot of Ashmore, who spent much of his time in London, relied on his principal tenant Samuel Hall to represent him locally and keep him informed by letters which he preserved. In 1826 Hall attended a meeting at the Crown Inn, Blandford, which he reported to Eliot.

From his letter we learn that there was a general agreement that the annual sum of £1800, required by Lord Rivers, should be 'levied on the coppices and fences round the enclosed land where the deer feedeth up to' – that is to say, on woodlands and arable land. Hall added 'The proprietors of coppices in what we call the out-bounds is agreeable to pay their quota equal with the In Bounds. I believe that the commons and down lands that is exposed to the Deer is not to be included in the fine'.

The basis of assessment approved at the final public meeting at the Crown Inn, August 1827, was five shillings per acre of woodland and £10 per mile of buck-fence. Eliot had 1475 perches of fences to protect his corn: his coppices amounted to 325 acres in Ashmore and 63 acres in Iwerne Minster. He was therefore a major contributor.

The only discordant note came from Lord Pembroke whose assessment amounted to £395 but who refused to pay more than £200. To prevent a last-minute collapse of the scheme the other landowners agreed to share responsibility for the short-fall of £195, since neither Pembroke nor Rivers would give way.

Over the years the 'Chase Rent', as it was called, became a

recognised charge on land, like ground-rent or ecclesiastical tithe. By degrees it was extinguished on payment of a suitable capital sum, but not in every case. In 1980 a well-known Shaftesbury lawyer, Stephen Rutter, told me that one of his clients continued to make the annual payment.

As soon as the parliamentary process for disfranchisement was complete, Lord Rivers set about the killing of the deer while they were still his property and before the inevitable free-for-all that would follow the terminal date – 10 October 1830. In the July of that year Samuel Hall wrote to John Eliot:

> As for the quantity of deer that will be left after the 10th of Oct. next we cannot at present say as the keepers are very busily employed in destroying of them and gets all the help they can so that they beset a coppice all round and turns the hounds in and as they come out they endeavour to shoot them and then they go to another.

Hunting enthusiasts outside the Chase were eager to join in on the first permissible day. Typically Sawbridge Erle Drax of Charborough Park sought leave from John Eliot to hunt the deer over his land. The local tenants were also eager to 'get Deer destroyed as soon as possible . . . if not they may increase and do us considerable damage'. Within nine days of the disfranchisement a party of guns at Ashmore, intent on shooting deer in Stickway coppice, contrived to add to their bag Samuel Stainer of Tollard Royal who died the following day of gunshot wounds. The perils of indiscriminate shooting must have been considerable in that autumn.

The Mediaeval Chase

Smart's section on the early history of hunting (pp 99 – 108) is typical of the period in which it was written and should be regarded – or disregarded – as such. The so-called Law of Canute is now discredited as a forgery and Manwood is not the unquestioned oracle that he once was. The general picture of Norman harshness and oppression under forest law was an accepted part of the stock-in-trade of Victorian authors. John

Wise followed a similar line in his history of the New Forest. Recent research suggests a more balanced and complex organisation of social life which reconciled hunting with farming and the other activities of normal human settlements. David Stagg, for example, in his introduction to *New Forest Documents* in 1979 commented that 'For the smaller crown tenant the advantages of life within the forest may have been such as to outweigh the disadvantages.' The period to which this refers is 1244 – 1334 (Henry III – Edward III).

What distinguishes Smart's work therefore is not the conventional denunciation of sadistic tyranny but the patient accumulation of documentary detail which by degrees yields a comprehensive picture of how Cranborne Chase was organised. The Court Rolls show Chettered and Alderholt as having separate identities, distinct from the inner Chase which was traditionally divided into the East Buckden and West Buckden. The two Buckdens become more clearly defined in the names of their individual lodges and walks – West, Burseystool, Rushmore, Staplefoot, Cobley and Fernditch or Vernditch. The last-named is different in character from the rest. It forms the eastern extremity and would always have been dominated by Wilton – originally by the abbess of Wilton and after the Dissolution by the Pembrokes to whom the abbey lands passed.

In 1551 Edward VI gave the Lordship of the Chase for 21 years to Sir William Herbert, the first Earl of Pembroke. When Pembroke died in 1570, Elizabeth I made his son 'Seneschal of our manor of Cranborne and warden and keeper of our chase of Cranborne' – offices that he held until his death in 1601. It is easy therefore to understand that not only the woodlands of Fernditch but the deer in them as well came to be regarded as belonging of right to the Pembrokes. Smart's assertion that as early as 1610-11 Robert Cecil was doing a deal with the third Earl of Pembroke to alienate Fernditch from the general franchise is extremely interesting.

It suggests that the newcomer – for all his political power – had to come to terms with the sitting grandee and it emphasizes the apartness of Fernditch. When subsequently the Lordship of the Chase was acquired by the Earl of Shaftesbury he gave Pembroke a disclaimer in respect of Fernditch (quoted by Smart, p. 269). According to Hutchins's *History of Dorset* Ferndith was disfranchised separately, by the voluntary act of the then Lord Pembroke in 1802, which perhaps explains his son's reluctance to pay his full contribution to the compensation demanded by Lord Rivers for the disfranchisement of the remainder of the Chase.

The Parish of Cranborne

The wealth of historical material associated with the Chase, and the controversies surrounding it, account for a great part of Smart's work but he certainly did not neglect the more normal lines of enquiry about his native place. The ecclesiastical history of Cranborne, its prehistoric relics, its communications and the changing fortunes of its trade and commerce – in these and kindred subjects he made a valuable contribution to our knowledge. His account of the contemporary pottery industry, for instance, is an important record of what in recent years has become a subject for intensive research.

After the publication of his *Chronicle* Smart continued to make notes of topics and events associated with Cranborne. Some of these memoranda were preserved by one of his granddaughters who communicated them to her friend, Miss Gladys Stanford of Cranborne: I am indebted to Miss Stanford for the opportunity to read and quote from them, and also for the photo of Dr. Smart which she kindly loaned me. His notes include some made prior to the publication of his book but omitted from it. During the agrarian riots of 1830 he noted that sixteen mounted men kept guard at the manor house from November 24 to December 7, being relieved daily: the need for this was evidently precipitated by 'the mob' which came to Boveridge on November 24.

His interest in the development of communications, by

turnpike roads and later by railways, sprang from his alert recognition that the decay of 'this once flourishing little Town' could be largely attributed to 'the formation of the Western Turnpike in 1757 . . . facilitating the means of access to Towns of greater note.' (p. 12). In pre-turnpike days the main road from London through Salisbury to Dorchester and Weymouth passed through Cranborne: so did the Salisbury-Wimborne-Poole road. It was doubtless Cranborne's role as the administrative centre of the Chase which sustained its importance as a road-centre.

It is difficult now to imagine a main long-distance route passing Londonwards through Cranborne and Martin Wood to cross the Allen River at Tidpit, climb over Toyd Down and head for a bridge over the Ebble at Homington or Coombe Bissett; yet this was the normal course until the middle of the eighteenth century. Even when the Great Western Turnpike was authorised in 1755-56 there was a simultaneous plan by the Poole, Wimborne and Cranborne Trust to compete by developing the Tidpit-Toyd Down section. The Trust must have had second thoughts, however, as it did not exercise its option to take over the road beyond Cranborne to Tidpit. According to Professor Ronald Good in *The Old Roads of Dorset* a later Act of 1817-18 expressly adopted this section, but no repairs were undertaken and it was finally abandoned in an Act of 1835-36. This last Act also abandoned the Trust's proposed link from Cranborne to a junction with the successful Great Western Turnpike, and its only remaining connection was the Wimborne-Cranborne road – the present B3078 – which that well-known cyclist, Thomas Hardy, praised for the excellence of its surface.

The historic route from Cranborne to Blandford was made redundant by the Great Western Turnpike and has disappeared: it ran over Creech Hill to All Hallows Farm and Gussage St. Michael; thence via Crichel Down and the pack-horse bridge at Tarrant Monkton to Blandford race-course. As a route from Salisbury to Blandford and the west it was superseded by the turnpike we now know as the A354.

A new turnpike which brought some hope to Cranborne was the Cranborne Chase and New Forest Trust, established in 1832 as part of a larger plan to improve communications between the Bristol Channel and the Hampshire coast. A letter from Sam Hall of Ashmore to Robert Howard, dated 8 December 1830, reads – 'Mr. Stephens is coming as soon as the weather will admit . . . he has been lately engaged in surveying and making a plan of a new road from Shaftesbury to Southampton'. This was, in effect, today's B3081 in the section from Tollard Royal to Cranborne, and it thus linked two existing turnpikes to form a new through-route from Salisbury to Poole, via Handley Cross, Cranborne and Wimborne: at least I assume it was this innovation which lay behind Wake Smart's note of April 7, 1835 – 'The turnpike through Cranborne opened', followed by a further note on May 8, 1838 – 'The "Star" stage coach passed through the turnpike gate at Cranborne from London to Poole'. A week later the "Star" began to run through Cranborne from Salisbury to Poole on alternate days, the fare from Salisbury being sixteen shillings outside and thirty shillings inside.

Whatever success the "Star" had was short-lived. The Salisbury and Dorset Railway opened in 1866, linking Salisbury to Wimborne and precipitating the decline of the turnpike road system. Cranborne was ignored by the railroad which established its intermediate stations at Verwood and West Moors. Wake Smart's assessment of the fading fortunes of Cranborne was increasingly justified as the century wore on. What he had no reason to doubt was the firm foundation that agriculture provided for the well-being of the little township. In his examination of the census of 1831 he noted that, of the parish's 2158 inhabitants, no less than 800 were agricultural labourers: there could hardly be a more telling illustration of the changing structure of rural life between Wake Smart's time and our own. The point is emphasized by his comment that 'a large portion of the land being of a sterile nature and uncultivated, the population of the parish is scanty in proportion to its extent.'

This sterile, uncultivated land was the acid, sandy heath in the south-eastern sector of the parish. In his analysis of the 13000 acres which made up the whole parish (before the partition of 1894) Smart described more than a third of the area as 'Commons and heath lands.' Today much of the heathland is planted to conifers, reclaimed for small-holdings or built over in the development of Verwood – and how much common land has escaped annexation?

With the hindsight of a further hundred-and-forty-odd years we can see that Smart had fully grasped the essential character and underlying problems of his native place. It had not enjoyed the prestige of a powerful governor in residence – an abbot, say, or a princeling or baron – but it had for centuries had a subordinate bureaucracy under royal or near-royal patronage to administer the Chase. It was that bureaucracy which guaranteed its significance as a centre of communications. When Cranborne lost its administrative role, as it had earlier lost its monastic role to Tewkesbury, its communications began to wither; it was by-passed by the turnpike development of the eighteenth century and the railway of the nineteenth. Like many another Dorset village it has to define a new role for itself in the next millenium if its decline is to be arrested.

A NOTE ON THE MAPS

In his *Chronicle of Cranborne* Wake Smart included a map, the provenance of which is described in pp. 222 – 224. The purpose of the map was to illustrate the conflicting views held in 1618 of the bounds of the Chase. As Smart's narrative shows, Lord Salisbury had had the worst of a dispute in 1616 in the traditionally contentious area on the Wiltshire side of the county border and he was using a sophisticated legal strategy to strengthen his position by involving the King and the Exchequer court.

At the time two maps were commissioned – one to be prepared by the plaintiff's surveyor, Thomas Aldwell, the other by the defendant's, Robert Corbett. The plaintiff, Lord Salisbury, subsequently withdrew his surveyor over what appears to be a legal quibble: the commissioners therefore instructed Corbett to prepare a composite map showing both the conflicting versions of the bounds. It is this map that was filed in the Exchequer, according to Smart, an attested copy being made at the time by Walter Hardinge of Blandford. The map, in the form that Smart reproduced, names the original copier as, not Walter, but Richard Hardinge and indicates that it was freshly copied in 1677 by Matthew Hardinge.

Corbett's name does not appear: perhaps he employed Hardinge senior as his draughtsman. There is no reason to doubt the authenticity of the map in its essentials although a later hand – possibly the engraver's – has inserted at least one item that did not exist in 1618. The course of the Great Western Turnpike from Blandford to Salisbury, which by-passed Cranborne in the mid-eighteenth century, has been incorporated.

What meanwhile of Thomas Aldwell and his employer, Lord Salisbury? A map was indeed prepared by Aldwell and eventually published privately in 1890 by General Pitt-Rivers in his book *King John's House.* This map also incorporated later details but may be presumed to have originated in 1618. In the legal action two years earlier Lord Salisbury had relied on the map made for his father, the first Earl, by John Norden. As early as 1597 Robert Cecil had begun to take an interest in Cranborne and was buying property there by 1602. The survey, or terrier, made for him by Norden is dated 1605. Wake Smart quotes (p276) an important testimony by Joseph Compton to the effect that, in about 1608, when he was deputy ranger he was instructed by Lord Salisbury to accompany Norden to make a map of the inner bounds in connection with a dispute between Lords Salisbury and Pembroke. The Pembrokes had virtually ruled the Chase under Queen Elizabeth: the change from Tudor to Stuart patronage must have come as a shock.

Correspondence in the Cecil family archives at Hatfield throws an interesting and rather amusing light on this map of Norden's. When the second Lord Salisbury was contesting the legal action of 1616, his steward, Christopher Keighley, was evidently unable to find the map and urged Norden to make a new one for the use of the Chancellor of the Duchy of Lancaster, Sir John Dackombe. Norden replied, in a letter from Hendon, that a new perambulation 'will be too tedious to do in the time required.' With a renewed searching Keighley found the missing map and entreated Norden to 'be at Westminster tomorrow' to testify that he drew the map. Some show of reluctance was considered advisable: Keighley's letter concludes with these words – 'and leaste it might be objected that yowe came voluntarilie I have sente yowe his majesty's writ of suppenas by this bearer'.

That was in 1616. For the new map in 1618 Lord Salisbury employed Aldwell. Whether or not it was, after all, submitted to the Exchequer court I do not know. Smart gives no sign of having seen it when he wrote his book; at a much later date Pitt-Rivers may have shown it to him. Taken together with the Corbett/Hardinge map, it gives us an unusually detailed picture of the Chase in the first quarter of the seventeenth century.

ACKNOWLEDGEMENTS

Any local historian must always be greatly indebted to the goodwill and friendly support of residents in the locality who generously offer their family papers, photo albums and personal anecdotes. I acknowledge with sincere gratitude such assistance from Miss Gladys Stanford of Cranborne, in whom I found a direct link with the Smart family through her friendship with Dr. Smart's granddaughters; from Mr. Raymond Sturge of Ashmore, whose family correspondence includes the letters of Sam Hall and William West from which I have quoted extracts; and from a Cranborne physician of more recent vintage than Wake Smart but in the same tradition as a storehouse of local knowledge, Dr. Kenneth Rooke, to whom I turn instinctively with any and every sort of enquiry about his locality. I also wish to acknowledge the kindness of the Marquis of Salisbury in allowing me to avail myself of the Cecil family archives at Hatfield, where I received every assistance from the archivist, Mr. Harcourt-Williams. Mr. Michael Pitt-Rivers, as always, takes a benevolent view of my enquiries into Chase history and has most kindly made available for reproduction the map drawn by Thomas Aldwell in 1618. The staff of the Dorset County Library Service, at Dorchester and Blandford, have put me yet deeper into their debt by their unfailing assistance; and Roger Peers, curator of the County Museum at Dorchester, promptly gave me a full account of Wake Smart's association with the Dorset Natural History and Archaeological Society for which I thank him.

THE TEXT

Dr. Smart was not well served by his printers. The lay-out of separate sections could have been more felicitously arranged, with a table of contents (a table of contents has been drawn up and included in this second edition); and the printing errors are at times distracting. The original edition contained an *errata* slip, but it must be described as representative rather than comprehensive. I have added considerably to it and hope that very few errors have now escaped detection: in saying which I should emphasize that I have not presumed to correct Dr. Smart in matters of fact or opinion. This is his book, not mine: the intention is to offer it as he wrote it.

Errata

p 24 line 8, for 'caracute' read 'carucate'

p 34 line 13, for 'co-heireses' read 'co-heiresses': and for 'Hantshire' read 'Hampshire'.

p 53 footnote, for 'yarland' read 'yardland'.

p 75 line 15, for 'Fracade' read 'Facade'.

p 87 last line, for 'devises' read 'devised'.

p 92 footnote, for 'strawing' read 'straying'.

p 95 line 23, for 'of a colony' read 'a colony of'

p 97 line 24, for 'Camp' read 'Lamp'.

p105 line 1, for 'stout' read 'short'.

p112 line 9 for 'swinmote' read 'swainmote'.

p117, erase the note ‡.

p129 line 11, for 'Canstantial' read 'Constantine'.

p133 line 25, for 'when' read 'where'.

p141 line 11, for 'profitably' read 'profitable'.

p142 last line, for 'Townes' read 'Fownes' and for 'Stapleton' read 'Stepleton'.

p155 line 16, for 'emerced' read 'amerced'.

p166 line 15, erase 'to'.
p168 line 26, et seq. It is easier to detect an error here than to suggest a correction.
p174, footnote, for 'Marrington' read 'Mannington'.
p179 line 13, for 'to' read 'they'.
p182 line 4, for 'Bedewgude' read 'Bedewn'.
p185 footnote, for 'Perden' read 'Verden'.
p201 line 5, for 'where' read 'were'.
p208 line 16, for 'prejudicial' read 'prejudiced'.
p210 line 6, for 'rescinded' read 'recorded'.
p211 line 5, for 'chimenage' read 'cheminage' and in l.14 erase 'been'.
p213 line 25, for 'of' read 'or'.
p214 line 2, 'not guilty' ought surely to read 'guilty'.
p222 line 3, for 'Tulk' read 'Fulk'.
p227 line 13, for 'Swayre's' read 'Swayne's'.
p238 line 6, for 'where' read 'were'.
p245 line 17, for 'sad extension' read 'such extensive'.
p261 line 30, for 'this' read 'his'.
p262 line 23, for 'Henry IV' read 'Henry VI'.
p288 line 16 et seq. for 'Saccario' read 'Scaccario'.
p296 line 29, for 'loss of the church' read 'loss the church'.
pp310/311: The pagination of the subsequent pages is confused, though the text proceeds in an orderly fashion to its conclusion on what should be p319 but is numbered 316.

A
CHRONICLE OF CRANBORNE,

BEING AN ACCOUNT OF THE

ANCIENT TOWN, LORDSHIP,

AND

CHASE OF CRANBORNE,

IN THE

COUNTY OF DORSET.

COLLECTED FROM ORIGINAL RECORDS AND OTHER AUTHENTIC SOURCES OF INFORMATION.

"VETERISQUE FAMÆ LATE VESTIGIA MANENT."
TACIT: DE GERM:

LONDON:—

NICHOLS AND SON, PARLIAMENT STREET—WHITTAKER AND CO., AVE MARIA LANE—BRODIE AND CO., SALISBURY—W. SHIPP, BLANDFORD.

1841.

The Town of Cranborne.

The Ancient Town of Cranborne is situated in the North-eastern part of Dorsetshire, near the boundaries of the adjacent Counties of Wilts and Hants, twelve miles south of Salisbury.* Its name is derived from that of the stream which, rising in its immediate vicinity, flows through the Town, and continues its meandering course through the vale to Hurn, near Christchurch, where it falls into the Stour, and soon afterwards enters the Sea. The Saxons called this, Cran-burn, the Crane-stream, from the circumstance, in all probability, of having been a favourite resort of that species of bird, which, without doubt, was accustomed in ancient times to frequent the marshy districts of this country very generally, and in great numbers, but has disappeared, like many other races of the animal kingdom, before the compelling tide of in-

* There is a Hamlet of this Name situated on a small stream between Stockbridge and Basingstoke.

creasing population.† Leland, who wrote in 1550, thus characterizes Cranborne, "it is a praty thoroughfare and for one streat meatly welle buildid. Ther runnith a fleting bek thorough it, and passid doun thorough the streat self on the right hond. I gessid it resort to Horton, but am not sure of thot." Camden, states it to be a place of high Antiquity, and "well watered." Seventy years ago, this once flourishing little Town could boast of a thriving trade ; here were Ribbon-manufactures, Glovers, Tanners, Malsters, a well supplied Corn Market, and large Cattle Fairs ; but the changes and chances which occasionally alter the condition of places as of persons, have fallen to it's lot, and left but the bare remembrance of the days of its prosperity.* The causes of its decay may not be very obvious, we are however, in clined to the opinion, that the formation of the Western Turnpike in 1757, mainly contributed towards this by facilitating the means of access to Towns of greater note and more extensive commercial relations, and by thereby diverting the streams of industry into a new and more advantageous channel. Thus Cranborne lost its Market, became unfrequented, and soon comparatively unknown as a place of trade or commerce. The Market was of very ancient

† See note *a* in Appendix. * See note *b* in App.

date, for in a record of the time of Edward I. it is stated that, "Gilbert de Clare, claims to have in Cranborne a Market every week on Thursday, and a Fair annually on St. Nicholas' day, and on the vigil thereof; and the jury found that such had been the custom from the time of which the memory does not exist." The Market-house was pulled down a few years ago. Fairs are still held on St. Bartholomew's, and St. Nicholas' days, *Aug.* 24*th.*, and *Dec.* 6*th.* A free Grammar-school in which the sons of twenty tradesmen were instructed for three years, formerly existed here, but Alma Mater has descended to the humbler and more useful task of educating the children of the poor in the principles of the Christian religion, as taught in the National schools.

The Town consists of the Borough,* Tything, and Priory, each having its respective Officers, *viz.* two High-bailiffs of the Borough, two Tythingmen, a Surveyor of the heaths, and turf-cutter of the Priory Manor, who are annually appointed at the courts held at the Manor house, and at a house belonging to the Priory appointed for that purpose.

The Streets are thus named; Salisbury street, Wimborne street, East or Castle street, (now called Dry street, in contradistinction to) Water street, Church street, and Shaftesbury

* See note *c* in App.

street, now called the Alley, where in former times the pauper class of the inhabitants were wholly located. The population of the Town is at present

Males,	- - -	336
Females,	- - -	385
Total	- - -	721

The Property is chiefly lifehold under the Marquess of Salisbury. Attempts have been made to improve the lines of communication with the neighbouring towns. A clause was inserted in an act 58. Geo. 3. to carry on the Poole turnpike through Cranborne and Martin to Salisbury, but the project was abandoned for want of adequate support. An Act has been lately passed for carrying a turnpike road through the town from Shaftesbury to Southampton, which, when completed will be a great accommodation to the Public. *Oct.* 14*th.*, 1748, a fire broke out accidentally in Water street, which spread in a South westerly direction, and caused a destruction of property to the amount of two thousand six hundred Pounds.* Contiguous to the town stands a large and handsome Mansion called Cranborne Lodge, which was built by one of the Stillingfleets, afterwards enlarged by Thomas Erle Drax Esq. and is now the property and residence of

* Hutchins.

John Tregonwell Esq. In digging for the foundation of the garden walls, which were built by Mr. Drax, a large quantity of human bones were disintered, and were supposed to be the remains of persons who had perished by plague. This destructive scourge was a frequent visitant of this country in former ages, and one of unusual fatality is recorded to have occured in the years 1348-49, to which we are inclined to attribute the circumstance of this deposit. Having traversed the continent of Asia, where it originated, and that of Europe also, this great plague, whose symptoms are said to have resembled the Asiatic Cholera, first appeared in England on the coast of Dorsetshire, from whence it rapidly spread over the whole length and breadth of the land, desolating many villages in its fatal career, and sweeping off at least one half of the total population. It is said "the church-yards were not large enough to bury the dead, and other places were appointed for the purpose." Now the spot where this discovery was made is part of a field called "New Litten" or new burying ground, which name it bore in the early part of the reign of James I. as appears in a survey of that date. If the term "New" has been retained for the last two hundred and thirty five years, it might have been also retained for two hundred and fifty six years previously, which is the time that had elapsed since the occurrence of the plague to the æra of James I.

The Parish.

The Parish is the largest in the county, being nearly forty miles in circumference, and containing upwards of 13000 acres :—*viz.*

	ACRES.	R.	P.
Of Commons and Heath Land	4604	1	5
Woodlands - -	1347	1	28
Arable - - -	5006	1	37
Pasture - - -	2093	3	13
Total - - -	13052	0	3 *

The annual value of the parish by the assessment of 1839, is £7712.

A Poor Law Union was formed in 1835, comprising fourteen parishes, and having Cranborne as its centre which was in the following year annexed to that of Wimborne, under the title of the Wimborne and Cranborne Union. The average annual expenditure during the last three years for the maintenance of the poor of this parish, including all charges, has been £1030, during the three years preceeding the formation of the Union, when the poor were managed under Gilbert's act, £1170,

* Okeden's Report.

and previously to that, it often amounted to £1500 per annum. In the years 1783-86, it was £600. The county rates are about £100 per annum, Land Tax £380 14*s.* 2*d.* A large portion of the Land being of a sterile nature, and uncultivated, the population of the parish is scanty in proportion to its extent. By the census of 1831, the number of inhabitants was 2158, 800 of whom were agricultural labourers. By the census of 1801 the number was 1402; by that of 1811, 1605; and by that of 1821, 1823 persons.

The Hundred.

The Hundred, which always has belonged to the Lords of the Manor, is extensive and scattered, and comprizes the following Tythings, *viz.*, Fifehead-Quintin, Edmonsham, Farnham, West-Parley, Pentridge, Witchampton, Upwimborn-All-Saints *(All-Hallows in Wimborn St. Giles.)* Rushton, Ashmore, Lovetown, Petersham, *(Farms in the Parish of Wimborn-Minster.)* Gunville, Bagber, *(a Hamlet one mile from Sturminster-Newton.)* Okeford with Keysworth, *(Shillingston, and a Farm two miles from Wareham.)* Holwell, Alderholt, Cranborne.

These are divided into two districts, the three last forming the in-hundred, and the rest forming the out-hundred, which is subdivided into the East and West districts; to each of them a constable is appointed, as well as one to the in-hundred, who resides in Cranborne. 14 Henry II. 1168, the Sheriff accounted to the King for twenty marks of Cranborne hundred for one Murder. The privilege of appointing a coroner is attached to it. The Lawday silver amounts to £5 4*s.* 2*d.*

Antiquity.

The Antiquity of Cranborne is proved by the testimony of ancient records, and demonstrated by the objects that reveal themselves to the notice of the most cursory observer, which are, the Church, the Manor house, and the entrenchment called Castle hill, the memorials of its feudal and Ecclesiastical history. To each of them we propose to devote a few remarks.

Ecclesiastical History.

The Church.

A stranger is naturally struck by its large dimensions, and asks whether Cranborne were more populous in ancient times than it is now? We have no reason to uphold such an opinion, but find no difficulty in accounting for the apparent inconsistency in respect to the disproportionate size of the church, when informed that, the wealthiest of the nobles and the richest of the ecclesiastical establishments of the land, were its nursing-father and nursing-mother. Alas! how many of the splendid triumphs of human genius have originated in motives and feelings that cannot stand the test of a deep and searching inspection! would that one pure motive alone had actuated the minds of those beneath whose fostering care the fane and the sanctuary were upreared in all the perfection and magnificence of art! This truth however we are constrained to admit, that, whatsoever the motive may have been, yet the regard paid to the spiritual condition of the people in the dark day of popish supremacy, may well put to shame the supineness and neglect unhappily too prevalent in these brighter days of protestant ascendancy. In illustration of our position we may adduce the fact, that, there were formerly four chapels at least in distant parts of this parish, in connexion with the church, three of which have been allowed to fall into decay, and are totally lost, *viz.*, at Alderholt, Monkton, and St. Leonard's. The earliest record relating to the church is found in the chronicle of Tewkesbury Abbey, and translated from the Latin is as follows; "about the year of Grace 930 in the reign of the first and famous King Athelstan, there lived a noble Knight named Aylward Sneaw, or Snow, (so called from his fair complexion) a descendant of the illustrious family of King Edward the elder.* He was a man of great bravery, distinction, and spotless integrity. Being mindful of his death, he founded a small monastery for himself and his wife Algiva, in the time of King Ethelred and St. Dunstan, in honor of God, our Lord Jesus Christ and his mother, and of St. Bartholomew, in his demesne at Cranborne, and endowed it with lands and

* Son of Alfred the great. A.D. 901 he encamped at Badbury.

estates. Having collected there some brethren under an Abbot, who should strictly obey the rule of our holy father St. Benedict, he made the Priory of Tewkesbury* of which he was the patron, entirely subordinate to the church of Cranborne. These things were transacted about the year 980. Aylward the first Lord having departed this life, was honorably buried in the church which he had founded; and his son Algar, with his wife Algiva were his heirs.—To Algar succeeded Brictric, both of them were good representatives (testes idonei) of the faith and nobility of their ancestors, and being actuated by a like spirit, completed the vow of their parents by enlarging with suitable magnificence the church they had begun to build. In the year 1102, Robert Fitz-Haymon, being led by the Holy Spirit, resolved at the entreaty of his good wife Sybil, and Gerald Abbot of Cranborne, that the church of Tewkesbury should be rebuilt to the honor of God and the blessed virgin, and he endowed it with rents, lands, and large estates.‡—And forasmuch as that spot seemed much superior to the monastery of Cranborne, as regarded the fertility of the soil, and the pleasantness of the situation, he translated the brethren with their Abbot Gerald,§ and certain estates

* See note *d* in App. ‡ See note *e* in App.

§ See note *f* in App.

to Tewkesbury, in the year of Grace beforementioned, leaving here a Prior and two brethren, for the sake of preserving the founders memory to posterity; thus changing the Abbey of Cranborne into a Priory he made it entirely subordinate to the Abbey of Tewkesbury, and raised the Priory of Tewkesbury, with great splendour to the dignity of an Abbey."* Thus in the short period of one hundred and twenty years did this once rich and flourishing Abbey of Cranborne sink into comparative poverty and insignificance, whilst its more fortunate rival sprang up to rank and favor, and finally became one of the most wealthy and distinguished of the monastic institutions of this kingdom. But the glory of Tewkesbury was destined in its turn to suffer an eclipse, when four centuries later the will of a despotic Monarch compelled it to disgorge the riches of its treasury into the coffers of the State; still we fear that the humble benefice of the poor Benedictines of Cranborne has not been much enriched by that grand and sweeping revolution. A.D. 1150 William Earl of Gloster confirmed the gifts which Robert Fitz-Haymon made to the church of St. Mary, and St. Peter, and St. Bartholomew, of Cranborne, to wit, of the tithes of all the demesne in the Manor of Cranborne, that is, of cheese, lambs, calves, pigs, wool,

* Dugdale's Monasticon.

hemp, foals, bees, hay, grass, pannage,* cyder, mills, *venison,* and of all things brought from off the same manor for which tythe should and hath been paid; and he granted to them pasture as well in wood as in plain, in all his demense, and from his coppices, housebote and haybote,‡ and for fuel when necessary upon the view of a Forester.§ In 1293 the lands of the Abbot of Tewkesbury here were valued at 102*s.* 13 Richard II. 1389, Thomas Chesterton, Abbot of Tewkesbury held at his death the manor of Tarrant-Monkton, Cranborne, (Priory) Chettle, Upwimborne, Boveridge, parcel of the foundation of his church of the manor of Cranborne, £1. 6*s.* 8*d.* rent in Le Gore juxta Shaston, and several messuages and lands in that will; and forty acres of land in Tarrant Launceston.

The Priory.

It stood in the present Vicarage garden and was pulled down in 1703. According to the valor 26 Henry VIII. the cell of Cran-

* Pannage, Beech Mast on which Swine were fed.

‡ Wood for repairs and fences.

§ In the Exchequer, the original deed of Fitz-Haymon is in the augmentation office.

borne was possessed of revenues to the gross amount of £55. 6*s.* 1*d.* clear value £37. 19*s.* 5*d.* The names of very few of the Priors in all probability are now recoverable. Adam de Preston is recorded to have died in the office *Nov.* 15*th.* 1262. Henry Bromall, occurs in 1535, and William Didcote, the last Prior 31 Henry VIII. 1540, had a pension of £10. per annum allowed him on the dissolution of the Priory. The Prior was one of those persons who upon apprehension of the descent of a foreign army on the coast of Dorset, was directed by the king's writ in the 12 Edward III. 1339, to repair to the sea coast with an armed force to repel the enemy.* By inquisition of the 2 and 3 Philip and Mary, the Priory manor consisted of the manor and farm of Rushton, *viz.* 76 acres of land, value 62*s.* the farm of Hide, county of Wilts; a warren of conies in Blagden Park; some lands and tenements in the Town of Cranborne, and St. Leonard's common of 300 acres, where the occupiers of the tenements belonging to the Priory have the liberty of free turbary; the annual value of the manor was rated at £14. 13*s.* 3*d.* and it was sold to Robert Freke, for £351, at twenty years purchase. Subsequently the manor and its appendages appear to have been vested in the crown, and were leased out from time to

* Dugdale's Monasticon.

time for different terms. In 5 James I. it was granted to Robert Earl of Salisbury, and now belongs to the Marquess of Salisbury.

But to return to the church,—Domesday-book* gives the following information concerning the property belonging to it. "The church of St. Mary at Cranborne, holds Ingeligeham (Gillingham.) The land is two carucates. There are five borderers, and seven acres of meadow. It was valued at 60*s.* now 20*s.* Hugo rented this land of the king and gave it to the church. The same church holds Bovehric (Boveridge.) Brictric held it in the time of king Edward (the confessor). It was assessed at five hides. The land is seven carucates, two and a half of which are demesne. There are two ploughs, and ten serfs, and five villeins, and nine borderers, with three ploughs. A mill there returns 6*s.* Pasture nine and a half furlongs in length and breadth; heath two leagues long and wide.—its value 100*s.*—of this land John holds two and a half virgates,—the same church holds Wimburne (Monkton,)—in the time of king Edward it was assessed at five hides,—the land is six carucates, of this one hide is demesne, and there are two ploughs, seven serfs, and seven borderers with four ploughs. There are ten acres of meadow; pasture a league long and a half a league

* See note *g* in App. for explanation of terms.

wide, wood four furlongs long and two wide,—of this Radolph holds two hides, its value 100*s.* The same church holds Levetesford.* There is half a hide and two ploughs, with four villeins, and one borderer, and four acres of meadow, value 15*s.*—the same church holds half a hide in Langeford,||—the land is one caracute, this two villeins occupy, pasture two furlongs in length and breadth, value 5*s.*—the same church holds Tarente (Tarrant Monkton). In king Edward's time it was assessed at ten hides,—the land is eight carucates, of this four and a half hides are demesne,—there is one plough, four serfs, twelve villeins, and twelve borderers with three ploughs. A mill returns 5*s.*—thirty-five acres of meadow, pasture, one and a half league in length and breadth,—wood ten furlongs in length and breadth, valued at £12, now £10.§

The church of Cranborne according to the annals of Tewkesbury, was dedicated to St. Mary, and St. Bartholomew, *Dec.* 6*th.* 1252,† which is probably the date of the completion of the building, and corresponds with

* In a fine levied 9 Henry VI. tenements at Boveridge, Fairwood, and Lestisford are mentioned. Estford occurs in a record 8 Edward I. and refers to a place near Westworth.

|| Langeford, a small Farm in the Parish of Stratton, near Dorchester.

§ See note *h* in App.

† Dugdale's Monasticon.

the architectural style of the principal part of the structure. But there can be no doubt of its having been preceded by one of higher Antiquity, that has left us the memorial of its existence in the fine specimen of a Saxon arch,* which forms the inner entrance to the church from the north Porch. The entrance to the Porch itself presents an equally characteristic example of the early Gothic, which is the style prevalent throughout the body of the church. The chancel is unquestionably the addition of a later æra, and was probably built by Thomas Parker, Abbot of Tewkesbury, whose cypher is seen in the moulding of the parapet above the eastern window, as well as on the pulpit. This gives the date of the beginning of the fifteenth century. The Tower was built in 1440 by an indulgence from the Bishop of Sarum. On either side of the belfry door is an escutcheon, the one on the south side being the arms of Richard Duke of York, who was Lord of the Manor of Cranborne; and the one on the north side, the arms of his wife Cecilia, daughter of Ralph Neville, Earl of Westmoreland. Attached to the north wall of the chancel, is a small ancient building, now used as a vestry room, which was in its original state most probably apart from the church, and used as a chapel. The cha-

* See note *i* in App.

pel of the cemetery is mentioned in an early record. The body of the church interiorly, is sixty-five feet long and forty-two feet broad, and has two aisles separated from it by a range of six plain pointed arches on each side. The south aisle is much narrower than the other. In one of the windows are the arms of Clare, Earl of Gloucester; a female head crowned; and remains of other paintings.—The chancel is forty-six feet long and twenty-one broad. The belfry thirty-three feet long, total length of the church inside, one-hundred and forty-four feet. The height of the walls twenty-nine feet, those of the aisles and chancel seventeen feet. Height of the tower seventy-four feet. There are five bells, very much injured. One of them has this motto "Prayse ye the Lord. I. W. 1610." another, "Clement Tosier cast me in the 12*th.* yere of Queen Anne's raine 1713." Another dated 1608. A.D. 1550 the commissioners appointed to make an inventory of church utensils, &c., returned four bells for this church. The font is coeval with the body of the building. The sacramental vessels consist of three chalices, and three patens. On the largest chalice is the following inscription.

"Quæ dedit hoc Christo scriptum pia fæmina nomen,
In libro vitæ gaudet habere suum 1632."

"The Lady who gave this has her name written in the book of life." On the largest paten this inscription, "Ex dono Edvardi Hooper Armig et dom Dorotheæ ux. Anno. 1715. Given by Edward Hooper Esqr. and Dorothy his wife 1715." On the smaller, this, "Pater tuus qui videt in occulto ipse reddet tibi in propatulo. MATH. 6. 1632. God who seeth in secret will reward thee openly."

The Chancel contains many monuments chiefly belonging to the Hooper, Hawles, and Stillingfleet families. On the south side of the Altar in the wall is the Piscina or sink which conveyed away the consecrated water in which the Priest had washed his hands, or the sacramental vessels. Under a low arch in the wall on the north side is an altar tomb of black marble, ornamented with quatrefoils and shields, but the brass is lost. There appears to have been a communication with the vestry room adjoining, by a quatrefoil aperture within this arch. On the north side of the east window, is the following monument. A figure, in Alabaster, of a youth seated, leaning his head on the right hand, the elbow supported by a scull on his knee, the left arm resting on the thigh and holding a bunch of flowers. Above the head is the following inscription, surmounted with the arms of Elliot with eleven quarterings.

M. S.

Desideratissimi capitis Iohannis Elliott, Io. F. Cornubiensis Armigeri, Ex Honora F. Danielis

Norton Militis South. Qui dum hic vernaculis literis incubuit repentina vi morbi oppressus occubuit 2 Februar MDCXLI.—thus rendered;—Sacred to the memory of the much lamented John Elliott, Son of John Elliott Esqr. of Cornwall, by Honor daughter of John Norton, of Southampton, Knight, who died suddenly whilst at school in this town, February 2. 1641. (Tradition assigns his death to the swallowing a bone which caused suffocation.) Underneath the Statue is the following.—At qualis adolescentulus quantæ spei in ætate jam puerili, vix uspiam majus exemplum memoriæ, comitatis, ingenii, dotum denique naturæ omnium, quas dum arte sedulo et studiose perpolire conatur, supergressus fere modum humanum, Angelorum inseritur choro. Avia D. N. nepoti bene merenti mærens P. P.—thus rendered;—What a remarkable boy he was! of how great promise even in early youth! there has scarcely ever been a more extraordinary instance of the powers of memory, of amiability, of intelligence, in a word, of all the gifts of nature. Whilst striving to improve them by care and study, and having made an almost supernatural progress, he was taken into the company of angels. His sorrowing grandmother Lady Norton, has caused this to be erected to her well-deserving grandson.—Below that again,—

Parvus avos referens, puer hic non degener ambos
Nortonum vivos, Eliotumque dedit.
Septenni incidit vitam laudesque parentum
Mors vitæ victrix laudibus inferior;
Quæ tamen immodicos virtutis crescere fructus
In teneris annis imperiosa vetat.

which we endeavour to imitate thus,—

The undegen'rate scion of his line
Norton and Elliott in his likeness shine,
But seven suns told, all conquering death laid low,
His Parents' hopes, and him at one fell blow.
Despotic death, that comes with blighting wing
To spoil the rich luxuriance of spring.

On the other side of the window is a tablet to the memory of the Rev. Henry Donne, B. D. one of his Majesty's justices of the peace, and forty-four years vicar of this parish, who died Aug. 17*th.* 1830, æt 67.—Also of Catherine his wife, obt, July 29*th.* 1820, æt 65.

Against the south wall is a monument in the bizarre style of James the first's æra, representing a male and female figure lying on a bier beneath a canopy. There is no date, but the coat of arms identify it as belonging to the Hoopers. Further on is a tablet of dark grey marble, above an altar tomb of the same material, with this inscription.—

Iohanni Hawles, armigero marito charissima uxor Margarita superstes posuit, 1571. Iacet sub hocce lector amice marmore Iohannes

Hawles armiger charissimi maritus conjugis octo liberorum pater vir justus, innocuus, castus, probus, pius, magno consilio candida plenus fide cultorque diligens supremi numinis nunc ergo mortali relicto corpore Christo suo fruitur Christique gloria.

Erected to John Hawles Esqr. by his beloved wife Margaret, who survives him 1751. Beneath this marble, reader! friend! lieth John Hawles, Esqr., the husband of a most beloved wife, the father of eight children; he was just, pure, chaste, honest, pious, of sound judgment, full of integrity, a diligent worshipper of the Supreme Being. Having cast off his mortal body he lives with Christ in glory.

The next is a Tablet to the memory of Samuel Stillingfleet Esqr., and Mary Symonds, his wife. She died July 11*th.* 1740, æt 68.—He, March 13*th.* 1750, æt 85.—He was nephew to the Bishop of Worcester.

A handsome tablet over the door to the memory of Susanna wife of Samuel Stillingfleet, gent, and daughter of Edward Morris of Petworth, Sussex, gent. She was a most faithful and loving wife, a religious, wise, virtuous and modest woman, during the space of thirty years of her marriage, being the mother of thirteen children, she was very careful to bring them up in the nurture and fear of the Lord, and to her poor neighbours she was both pitiful and charitable. She patiently and christianly ended this mortal life the 18*th.* day of February 1647, in the 51*st.* year of her age.

> Here lyes a pious, prudent and a virtuous wife,
> Godly she lived and so expired this life.

Thomas Stillingfleet, died 17*th.* Oct. 1789, æt 84.—Rebecca his wife died April 3*rd.* 1803, æt 83.

George Frederic only son of Thomas and Elizabeth Stillingfleet, died Nov. 25, 1811, æt 16.

Thomas Stillingfleet Esqr. obt, Dec. 31*st.* 1815, æt 63,—His widow Elizabeth, daughter of the Rev. J. Griffiths, of Caermarthenshire, obt, Nov. 23*rd.* 1830, æt 74.—This gentleman was a page of the back stairs, to his majesty George III. and was a great favourite of his royal master.

On the floor of this chancel there are several more inscriptions to members of this family.

1. Cuthbert Stillingfleet late of Westminster obt. 9*th.* July 1627, æt 70.—Samuel his son obt. 15*th.* July, 1661, æt 73.—George, son of Samuel 11*th.* August, 1694, æt 67.

2. George, son of George Stillingfleet, July 9*th.* 1701,—James Stillingfleet, 1738, æt 50.

3. Mary, wife to George Stillingfleet, gent, who enjoyed a blessed remove from this world, to a better on the 6*th.* day of July, 1710, æt 89.

4. Dorothy, wife of Robert Stillingfleet, obt, Oct. 12*th.* 1732, æt 32.—William, their son, April 12*th.* 1731, æt $3\frac{1}{4}$

5. Grace, wife of Robert Stillingfleet, obt, July 25*th*. 1749, æt 47.—The ancestor of this family was descended from Cuthbert, last Abbot of York, and originally came from Stillingfleet, in Yorkshire. Cuthbert Stillingfleet was probably the first of the family located here, in the time of James I. as Steward of the Earl of Salisbury, an office which his descendants enjoyed for several generations.—Edward, son of Samuel and Susanna Stillingfleet, was born here April 17*th*. 1635, and received the first rudiments of his education in the grammar school of Mr. Garden.* He was a student of St. John's, Cambridge, and in 1657, appointed to the Rectory, of Sutton, Bedfordshire; afterwards, of St. Andrew's, Holborn. He was then instituted to the preachership of the Rolls chapel, and to a stall in St. Paul's :—was appointed chaplain to Charles II.,—archdeacon of London in 1677,—dean of St. Paul's 1678, and Bishop of Worcester, Oct. 3*rd*. 1689. He died March 27*th*. 1699, and was buried in his cathedral, where there is a long inscription to his memory. He was a prelate of great learning, and is known as the author of various theological works, particularly "Origines Sacræ," and "Origines Britanicæ," or "Antiquities of the churches of Great Britain," 1685. The following anecdote has been related of him: at

* Hutchin's.

a visitation of the Bishop of Worcester, when Mr. Stillingfleet's name was called over, he advanced towards the Bishop, who, seeing before him a very youthful looking divine, enquired whether he was a descendant of the learned author of the "Origines Sacræ," or, a rational account of the grounds of natural and revealed religion. The young divine was puzzled what reply to make, when a clerical friend relieved him from the difficulty, by assuring the Bishop, that the author himself stood before him. Not long afterwards, on the Bishops decease, he was appointed to the vacant see. A short time before his death he engaged in a controversy with Locke repecting some points in the Philosopher's writings, which were thought to lean towards materialism, and scepticism, but his objections were met by a masterly refutation. It is said that the defeat tended to shorten his days. Locke in his reply writes "nothing I know, but truth on my side, can support me against so great a man; whose very name in writing and Authority, in the learned world, is of weight enough to crush and sink whatever opinion has not that solid basis to bear it up."

Bishop Burnet has left this character of him, "he was a man of much more learning than Tillotson, but of a more reserved and haughtier temper. He was a great man in many respects,—he knew the world well and was esteemed a very wise man,—he applied himself much to the study of the law and records, and the original of our constitution, and was a very extraordinary man."—Archbishop Tillotson said of him "he is the glory of our church."

Against the north wall is a large monument of some pretension, in a style peculiar to the architect, containing three tablets to the memory of some of the Hooper family, *viz.*

1. "Of Anne, one of the daughters and coheireses of John Moore, of Hantshire, Sergeant at law, wife to Edward Hooper, of Boveridge, Esqr., who there died in the Lord, 15*th.*, *Jan.* 1637, æt 30 years."

2. "Katherine, wife of Thomas Hooper, of Boveridge, Esqr., there departed this life 11*th.*, *Mar.* 1637, in an assured hope of a better. He likewise on 14*th.*, *Sept.* 1638. Either of them aged 66 years; both here beneath buried, leaving behinde virtuous memories."

3. "In expectation of a joyful resurrection, the body of Thomas Hooper Esqr., of Boveridge, second brother to the above said Thomas Hooper, obt, 30*th.*, *Sept.* 1654, æt 78."

4. "Edward Hooper, of Boveridge, Esqr., who died 11*th.*, *June*, æt 73, A. D. 1664."

5. "Sir Edward Hooper, Knight, son of the above said Edward Hooper, obt, *June* 12*th.*, 1671, æt 48."

6. "Katherine, daughter of Thomas Fleming, of North Stoneham, in the county of Southampton, Esqr., who was first married to the above said Sir Edward Hooper, and afterwards to Sir Hugh Wyndham, Judge of the Common Pleas, and died *Oct.* 3*rd.*, 1693, an. æt. suæ 58." Over these inscriptions the arms of Hooper, quartered with Port, of Poole, and Fleming of North Stoneham. This monument has been lately repaired by the Earl of Malmesbury.

The next is a plain marble tablet, on which is inscribed, "Lady Catherine Noel, obt, 15*th.*, *Dec.* 1779, is interred in the vault of Robert Prower, M. D. Robert Prower, M. D. died *Aug.* 30*th.*, 1793. Fanny his wife died 9*th. Jan.* 1789. The Rev. W. Storey, A. M. died *Oct.* 1*st.*, 1797. Harriett Rigby, and daughter of Robert Prower, M. D. died 13*th.*, *Aug.* 1816. Fanny, widow of the Rev. Henry Rigby, daughter of R. Prower, M. D. died *March* 6*th.*, 1827.

Over the vestry door, an elegantly sculptured tablet, to the memory of Mariana, daughter of the Rev. C. W. Shuckburgh, of the Moot, Downton, Wilts, and wife of Richard Brouncker, Esqr., of Boveridge, who died *Nov.* 29*th.*, 1833, æt 23.

A tablet to William Miles, obt 4*th.*, *April*, 1806, æt 44. William his son, 29*th.*, *Nov.* 1821, æt 20.

1. On the floor, on a slab of white marble was the following inscription in Hutchins's time, now effaced "Here lieth buried the body of Elizabeth, wife of Edward Hawles, of Monkton Esqr., who towards her God lived in verity, and towards her neighbour in Christianity, and towards her husband lovingly, and dying 25*th.*, *Feb.* 1642, she desired to be interred next to her said husband on the left side.

2. "Edmund Hawles buried *Sep.* 10*th.*, 1660."

3. "Elizabeth the wife of Edmund Hawles, of Monkton, Esqr., daughter of William Frampton, of Moreton, of this county, Esqr., who died 28*th.*, *May* 1652."

4. "Edmund Hawles, of Lincoln's Inn, London, only son of the first mentioned Edmund Hawles, by Elizabeth his wife, daughter of William Basset of Claveton, in the county of Somerset, Esqr., who died 28*th.*, *May*, 1678, æt 22."

5. On a brass plate in old English letters. "Here lieth Margaret daughter of Henrie Ashlie Esqr., the wife of William Waller Esqr., and before the wife of John Hawles Esqr., who had by the said John 8 children, *viz*, John, Henry, and Nicholas, Anne, Catherine, Mary, Avice, and Dorothea, and departed this life 21*st.*, *Oct.* 1582."

6. "Edward Holles, son of Edmund Holles, of Monkton, Esqr., who died the 30*th.*, *Jan.* 1636, æt 35."

7. "Here lieth the body of Lady Katherine, wife of Sir Thomas Leigh, Knight, daughter of Edward Hooper, of Boveridge, obt, 19*th.*, *Nov.* 1681, æt 48."

8. Mrs. Elizabeth Mortlock, daughter of George Stillingfleet, gent, relict of Henry Mortlock, late citizen of London, obt, 18*th.*, *March* 1727, æt 76."

9. "Mary Anne Symonds, relict of Samuel Symonds, citizen of London, obt, 29*th.*, *Sep.* 1726, æt 97."

There are many more grave stones in the church, as well as chancel, with effaced inscriptions. On one in the north aisle, Thomas Bartlett, died 24*th.*, *May,* 1718, æt 74.

In Hutchins's time this inscription was to be seen on a brass plate, under the wall of the south aisle, on the chancel, "Pray for the soul of Thomas Pa . . . whose soul . . ." and he suggests whether it might be the Thomas Parker, Abbot of Tewkesbury, whose cypher occurs on the pulpit, &c.

The Registers begin in 1602.* The following memoranda occur, "no Register from 1649 to 1653, things were in great confusion

* Parish Registers first introduced about 8 Henry VIII. A. D. 1500.

during this interval; there was an ordinance of Parliament made for Registering, which took place in 1653.*

"Of the four chapels belonging to the mother church of Cranborne.

1. Hannibal Chater ye last reader at Alderholt chapel, about the year 1670, the chapel demolished in twenty years after: sited in chapel Hays, now Blomels, near ye middle of ye streat.

2. The ruins of the chapel of Fairwood, to be seen about the year 1666, no service remembered; sited in a field near Mr. Cray's Farm-house, (now called chapel close.)

3. The chapel of Monkton, served since either of them by Mr. Rivers, Minister of Allhallows, probably the last who enjoyed it separately, demolished 1742; sited adjoining to ye Mansion-house.

4. St. Leonard's was near ye Farm-house: so says Thomas Hayward, sen., *July* 16*th.*, 1739. (Hamlets in other places maintain their own chapels and pay to the mother church too, as Hatherfaye in Derbyshire, whose chapels of ease are Middleton, and Darwent.)

Priory house pulled down about 1703, last inhabitants Samuel Stillingfleet, gent, and his wife. The Limes planted in the church-yard, anno. 1724.

*** See note *k* in App.**

A list of the vicars of Cranborne since ye dissolution of the Priory, as far as appears by the Registers.

George Richards,	Anno.	1602.
George Fyler,	—	1626.
William Swayne,	—	1636.
Thomas Payne,	—	1648.
Thomas Anstey,	—	1649.
Nathaniel Johnston,	—	1658.
John Edwards,	—	1672.
William Newton,	—	1690.
Richard Wynne,	—	1720.
Edward Hickman,	—	1730.
M. Keet,	—	1780.
to which we may add		
Henry Donne,	—	1787.
Frederic Pare,	—	1831.

The following list of vicars prior to the dissolution, is taken from Hutchins.—

Patrons.	Vicars.
The Abbot and convent of Tewkesbury.	John de Cotes, inst. 9 Mar. 1308.
	Nicholas de Pedingho, Sept. 1312.
	Thos. de Craneborn, 17 Oct. 1314.
	John Dowdeswell, 5 June, 1315.
	John de Saudeswel, probably the same.
	John Goitteby, perpetual chaplain of Li̇tchet Maltravers, 11 Nov. 1340, exchanged with

Thomas Cocks, rector of Ashemere, 14 Oct. 1346.

Robert Seaward, exchanged with

Stephen Hallen or Hatten, rector of Wokesby, Wilts, 20 April, 1378.

John Rygges, 24 Feb. 1391, exchanged with

Peter Mighel, rector of Holy Trinity, Dorchester, 1 May, 1393.

John Ilmyngdon, rector of Sutton Walrond, Oct. 30, 1393.

John Alfred, deacon, 16 April, 1411.

Richard Smithland, 3 Oct. 1415.

John Goderyche, on the resignation of Smithland, 27 Sept. 1430, exchanged with

William Gerveys, rector of Glanville Wotton, 6 Sept. 1433.

John Durant, on the death of Gerveys, 19 March, 1436.

John Costomb.

John Cutteberd, on the resignation of John Costomb, 2 July, 1472.

Thomas Shirwood, on the death of Cutteberd, 23 May, 1480.

Thomas Ormus, on the death of Shirwood, 1 March, 1492.

Roger Nicolson, on the death of Ormes, 13 Feb. 1506.

Collated per Lapsum. Richard Casewell, L.L.B. on the deprivation of Nicholson 25 Sept. 1509.

Robert Saunders, M.A. on the resignation of Casewell, 27 June, 1514.

Thomas Bagshaw, on the death of Saunders, 27 Sept. 1525. Obt, 1566.

Memorandum in the Register, "*March, 2nd.*, 1660. A Lysense was then granted to Edward Hooper, of Boveridge, in the parish of Cranborne, Esqr., to eate flesh in the time of Lent, and att other times duringe his infirmity, according to such provisors as by Law is appointed, and hath paid to the use of the poore of the parish aforesaid 6*s.* 8*d.*"* "*Oct. 3rd.*, 1680, collected in the parish of Cranborne, for the redemption of poor slaves in Turkey, the sum of 2*s.* 8*d.*

"Edward, sonne of Samuel Stillingfleet, and Susanna his wife, baptized *May 28th.*, 1635."

The Rectory.

After the dissolution it was frequently granted for life, or for a term of years. 1 Elizabeth, (1558.) The Rectory, advowson of the

* See note *l* in App.

vicarage, and priory manor, with tithes in Cranborne, Upwinborne, Farnham, Blagden, Tarrant-Rushton, Edmonsham, Hampreston, Tarrant-Gunville, Chettle, Bagber, Steple, Knoll, Milborne, Dewlish, Boveridge, late parcel of Cranborne cell, and Tewkesbury priory, were granted to Robert Francis in consideration of 100 marks, and paying yearly £28. 6*s*. 10*d*.—20 Elizabeth, on the demise of Francis, the same was granted to Edward Horsey.—32 Elizabeth, to Thomas Swetman.—40 Elizabeth, to Henry Sterr, and Thomas Hacker.—43 Elizabeth, to Miles Whittaker.—2 Jac. 1. to the Queen Anne, with a Fee-farm of £28. 6*s*. 10*d*. and £27. 6*s*. 8*d*. issuing therefrom, and some tenements,—5 Jac 1. (1608,) to Robert Earl of Salisbury, and now belongs to the Marquis of Salisbury. In 1291 this rectory with a chapel was valued at 12 marks. The Rectorial tithes of the Parish are now worth about £2500 per annum. James Marquis of Salisbury, sold the tithes with the exception of those of his own estate, to John Ford Esqr., and other landholders in the Parish.

The Vicarage.

It is a discharged living in Pimperne Deanery, value £6. 13*s.* 4*d.* formerly in the Diocese of Bristol, now, in that of Salisbury. In 1291, value, six and a half marks. The cause between Alan, Abbot of Tewkesbury, (obt, A.D. 1202,) and Herebert, the chaplain, concerning this vicarage, was decided by a commission from Pope Celestine, to William Bishop to Hereford &c. Herebert claimed the perpetual vicarage, and a Chapel in the Earl's Court,* which he alledged he held of the Earl, and not of the Abbot. After two years contest Herebert acknowledged his error and asked pardon, on which the Abbot permitted him to hold the vicarage for life, or so long as he behaved well; to serve the church of Cranborne, and its chapel, *viz.* the chapel of the cemetry,|| and the chapel of the Earl's Court, and the chapel of Winborne Abbas, not presuming to do any thing in them contrary to the Abbot's will. He was to have his diet at the Prior's table every day, unless prevented by sickness, also a third part of the offerings on Christmas day,

* There are no traces of a chapel in the Manor-house, which has been built subsequently to the "Earl's Court" here mentioned.

|| In all probability the present vestry room.

Good-Friday, and Easter day; the offerings of the second mass, all above 12*d.* to be equally divided between the Prior and him: also the fees for confession. He was to have one virgate of land, which he held in Cranborne, with the houses belonging to it; also the whole tithe of the villainage of Wimborne Abbas, with the third part of the Lordship, except the tithe of wool. Every penny offered in mass to be his own, and he might claim a third part of the wedding fees, but not retain a chaplain under him without the Prior's consent. By a composition made between the Abbot of Tewkesbury and John Durant vicar in 1437, the Abbot agreed to pay four marks and 6*s.* 8*d.* in lieu of tithes in the Chapelry of Wimborne Abbas; the vicar to serve that chapel, and to have his diet with the Prior of Cranborne, and when infirm, to be allowed in lieu 14*d.* weekly, and to have a house on the south side of the Cemetry, rent free.* By the return to the Commission of 1650, the vicarage was worth 20 marks per annum; there were three chapels of ease, *viz.* one at Alderholt, but had no minister or maintenance: another at Monkton, supplied with a minister by Mr. Hawles, who was obliged to do it by his lease from the Earl of Salisbury, for the tithes there, which are part of the impropriation; another

* Dugdale's Monasticon.

at Boveridge, but had no minister or maintenance: Alderholt chapel only fit to be made a church, there being many souls there.

"Terrier of glebe lands, houses, buildings, gardens, offerings, and pensions due to the vicarage of Cranborne in the Diocese of Bristol, deanery of Pimperne, County of Dorset, taken the *20th.*, day of *Sept.*, in the year of our Lord 1784.

1. A vicarage house, garden, stable, and fuel house.

2. 70 acres of glebe lands: 30 whereof lie between a lane leading from Cranborne to Wimborne Minster, and a lane which leadeth from Cranborne to Edmonsham, called "middle field," all enclosed.

3. 20 acres in Castle Hill field, abutting on Ensham lane, enclosed.

4. 20 acres in White Hill field abutting on Wimborne and Blandford lanes, enclosed.

5. A pension of £40. per annum, by the impropriator of the rectory of Cranborne, to the vicar."

By the aid of Queen Anne's bounty, this sum has received an augmentation, and the vicarage is now worth about £125 per annum, without glebe. The vicarage house was built by the Rev. Henry Donne, assisted by funds derived from Queen Anne's bounty, on land given for that purpose by the Marquis of Salisbury.

From the preceding records we learn that there have existed at different periods six chapels, within the precincts of this extensive parish; another remains to be mentioned, that of Boveridge, which was founded by the Hooper family, and has been recently rebuilt on a more commodious site by Richard Brouncker Esqr. There is a small stipend attached to it, but it has hitherto been very irregularly served. This and the newly erected chapel at Verwood, are the only chapels now remaining in connexion with the church of Cranborne.

Church Lands.

These consist of two tenements, and a small garden in Shaftesbury Street; two tenements and gardens in Wimborne Street; one barn and garden, in Salisbury Street; and a tenement in Castle Street, near the Fleur de Lis Inn, all on lives; annual value £12.

Church Rates are about £42. per annum. The priory, lands, and tenements, are in general, exempt from the payment of them.

Charitable Benefactions.

1. Mr. Richard Carter, bequeathed in 1694, £60. the interest whereof is distributed in bread to poor persons annually, on St. Thomas's Day. Vested in Mr. Richard Carter,—a house and garden, in Castle Street, and three acres of land were purchased about fifty years after the testator's decease, which now produce the net annual income £4.*

2. The Rev. Mr. Wynne, bequeathed in 1729, £20. in money, the interest thereof to be distributed in bread on St. Thomas's Day annually, by the churchwardens.—Vested in the parish stock,—annual produce £1. §

3. Thomas Hooper Esq., late of Boveridge, bequeathed in 1661, £30. in money, to be lent gratis, to poor tradesmen, at £3. each for one year only, at the discretion of the minister and churchwardens,—Vested in the parish stock.†

4. Elizabeth Hutchins, widow, of Pennington, in the parish of Milford, county of Southampton, bequeathed in 1676, £60. to purchase so much land as the rent thereof may

* The Will is lost.—the House is gone.

§ This charity is discontinued.

† This charity is lost. In 1786, £18 of the stock remained.

buy for poor men and women, that have no relief of the parish, by weekly collection, Coats, (each of them having the letters J. H. on the right shoulder,) to be given them by the minister and churchwardens, at their discretion, on the feast of All-saints every year for ever. After her death, a house, garden, stable, &c., called Melledge's, situate in Salisbury Street, and three acres of land, called Holdings, were purchased, and now produce a net annual income £10. which is distributed to poor men in great Coats, annually.*

5. Thomas Hooper Esqr., late of Boveridge, bequeathed a grant in land for the establishment and support of an Alms-house, (Bouveridge) by which three single persons, particularly old servants and tenants of the family, have been from time to time, and are maintained by an annual income arising out of the land, called Overthatcher's lease, in the parish of Manston. —Vested in Edward Hooper, Esqr., annual produce £23. out of which the minister of Cranborne is paid £6. for instucting the Alms-house people in the Protestant religion; also in land an annual income for the Alms-house steward issuing from a field contiguous to the Alms-house garden, to the amount of £6. §

* This charity is incorrectly stated in the return made to Parliament in 1786, (Hutchins' 2*nd*. Edit.) The testatrix left the same to Ringwood Parish.

§ Hutchins' 2*nd*. Edit.

Feudal History.

The Manor.

The Manor, including the Borough of Cranborne, was for several centuries comprised in the Honour of Gloucester,* and has been, with its appurtenances, anciently styled an Honour itself. There is a survey of the manor in the manor house, of the date 9 Jac 1. by which it is shewn to consist of 7799 acres, much of which is uncultivated; the whole varying between a gravelly and a chalky soil. The following records give some curious particulars relating to it.

1. An Inquisition † of the lands and tenements of which Gilbert de Clare, Earl of Gloucester and Hertford, was seized on the day on which he died, taken at Cranborne, in the 24 Edward I. (1296.) The Jurors say, that the Close of the Court of Cranborne in itself

* See note *m* in App. † See note *n* in App.

five and a half acres is worth with the easement of the houses, by the year 5*s.* that in the field on the west side of the aforesaid Court are 285½ acres of arable land, whereof 170½ are of the price of 3*d.* per acre, and 115 acres of the price of 4*d.* sum 80*s.* 11¼*d.* that the croft of the sheepcote contains in itself 2 acres worth 12*d.* and besides these there are on the north side 2 acres of pasture, by the year 6*d.* 187 acres of arable land, the price of the acre 3*d.* sum 46*s.* 9*d.* also, 31 acres of meadow, price of the acre 12*d.* sum 31*s.* also, 458 acres of upland pasture, price per acre, 1*d.* sum 38*s.* 2*d.* also, 33 acres of land newly broken up, price per acre 1*d.* sum 2*s.* 9*d.* also 1433 acres of wood, where the pasture in the same wood is worth by the year 100*s.* but it cannot be sold on account of the Deer (feræ); they say, that the pleas and perquisites of the Chace are worth by the year 60*s.* also, they say that the perquisites and pleas of the Hundred are worth by the year £10. also of the manorial court (curiæ intrinsecæ) are worth by the year 100*s.* also, there are rents of assize of customary tenants* by the year £28. 17*s.* 3*d.* also, rents of lands let to farm by the year £4. 19*s.* 6¾*d.* also the works of villains are put at £8. 17*s.* 11½*d.* by the year; also there are of rents by the year, 1 lb. of

*** See note *o* in App. "tenure."**

pepper; 3 lbs. of cummin, and 1 lb. of wax; also of rents by the year, 28 coulters, which are put at 14*s.*—also they say that Gilbert de Clare, Earl of Gloucester, and Hertford, held the aforesaid manor of Cranborne, with the appurtenances, of the Lord the King in chief, but by what service they are ignorant; and they say that Gilbert, the eldest son of the said Earl, is the next heir, and of the age of five years; sum of the extent £78. 12*s.* and 1 lb. of pepper, the price of 8*d.* 3 lbs. of cummin, price 3*d.* 1 lb. of wax, price 5*d.**

34 Edward III. (1361.) an inquisition of the lands &c., of which Elizabeth de Burgh, was seized on the day, on which she died, taken at Cranborne, before John de Blekynton, &c. The Jurors say upon oath, that Elizabeth de Burgh, held in her demesne, as of fee on the day on which she died, of the Lord the King in chief by Knight service,§ the manor of Cranborne, with the appurtenances which is worth by the year in all issues £70. &c.||

35 Edward III. (1362.) *May* 28*th.*, Inquisition made at Dorchester, of the lands &c., held by Gilbert de Clare, in the county of Dorset, on the day of his death &c.

* Record in the Tower.

§ See note *p* in App. "tenure."

|| Record in the Tower.

The Jurors say, that the Earl held in his demesne as of fee, the manor of Cranborne, with its appurtenances of the Lord the King in chief by the service of two Knight's fees, which manor belongs to the Earldom of Gloucester. There is therein a capital messuage which is worth with the fruit and herbage 12*d.* also, 110 acres of arable land, worth by the year 27*s.* 6*d.* the price of the acre 3*d.* and 150 acres of arable land, worth by the year 25*s.* the price of the acre 2*d.* and 47 acres of meadow, worth by the year 47*s.* the price of the acre 12*d.* and there is a certain separate Pasture, worth by the year 6*s.* and a Hundred which is worth by the year 20*s.* and a (baronial) court, worth by the year 26*s.* 8*d.* and there is a certain chase worth nothing by the year beyond the sustenance of Deer (ferarum.) Total £7. 13*s.* 2*d.*—And there are there fifty-one free tenants who pay annually, every quarter, in equal portions £8. 12*s.* 6*d.* and three free tenants who pay annually at Easter and Michaelmas, in equal portions 39*s.* 6*d.* and one free tenant who pays annually at Michaelmas, half a pound of wax, the price 3*d.* and one who pays at the same time 1 lb. of pepper, price 12*d.* and one who pays 1 lb. of cummin, price 1*d.* and one who pays 18*d.* and one who pays 6*s.* and one who pays annually by equal portions every quarter 16*s*. Total paid by free tenants £11. 16*s*. 10*d*.—And there are six customary tenants, each of whom holds a virgate of land,‡ in villainage, paying annually in equal portions every quarter 7*s*. 6*d*. and each of them pays annually in lieu of work (pro operibus) at Christmas, Easter, and Midsummer, in equal portions 3*s*. 5¼*d*. and there are thirty-one customary tenants, each of whom holds half a virgate of lands in villainage, paying every year in equal portions, quarterly, 2*s*. 6*d*. and each of them pays annually in lieu of work every quarter, in equal portions, 3*s*. 5¼*d*. and there are twenty-two customary tenants each of whom holds a fardel* of land, paying every year, in equal portions quarterly 2*s*. and each of them pays annually in lieu of work, at the three quarters, in equal portions 3*s*. 0¾*d*. and each of the aforesaid tenants work from the 1*st*. *Aug*. (â Gulâ Augusti) to the feast of Michaelmas, three days every week, and the day's work is worth 1*d*. and there are three customary tenants each of whom holds 6 acres of land in villainage, paying annually every quarter, in equal portions 3*s*. 1*d*. and one pays (in like manner) 5*s*. 1*d*. and —— pay (in like manner) 7*s*. 4*d*. and one who pays (in like manner) 2*s*. 5*d*. he mows four acres of

‡ A Yardland, varied in quantity from 15 to 40 acres.—Four virgates make a hide, and five hides a Knights fee.

* Generally accounted the fourth part of a Yarland; by some, however, the eighth.

corn in Autumn, and the value of the harvest is 12*d.* and there are nineteen customary tenants who pay annually, every quarter, in equal portions 76*s.* 3*d.* in lieu of all service; and there are there ninety cottagers, who pay annually, every quarter, in equal portions £11. 13*s.* 4*d.* in lieu of all service.—The total paid by customary tenants £25. 10*s.* 3*d.*—The total value of their work £16. 2*s.* 7*d.*—Total £61. 2*s.* 10*d.**

A. D. 1399, 22 Richard II. *Sept.* 16*th.* Inquisition made at Dorchester, of the lands &c., of Roger Mortimer, (de Mortuo Mari) Earl of March, &c.—The Jurors say, that the aforesaid Roger, Earl of March, held on the day of his death, in his demesne, as of fee of the Lord the King in chief, by Knight service, the manor of Cranborne, with its appurtenances, which is worth annually, in all outgoings about the true value beyond reprisals £90. and they say that the aforesaid Earl, a long while before his death, granted to the Lord, Edward Mortimer, his brother, for life, the office of Head Forester, and Keeper of his chase, of Cranborne &c., taking the accustomed fees and sureties.†

A. D. 1415, 43 Edward III. *July* 3*rd.* Inquisition made at Blandford, in the county of Dorset, before William Cheyne, escheator of the Lord the King, of the lands &c., held

* In the Tower. † In the Tower.

by Lionel, Duke of Clarence, on the day of his death.—The Jurors say, that the Duke held of our Lord the King, in chief by military service, to the end of his life, by the law of England, as of the inheritance of his wife Elizabeth, the manor of Cranborne, with its appurtenances, which is worth annually, in all outgoings £90. 3*s.**

A. D. 1542, 33 Henry VIII. The manor of Cranborne, was rated at £32. 16*s.* 10*d.* in the minister's accounts.‡

Grants of the Manor.

A. D. 1322, 15 Edward II. The King granted Cranborne Castle and Honor to Robert de Aston, this was by the King's right of Escheat,§ and was probably during the minority of Elizabeth, sister of Gilbert, the last Earl of Clare and Hertford, who was afterwards married to William de Burgh, Earl of Ulster, and inherited this manor.†

A. D. 1413, 1 Henry V. William Stourton, was seized of the manor. This was pro-

* In the Tower.

‡ Dugdale's Monasticon.

§ See note *q* in App.

† Hutchins' says, probably on some forfeiture or minority, of the Mortimers,—but this will not correspond with the date.

bably on the forfeiture of Richard, Earl of Cambridge, who married the daughter of Roger Mortimer. 9 Henry V. Sir John Arundel, chevalier, was seized of the manor,—this was also probably on forfeiture. It will be remembered that civil war was now raging in England, and that this manor was then in the possession of the leaders of the York party, who were in opposition to the crown,—but the two roses were united in Edward IV. who inherited together with his crown, the manor of Cranborne. After this period it was frequently granted by the reigning monarch, to persons for a term of years, or for life.

A. D. 1537, 28 Henry VIII. An act passed vesting the manor in the crown, and reciting that in the third year of the said King's reign, a fine had been levied by Katherine, Countess of Devon, and Thomas, Duke of Norfolk, and the Lady Anne, his wife, of the said manor &c., unto the King, his heirs and successors. These noble ladies were the only surviving issue of King Edward IV.—and King Henry VIII. was the only son and heir, of Elizabeth, his eldest daughter.

A. D. 1541, 32 Henry VIII. The manor, hundred, burgh, the forest or chase, park, and the office of Feodary of Cranborne,* were grant-

* See note *r* in App.

ed to Queen Catherine, being parcel of the jointure of Queen Jane.

A. D. 1551, 4 Edward VI. It was granted to Sir William Herbert for twenty-one years. 15 Elizabeth, (1573.) The manor, Castle hill coppice, twenty-eight acres; Burwood coppice, eighty acres, &c., were granted for twenty-one years to Robert Freke. 16 Elizabeth. It was granted with messuages and tenements in Daggens, St. Clement's chapel, and chapel close, (Alderholt,) to Robert, Earl of Leicester. And the same year to Edward Fitz Garret, for thirty-one years. 17 Elizabeth. The scite and capital messuage of the manor, and the profits of the Fairs were granted to Alice Johnstone, for fifty years in reversion. 29 Elizabeth. The Burgh to Richard Borde, for twenty-one years. 42 Elizabeth. The manor was granted to Thomas Bellott, value £34. 12*s.* 11*d.* 9 Jac 1. (1612.) To George Whitmore; and the same year, the Hundred, Lordship, and Manor, the Chase and Free-warren, the scite and capital messuage of the manor and demesne lands, the profits of the Fairs, Castle hill and Burwood coppices, were granted to Robert, Earl of Salisbury; whose descendant the Marquess of Salisbury is the present proprietor of all, excepting the Chase.

Lords of the Manor.

As the manor of Cranborne was originally included in the honor of Gloucester, the Lords of that honor, were the Lords of the manor of Cranborne. Aylward Meaw, or Sneaw, whose name has been mentioned in connection with the Ecclesiastical part of our History, is the earliest of the feudal Lords on record. We know little more of him, than the circumstance of his having been a Saxon noble of the Royal lineage, and a celebrated warrior; of having lived in King Athelstan's reign; died about A. D. 980, and was interred in the Abbey of Cranborne, which he had founded.* Concerning Algar his son, we are left in obscurity, excepting that we are told he enlarged the monastery of Cranborne. Of Algar's Son Brictric, we have more particulars; from the Domesday survey, he appears to have been a very

* "Aylward being possessed of Tewkesbury and Cranborne, and being patron of the religious houses there, which possession were parts of the royalty or honor of Gloucester for ages after, was certainly Lord of that honor."—*Seyer's Hist. Bristol.* Bristol was part of that honor. Aylward Street occurs there now.

wealthy noble,§ and doubtlessly on that account was selected by Edward the Confessor, to fill the office of Ambassador to the Court of Baldwin, Earl of Flanders; where he had the misfortune to attract the notice of Matilda, the Earl's daughter, who cherished an affection for him, that unhappily was not reciprocal. The disappointed Lady was sometime afterwards married to William, Duke of Normandy, and in consequence of the successful result of his enterprise, was raised to the high station of Queen of England. Having now the power, as well as the longing desire to revenge the slight her affections had sustained, she incited William to arrest Brictric, and seize his Estates; which suiting the policy of the rapacious conqueror, he readily assented to, and threw Brictric into prison at Winchester, where he died without issue, and was interred. This occured about A.D. 1070. The king gave the whole honors of Gloucester to Matilda, for her life, but she did not long survive the unhappy victim of her revenge, for she died A.D. 1083, whereupon the honor reverted to the king, who retained it during the remainder of his life.

"Lands which were held by Queen Matilda.* The King holds Cranborne. In the

§ He held the manors of Deverel, Litelfrome, Cranborne, Aishmore, and Wimborne; also manors and estates in Somerset, Devon, Cornwall, Gloucester, and Worcestershire.

* Domesday Book.

time of Edward, (the Confessor,) it was assessed for ten hides,—the land is ten carucates, three hides and a half are demesne. There are two ploughs, ten serfs, eight villeins, seven cottagers, with eight ploughs,—four mills, which return 18*s*. Twenty acres of meadow,—a pasture, two leagues long, and one furlong and one league wide,—woodland, two leagues long and two broad; it was valued at £24, now returns £30. Of the same land, there are three Thanes who hold three hides, which return £3. without service."

William Rufus granted the honor to his cousin, Robert Fitz-Haymon, Lord of Astramaville or Corbeille, in Normandy, as a reward for his services in the conquest of Glamorganshire. On the death of William, he espoused the cause of Henry, against his elder brother Robert, and continued steadfast to his cause when almost all the other nobles deserted him, and went over to Robert.* He was however, after a while, taken prisoner, and confined in the city of Bayeux, from whence he was released by King Henry, in 1106. In the following year he died, having been sometime before his death insane, according to William of Malmesbury, from a blow on the temple by a pole, at the battle of Falaise, in Normandy. He was buried in the Abbey of Tewkesbury, which he had

* Seyer Hist. of Bristol, vol. 1. p. 347.

enriched and ennobled, by despoiling the once favored monastery of Cranborne. His body was re-interred between two pillars on the right hand of the presbytery, about the year 1241, and afterwards in process of time Thomas Parker, the eighteenth Abbot in A. D. 1397, caused a chapel of stone, admirably carved, to be erected over him, and appointed a mass for the dead, to be celebrated every day with the collect for the founders, in perpetual memory for the founder and his wife.†

By his wife Sybil, or Isabella, daughter of Roger Montgomery, Earl of Arundel, he had four daughters, coheiresses; the eldest of whom king Henry I. gave in marriage to his illegitimate son Robert, and conferred on her the honor of Gloucester, "being unwilling that so great a Lordship should be divided amongst sisters,"§ and creating him Consul, and Earl of Gloucester.|| Robert was said to be the son of Nesta, or Nefla, daughter of Rees, King of South Wales, and was married to Mabel A. D. 1109. Robert, the rhyming Monk of Gloucester, gives the following particulars of this marriage,

† Chronicle of Tewkesbury.

§ Chronicle of Tewkesbury.

|| The title of Consul appears to have been commonly applied by the Roman—Britons, to persons of high distinction, superseding that of Cæsar. In the Saxon and Norman periods, it was used synonymously with Comes or Earl.—*Seyer*. Earl from the Saxon Jarl, signifies Governor of the county.

"When the King made the proposal that she should marry his son, she was against it, and long withstood it; and when the king often solicited her, she at last answered like a good and courteous maiden; Sir, said she, I see plainly that your heart is set on me, more for the sake of my inheritance than myself. My Father's name was Sir Robert le Fitz Hayme, and that inheritance ought not to be any man's that was not of his rank; therefore Sir, for God's love, let me have no man for a husband, who has not two names whereby he may be known. Damsel, quoth the King, thou sayest well in this case; thy Father's name was Robert le Fitz-Hayme, and I will take care that my son shall have one as fair, for his name shall be Sir Robert Fitz le Roy. Sir, said the maiden, that is a fair name and of great repute as long as he shall live, but what shall his son be called, or any other of his descendants? unless care be taken of that also, they may soon come to have no name. The King perceived that the maiden said nothing unreasonable, and knowing that Gloucester was the chief part of her heritage, Damsel, said he, thy Lord shall have a fair unobjectionable name for himself and his heirs; his name shall be Robert Earl of Gloucester; Sir, quoth the maiden, then I like this well; on these terms I consent that all my lands shall be his."

He was the richest, and most illustrious personage of that age, and signalized himself in supporting the claims of his half-sister Matilda, against the usurper Stephen, in a long continued warfare, terminating only in his death, which took place from fever, *Oct.* 31*st.* 1147, at Gloucester. He was buried in St. James's monastery at Bristol, which he founded. His son William, second Earl of Gloucester, succeeded him; "a man of gentle manners, who liked chambers better than warfare," yet was not wholly deficient of his father's warlike spirit, or of the piety of his ancestors, for "he confirmed all the charters, confirmations, liberties and donations, which his father or any of his ancestors had granted unto Tewkesbury."* He married Avisa, daughter of Robert Earl of Leicester, and had three daughters, the youngest of whom, Isabella, he betrothed to John, youngest son of King Henry II. he being but ten years old at the time, and her third cousin. The Earl died before the marriage was solemnized, A. D. 1183, and was buried in the priory of Keynsham, which he had founded. At his death, the honor lapsed into the hands of the King, (Henry II.) as his escheat, who held it six years; and afterwards it was held in like manner by Richard I. by whom it was granted to John, his brother, who having

* Chronicle of Tewkesbury.

attained the age of twenty-three, and received the title of Earl of Mortaigue, or Moreton, was married to Isabella, A. D. 1186, although Archbishop Baldwyn interdicted the union, on the plea of the consanguinity of the parties. § Ten years afterwards, when John had succeeded to the crown, he in the first year of his reign, availed himself of this plea, to procure a divorce, and married Isabella, daughter of the Earl of Angouleme. John permitted his ill-used and divorced wife, to marry Geoffrey de Mandeville, Earl of Essex, A. D. 1214, on his payment of twenty-thousand marks; ‡ but reserved the principal part of the honor of Gloucester to himself. It does not appear when John surrendered these possessions, † but he probably retained them until his death, A. D. 1216. Geoffrey de Mandeville was accidently killed at a tournament, the year before the King's death, and his widow again married Hugh de Burgh, Earl of Kent and chief Justiciary of England, but

§ "Richard now was king, and gave his brother John,
The Earldom of Gloucestre; and let him spousy anon
Isabel, that was heir; and great lands thereto
Gave him here in England, and beyond sea also."

Robert of Gloucester.

Afterwards John was disseized of all his lands in England, but on the mediation of Queen Eleanor, the brothers were reconciled, and John's lands restored.

‡ If we suppose the value of money to have been fifteen times greater than at present, the sum will amount to £200,000 of our money.—*Seyer.*

† Hutchins,—17 John 1216. Geoffrey de Mandeville, held the Chase of Cranborne.

soon afterward died without issue; * whereupon the Earldom and Honor of Gloucester devolved upon her nephew Almeric, son of the Earl of Evreaux, who had married her eldest sister Mabel; but upon his death soon afterwards without issue, they passed to Gilbert, son of Richard de Clare, Earl of Hertford, deceased, who had married her second sister Amicia, Gilbert, the first Earl of Gloucester and Hertford, who married Isabella, sister of the Earl of Pembroke, having been in the wardship of king Henry III. during a minority of nineteen years. He was one of the twenty-five Barons appointed under the *Great Charter*, to adjust any differences that might arise under its execution; and we find him joining Prince Richard, to compel the vacillating king Henry to confirm the Charter, which he seemed disposed to annul. Gilbert died, A. D. 1230, and was buried at Tewkesbury. His son Richard, then a minor, succeeded him, and was in the wardship of Henry fifteen years. In public life, we find him following his father's example,—strenuously endeavouring to secure the confirmation of the *Great Charter*; and was one of the twenty-four Barons, who, with that object in view, drew up the statutes of Oxford which the King swore to observe; but defeated their intention, by getting his oath annulled

* 1 Henry III. Hubert de Burgh, held the manor of of Cranborne and Wareham.—*Hutchins.*

by the Pope. The Earl appears to have been, upon the whole, a noble independent character, nevertheless his opposition to the ambitious aims of the Earl of Leicester, are not entirely free from the stain of unworthy motives.* He died about A. D. 1260, his body was buried at Tewkesbury, his heart at Tunbridge, and and his bowels at Canterbury.† Gilbert, his son succeeded to his title and estates. Animated with the spirit of his Father and Grandfather, he adopted still stronger measures for the attainment of the same objects, for which they had so perseveringly contended. He, with other Barons, took up arms against the hypocritical Monarch, and commanded one of the divisions of the Army at the battle of Lewes, where he took Richard, king of the Romans prisoner, and defeated the ambitious Leicester, at the battle of Evesham, where the latter was killed. He rendered himself obnoxious to the king by siding with the Welsh insurgents, and at their head took tower of London ; a reconciliation was howhowever effected between them, a short time before the king's decease. He married A. D. 1290, Joan, daughter of Edward I. Prior to this event, he had lost the king's favor by

* See Rapin.

† He held one-hundred and seventy-one Manors and Lordships in Dorsetshire, *viz.* Cranborne, and the places that are comprised in the Hundred ; Wareham, Wyke, Weymouth, Portland, &c.—*Hutchins.*

refusing to accompany him in an expedition against the king of France, on which account Edward seized all his estates, and forced him to marry Joan, without lands or money; but on her marriage, the king restored all to him and entailed them on her, and her issue by him. He died at Monmouth, A.D. 1295, and was buried at Tewkesbury. His widow married the next year Ralph de Monthermer, an Esqr. of her late husband, who took the title of the Earl of Gloucester. Her clandestine marriage incensed the king, who seized her lands, and threw Monthermer into prison at Bristol, but he was afterwards reconciled,—restored her property, and summoned Monthermer to parliament as Earl of Gloucester and Hertford, who so sat until 1 Edward II. A. D. 1307, in which year young Gilbert, being of age, was admitted to his lands and honors.† This Earl, the last of that surname and family, married Matilda, daughter of John de Burgh, son and heir of Richard de Burgh, Earl of Ulster, by whom he had issue, a son, who died.—Gilbert being with Edward II. in Scotland, to raise the seige of Sterling Castle, was there slain, A. D. 1313, whom the Scots would gladly have saved for ransom, had they known him, but he had neglected to put on his coat of Arms over his

† Ralph Brookes's Peerage, 1622.

armour. Robert Bruce, caused his body to be sent to the king, at Berwick, demanding no reward. He was buried at Tewkesbury.§ His lands and estates were divided between his three sisters, Eleanor, Margaret, and Elizabeth, A. D. 1318,* and this part of the honor of Gloucester, together with the other manors and lordships in Dorsetshire, fell to the share of Elizabeth, who was married to William de Burgh, Earl of Ulster.† She died A. D. 1361, leaving a sole daughter and heiress, Elizabeth, who married Lionel of Antwerp, Duke of Clarence, third son of Edward III. He died at Venice, A. D. 1368, leaving Philippa, his sole daughter and heiress, who married Edmund Mortimer, Earl of March. He died at Cork, A. D. 1382, leaving his son Roger, his heir. Roger Mortimer was nominated by Richard II. as his successor, but on the king's dethronement, resigned his right to Henry V. who was descended from John of Gaunt, fourth son of Edward III. He was killed in Ireland, A. D. 1398, and Edmund, his heir, died without issue A. D. 1425, whereupon his property was

§ Ralph Brooke's Peerage, 1622.

* Eleanor married Hugh de le Spencer; Margaret, Peter Gaveston, and afterwards Hugh Audley, Earl of Gloucester.

† She married secondly, Theobald de Verdun; and thirdly, Roger Damory, by whom she had one daughter, Elizabeth, who married Lord Bardolph, and died A. D. 1361, without issue.

inherited by Anne, his sister, who was married to Richard, Earl of Cambridge, second son of Edmund Langley, Duke of York, "a marriage that proved a fertile source of troubles, which long afflicted the kingdom,"* for their son Richard Plantagenet, Duke of York, inherited his uncle Edmund Mortimer's claim to the throne, and became the chief of the faction of the White Rose, waging a deadly war against the house of Lancaster. He won the battle of St. Alban's against Henry VI. and was made by Parliament heir apparent, and Lord Protector, but was slain at the battle of Wakefield, A.D. 1460, and was first buried at Pomfret, afterwards at Fotheringay.§ He married Cicely, daughter of Ralph Neville, Earl of Westmorland, and had twelve children, of whom the second Edward, inherited the crown, and united the two rival houses of York and Lancaster.

Having now arrived at the period when this manor with its appendages became vested in the crown, we shall bring our sketch of its descent to a close, by a brief memoir of the ancestor of its present noble proprietor, to whom it was granted by James I.

* Richard, Earl of Cambridge, was beheaded at Southampton, A. D. 1415.—*Rapin.*

§ 14 Henry VI. (1436.) License was granted to Richard, Duke of York, to have the manors of Cranborne, Pimperne, Tarrant-Gunville, Weymouth, Wyke, Portland, Wareham, Steple, and Crick.—*Hutchins.*

Sir Robert Cecil, was the second son of William Cecil, Lord Burleigh, and was born about A. D. 1550. He was created by James, A. D. 1603, Baron Essenden; in 1604, Viscount Cranborne, (being the first of that degree that ever used a coronet,) and in 1605, Earl of Salisbury, and a Knight of the Garter. He inherited the political sagacity of his father the great Lord Burleigh, and succeeded to his places and favor at court. Living in times when Elizabeth had need of the ablest persons, and being such a one himself, she employed him in negotiations and affairs of the highest consequence. In 1596 he was made second Secretary of state with Sir Francis Walsingham, after whose decease he was continued principal as long as he lived. He was in that office a craftsman in foreign intelligence, by which means he discovered enemies abroad, and private conspiracies at home. For this the Queen highly valued him, and the papists hated him. In 1597 he was made chancellor of the Duchy of Lancaster, and was also Lord Privy Seal. In 1598, he was one of the commissioners sent into France to negotiate peace between that crown and Spain. In 1599 he succeeded his late father as master of the Wards, also as Prime Minister, and from that time the public affairs were completely under his wisdom and controul, which he conducted with great capacity and integrity. Still "he adored the rising Sun," and kept up a correspondence with her successor, James, who took him into favor, and continued him in the office of prime minister. In 1608, he succeeded the Earl of Dorset, in the office of Lord High Treasurer. He was a great patron of art and manufactures. He advised the institution of the order of Baronets, by which project, he raised £200,000. for the service of the State. He died at Marlborough on his road to London, from Bath, where he had been to recover his health, *May* 24*th.*, 1612, and was buried at Hatfield, Herts.* "For his person, he was not much beholden to nature, though somewhat for his face, which was the best part of his outside; for his inside it may be said, that he was his father's own son, and a pregnant precedent in all his discipline of State. He was a courtier from the cradle,—though his little crooked person could not promise very great supportation, yet it carried thereon a head and a headpiece of vast content." †

* Biog. Britan.

† Harleian Miscellany.

Castle Hill.

Half a mile south of the Town there is an antient earthwork or entrenchment, called Castle Hill, constructed at the western extremity of a ridge of land, whose terminal escarpment has been rounded off and heightened so as to form a high mound, which, taken in connexion with the other parts of the earthwork, presents a great similarity to the Keep of antient Castles, and it is not improbable that some kind of superstructure may have been raised upon it, though no traces of a foundation have ever been discovered. A very deep fosse and rampart, enclosing an area about forty-five yards long, and fifteen broad, are continued around behind the mound or Keep, in a semicircular form, but do not abut upon it, which stands therefore isolated as it were from the rest of the work. On the south side the rampart is broken to admit of an entrance into the area, inner court, or ballium, being rounded off on the one side, and formed into a separate mound on the other, flanking the entrance, which is approached by a narrow causeway thrown across the fosse. Within the precincts of the Castle, is a small spot of swampy ground, which is called the well. The soil consists of a stratum of Shingle, the pebbles composing it being frequently found agglutinated together in large masses, by the agency of water impregnated with the oxyde of Iron. No relics of Antiquity are remembered to have been found here. In the adjoining field are traces of earthworks of a remote period, and a low tumulus, from which were obtained small fragments of coarse pottery, and bits of charcoal; hence we infer that this elevated spot, which commands an extensive and beautiful panoramic view, bounded on the East and South by the New Forest, the Isle of Wight, and the Purbeck Hills; and on the West, by the Wilts and Dorset range of hills, and Cranborne Chase, and having the hill-camps of Badbury, Chalbury, and Penbury,* as some of the most prominent features in the landscape, we infer that this spot so well adapted, as a station for security, or defence, was originally occupied by a branch of that Celtic Colony, which has left such numerous and indisputable evidences of its existence, in the tumuli and earthworks on the adjacent Downs.§ The work in question bears no resemblance in its present state, to such as are admitted by competent authority, to be of Celtic construction; but there is reason to suppose that, in its original plan, it consisted merely of a very strong single cir-

* See note *s* in App. § See note *t* in App.

cular entrenchment, and that its present form has resulted from the alterations and additions effected in a subsequent age. It cannot with any probability be referred to the Roman æra of this country; nor may we more reasonably attribute it to the Danes, who visited our coast as a marauding people, and made no permanent settlements in the interior of this part of the Island; we must therefore assign it to the Saxon or the Norman period of our history,* and as the form of the entrenchment undoubtedly resembles much the ground plan of the Castles of the latter people, being at the same time of much ruder construction, we are of opinion that it must be referred to a date antecedent to them; and that, in fact, it was the stronghold, fortress, or castle, of the Saxon chieftains who held the seignory of Cranborne, and the sovereignty of the surrounding country.

The Manor House.

This is an ancient building which stands conspicuously a little west of the church. In old records, it is styled "the Court," for it was the head lodge of the chase, wherein were held the chase-courts, as well as the court Leet and court Baron.† In other old

* See note *v* in App. † See note *w* in App.

records "the Castle" is mentioned, referring in all probability to a more ancient embattled building, that stood on the same site. The antiquity of the present house has no recorded date, we must therefore supply the want of positive testimony, by an appeal to the style of its architecture. At a glance we perceive that no unity of design embraced the entire structure, whence we infer that all its parts are not of equal age, and on nearer inspection we find their respective characters so distinctly marked, as to leave no doubt in the mind on the question of their relative antiquity. The main part of the building is characterized by a broad plain fraçade to the north, with embattled parapet; lofty, angular, grouped chimnies; high, broad mullioned windows; on the south or principal front, a square tower at either end, rising to about the height of the roof; the doorways crowned with the depressed or Tudor arch,—we do not hesitate to assign to this part the date of Henry the eight's reign; whereas the arcaded stone porches, that of the north entrance highly ornamented with a curious intermixture of Italian and Gothic devices, and surmounted by the arms of the first Earl of Salisbury; and that of the south entrance, rude and less ornamented, but surmounted by emblematic figures of Justice and Mercy, in circular niches,—these porches, and the pilasters which decorate the massy buttresses of the north front, evidently denote the æra of James I. when an incongruous style of architecture arising from the transition from the Gothic to the Italian, very generally prevailed. Again, the west wing bears the unequivocal stamp of a still later period, which is probably that of the reign of Charles I.* We will now ascend the flight of steps from the garden, (which appears to be an enclosure of later date than the house,) to the terrace, remarking the remains of a handsome balustrade; then by a shorter flight of steps enter the north porch, and pass on into the interior of the house itself. The interior of the body of the building, is divided into two unequal parts, by a very thick party wall, extending from the basement to the roof; on the one side are, the entrance hall, and the great hall, or court of Judicature, on the ground floor, together with the state apartments in the story above, which are reached by the grand staircase, constructed in the western Tower; on the other side are the apartments which were appropriated to the residence of the Major Domo, who also occupied the eastern Tower; and underneath them on the basement story, are vaulted rooms, one of which

* The Vanes which belonged to this wing, and now in the lumber-room, are dated 1647.

was the cellar, and the other the prison or dungeon. A few years ago, ere yet the genius of modern improvement, that has no sympathy with the old and the romantic, had waved over it his transforming wand, the ringbolts to which the prisoners' chains were wont to be locked, were still seen festering in the walls, but the metamorphosis is complete,—the dungeon is now converted into a larder. It is said that a subterranean passage extends from hence in a direction towards the church. The wall, before alluded to, is unquestionably the most ancient part of the house, and was in all likelihood, the extreme end of a building that existed antecedently to the present. The proof of its superior antiquity is derived from the circumstance of there being a circular stone staircase, partly formed within the thickness of the wall, and partly projecting exteriorly, ascending from basement to battlement, in which the pointed Gothic arch may be recognized, the only instance of its occurrence throughout the whole structure, which is, on the other hand, strongly characterized by the depressed or Tudor arch, seen in all its doorways and fire-places,—a fashion of much later introduction. The staircase in question was a medium of communication between the two divisions of the house, afforded a direct access to the vaults beneath, and to the rooms above; and was the way by which the prisoners were conducted from the dungeon, to the Hall of Justice at the time of trial, passing into the entrance hall by a doorway, now walled up and concealed by a modern partition. The great hall is a very lofty and spacious room thirty-two by twenty-four feet, and eighteen feet high; we remark in it the great height of the south window; the staircase ascending to the gallery over the entrance hall, which was originally open towards the great hall, and used as an orchestra on festive occasions; over the yawning hearth, a rusty array of halberts, antique swords, and armour, memorials of the pride and pomp, and circumstance of bye-gone days; leaving this room, and ascending by the grand staircase, we are shown the state chamber, hung around with faded arras, and containing the state bed with its embroidered curtains, whereon the head of Royalty hath many a time and oft been pillowed,—from hence we ascend and wander amongst a succession of noble apartments, but all dreary and tenantless now, and offering no attraction to arrest the stranger's gaze. Descending to the basement story, we visit that *sine quâ non* of an English mansion, the kitchen, which is a large crypt-like room, and its groined ceiling begrimed with the smoke of centuries, testifies most eloquently, to the good service rendered here to the gastronomic propensity of men of the "good old times." So much for the interior, and now pass we to its exterior, and notice the beautiful field spread out before the north front, called the Court-close, (clausum curiæ) down the middle of which a fine avenue of ash trees, formerly stretched almost up to the great gates of the front court or garden.—It was destroyed about sixty years ago. A park of one-hundred and fifty acres anciently surrounded the mansion, the bounds of which may be distinctly traced. We notice also, the fish-pond, the terraced walks, the effaced parterre, in front of the west wing, all indisputable evidences of original grandeur and importance; and the court-yard enclosing the south front, the entrance to it being through a spacious arched gateway, flanked on each side by an angularly-set tower, or porter's lodge.

The Lords of the manor never made Cranborne, their place of permanent residence, having possessed large estates, and more important castles in other parts of the kingdom,* still it is likely that they did reside here occasionally for the enjoyment of the chase. We have a record of the visits of king John to Cranborne,† who then held the manor in right of his wife Isabella. This restless and erratic monarch visited Cran-

* The castles of Cardiff, Dover, Canterbury, Marlborough, Holme near Tewkesbury, and Bristol, were the chief residences of the Earls of Gloucester.—*Seyer.*

† Itinerary of king John,—See note *x* in App.

borne fourteen times during his reign, *viz.*, in 1200, *Dec.* 10*th.*, *April* 15*th.*,—1205, *Jan.* 9*th.*, *Aug.* 17*th.*,—1206, *April* 16*th.*, 17*th.*, *May* 16*th.*, 1207, *Jan.* 20*th.*, *March* 27*th.*, 28*th.*, *Sept.*, 1*st.*, 3*rd.*,—1208, *Nov.*, 6*th.*,—1213, *July* 6*th.*, 8*th.*, 16*th.*, *Aug.*, 10*th.* We may suppose that he sometimes came for the purpose of hunting in the chase, although it is said that he had a hunting-seat at Tollard-Royal, in Wilts. There can be no doubt of the present house having been the honored receptacle of Royalty, on hunting excursions, at a later period.* The following narrative may be relied on.—

"A. D. 1607, the 24*th.*, day of *Aug.*, our kinge James was in Mr. Butler's walke, and roused the Buck, and killed him in Vernedich, in Sir Walter Vahen's walke, and from thence came to Mr Howles' walke and hunted ther, and killed a Buck under hanging Copes, and sometime after that came to our Mrs. Carren's and ther dined, and after dinner he tok his choch and came to the Quene's Majestie, at Tarante."§

"A. D. 1609, the 17*th.*, day of *Aug.*, our kinge James came to Cranborne, in the afternone, betwene the houres of five and six of the Clock, and so rested the night. The next day being the 18*th*, of *Aug.*, he came

* Rymer's Fædera.—*Hutchins.*

§ Which Tarrant?

into our chase, and hunted in Mr. Howles' walk, and killed a Buck, and in Mr. Rangers' walk, and killed a Buck, and so returned to Cranburne to the courte there, and the 19*th.*, day he did come into William Morgayne's walk, and ther he killed to (two) Bucks, and the same day he killed one in Mr. Howles' walk, and the hunting being ended he took his choch, (coach) and went to the Quene's majestie at the court at Tarante."*

"In our days Cranborne gave the honourable title of Viscount unto Robert Cecil, whose son William nowe enjoyes his honours and this place, where he hath a convenient house at which the king as often as he comes his western progresse, resides some days to take his pleasure of hunting both in the Park and Chase.† It was probably on similar occasions that the following circumstance occured."—

A. D. 1623, *Aug.*, 10*th.*, at Cranborne, the king dated thence three billets to Madrid, one to his "sweete boyes" jointly, another to the prince alone, and the third to the Marquess alone, wishing his son to return either with or without the Infanta, he writes, "the necessitie of my affairs enforcith me to tell you

* These memorandums are copied from the original M.S. on the fly leaf of a "breeches" Bible, purchased at Mr. Coker's sale at Woodcutts, and now in possession of the Rev. Edward Butt, of Wimborne, who politely obliged me with a copy.

† Coker's Survey of Dorsetshire. Blagden Park is meant.

that ye must præferre the obedience of a Father to the love ye carrie to a mistresse."—*Aug.*, 19*th.*, Sir John Bathe, knighted there.

A. D. 1621, *Aug.*, 11*th.*, James I. went from Salisbury to Cranborne, the seat of Sir. William Cecil, second Earl of Salisbury, and on the 14*th.*, Sir Hercules Pawlett, there received the honor of knighthood."* 8 Charles I. 1633, in a bill filed in the Exchequer to restrain John Cole, for hunting and killing Deer in Witchampton, it was stated "the king Charles I. when he repaired to Cranborne Chase, did chiefly delight to hunt in the said chase or walk (Chettered) as the late king James had done." Of the Chase Court which was formerly held here, we shall speak in a future page. At the Court Leet, and Court Baron, the following officers were annually appointed; *viz.* two high Bailiffs, two assizers of bread and tasters of ale,‡ two surveyors of hearths,|| two searchers, sealers and registrars of leather,† the three latter are now merely nominal appointments, retained for custom sake. In the time of Henry III. Richard, son of Alured de Wake, of the fee of the abbot of Tewkesbury, in the county of Dorset, was carried to

* Nichola' Progresses of James I. vol. 3. p. 491. from Harleian Miscellany 6987, and Camdens' Annals.

‡ See note *y* in App. || See note *z* in App.

† See note *a a* in App.

the Earl of Gloucester, and hanged, the Abbot's bailiffs, being ignorant of their privileges.¶— This transaction appears to have excited the Abbot's ire, for A. D. 1294, (34 Henry III.) Robert, Abbot of Tewkesbury, at a court held at Monkton, tried John Milksop, of Cranborne, for theft, being taken on the Abbot's land : Richard de Clare, Earl of Gloucester, denied the Abbot's right and insisted on the criminal's being tried at his Court at Cranborne, but he was condemned by the Abbot and executed, the unhappy victim of jealousy between the Lay and Ecclesiastical potentate.* In the time of Edward I. Gilbert, Earl of Gloucester, claimed the following liberties and franchises in his hundred and manor Cranborne, *viz.* return of writs, view of frankpledge, waifs, a gallows, pillory and tumbrel, pleas of blood, hue and cry, the trial of thieves, the assize of bread and beer, and pleas of distress.§

12 Elizabeth, (1570,) the Queen granted to the Earl of Pembroke, the office of head Seneschal of the manor of Cranborne, for which he was to receive 60*s.* 8*d.* per annum ; the office of bailiff of the manor and hundred, for which he was to receive 60*s.* per annum ; and the office of bailiff and harvester (messor) of Cranborne, for which he was to receive 22*s.* 5¾*d.* per annum.

¶ Hutchins. * Hutchins. § See note *bb* in App.

Of the Hamlets, Belonging to Cranborne.

The following Hamlets and Manors belonging to Cranborne, *viz.* ALDERHOLT, BLAGDEN, BOVERIDGE, CRENDALL AND DAGGINS, HOLWELL, MONKTON AND VERWOOD.

Alderholt.

Is a hamlet, manor, and tything, in the in-hundred, four miles east of Cranborne. It is situated in the most extensive ancient walk of the chase, which included all the country eastward, from the inner bounds, to the river Avon, and was called Alderholt walk. There was a Park here. A. D. 1315, 8 Edward II. Gilbert de Clare, held of the king in chief, the manor of Cranborne, and there were in the Park of Alderholt within the ditch, by estimation one-hundred and fifty-four acres.—It was disparked, and the deer destroyed, in the time of Henry VIII. but the term "Park" is still retained, and applied to the lands, which were enclosed, 8 James I. and granted to Anthony Gooche. The property has been lately purchased by J. M. Key Esqr. who resides in the mansion built on the Estate by the late George Reade Esq. St. Clements' chapel, which stood in Alderholt, was demolished about the year 1690.

Blagden.

A Manor, tything in Upwimborn hundred, and farm, two miles north of Cranborne; bounded on the north by the county of Wilts; the boundary being formed by an ancient earth-work, consisting of a very high and steep vallum, and fosse, called Bockerly ditch, which immerges from the chase woods, near Woodyatts Inn, is continued in a bold and sinuous course for two miles across an open down, and terminates on Blagden furze-hill. It is undoubtedly a work of very early construction, evidence being afforded of a date anterior to the formation of the Roman road or Ikenild-street, in the fact of its continuity having been broken, to give passage to the latter, in this part of its progress between Sorbiodunum, or Old Sarum, and the next station on its line, Vindogladia, which has been thought by eminent antiquarians, with great appearance of truth, to have been situated about four miles south, on Gussage Cowdown Bockerly ditch, as it is vulgarly called, is one of those protective territorial bulwarks, supposed to have been thrown up by the Belgæ, in the progress of their victorious invasions, of which the first is recorded to have taken place about three-hundred and fifty years before the Christian æra.* If we may be allowed to indulge in an etymological hypothesis, we would suggest, that the syllable "Bock" is a corruption of the word "Balc" which in the Erse language signifies "strong, mighty,"† and is synonimous with "Belg," the name applied to this Celto-Germanic nation, and is therefore indicative of the people by whom the work in question was constructed.§ Here was formerly a Park. A. D. 1321, 14 Edward II. Roger Damory, had liberty granted him to make a Park of his wood at Blakedon, within the chase of Cranborne, and it contained five-hundred acres. It is frequently mentioned in records relating to the chase. 12 Elizabeth, the Earl of Pembroke, had an allowance of 60*s*. 10*d*. per annum, for executing the office of keeper of this Park, and 10*s*. per annum, to be given for twelve cart loads of hay,

* A. M. 3650. Richard of Cirencester.

† "The genuine History of the Britons asserted," 1783. *Whitaker.*

§ It is said that a line drawn thirty miles inland, from the Dorset coast, northward, would intersect seven of these boundary ditches or bulwarks, as if the invaders won their way gradually and with difficulty.

bought for the sustenance of the deer. It was disparked about the year 1570.‡ The manor belongs to Richard Brouncker Esq.

Boveridge.

A Hamlet, manor, and tything in Upwimborne Hundred, one mile and a half north-east of Cranborne. In Domesday book, the church of Cranborne held Bovehric. Brictric held it in the reign of Edward the Confessor. It consisted of seven carucates worth 100*s.*—19 Henry VII. 1504, the free-warren of this manor was granted to the Abbot of Tewkesbury. 7 Edward VI. 1553, this manor belonging to Tewkesbury Abbey, was granted to William Earl of Pembroke. 2 and 3 Philip and Mary, it was held by Thomas Gardiner, William and Michael Hawtre, gents, who had license to alienate it to Giles and John Hooper, and the heirs of John, value £20. 5*s.* 3*d.* 14 Elibabeth, it was held by John Hooper, at his death. 16 Elizabeth, his son John, had living of his lands. Sir Edward Hooper, knight, obt. 1671, by will ordered his body to be buried at Cranborne, with his ancestors, and devises to Edward Hooper, of Hurn Court, Hants,

‡ See evidence in the cause, Salisbury v. Arundel, in App.

and his heirs, the manors of Boveridge, Eastworth, Blagden Park, Cranborne Farm, parcel of the manor of Cranborne, and lands there &c. He died A. D. 1750, and his Estates came to his son Edward Hooper, a commissioner of Customs, who sold the manors of Boveridge, Blagden, and Eastworth, to Henry Brouncker Esqr. about the year 1785, and afterwards retired to Hurn Court, where he died, a bachelor, at a very advanced age. He was the last male descendant of this ancient family, and was grandson of the third Earl of Shaftesbury, by Lady Dorothy Ashley, who married the Rev Edward Hooper, his father, then rector of Wimborne St. Giles.* The family mansion which appears to have been of the Elizebethan style, was pulled down some years ago, and an elegant modern mansion has been completed by Richard Brouncker Esqr. the present proprietor, who has also lately rebuilt the chapel and almshouse, on more commodious sites. This gentleman is the representative of an ancient and honorable family, who formerly possessed the Stoke property in Wiltshire, and is the lineal descendant of Henry Brouncker, knight, Lord President of the Province of Ulster, whose younger brother was created a Viscount by Charles II. and was the first President of the Royal Society on its incorporation. He was

* See note *c c* in App.

an eminent mathematician, and filled important offices in the State,—died in 1684,—The title is extinct.

Crendall and Daggens.

Small hamlets two miles east of Cranborne, where a strong blue clay is found, from which a great quantity of coarse earthen-ware is manufactured. Geologically considered, this useful material is a member of the plastic clay formation, which belongs to the Eocene or earliest period of the tertiary strata. Fossils are never found in it. Cranborne itself is situated on the chalk, near to its junction with the plastic clay, and probably on the shore of the ancient tertiary sea, which filled the Hampshire basin (as it is called,) and deposited the strata of this formation. Banks of sand and shingle are seen at Boveridge, Burwood, Castle Hill, and at other spots in the neighbourhood, marking the line of the ancient sea beach. Adjacent to the limits of the chalk, a bed of fossil oyster shells may be noticed in several places, throughout a line of some miles in length; and in some spots, where the green marl in which the shells are imbedded overlies the chalk, this has the appearance of having been drilled or perforated to the depth of several inches, which was no doubt effected by the agency of certain species of marine lithodomous mollusca. Clefts and cavities in the chalk, filled with sand and gravel may also be noticed, denoting the action of aqueous currents, as well as the gigantic throes of subterranean convulsion. The potteries employ one hundred men and ten boys.*—8 Jac I. two tenements called Daggens, and Prior's coppice, were granted to Antony Auchier. These hamlets now belong to the Marquess of Salisbury.

Hollwell.

A Manor, hamlet, and tything in Cranborne hundred, one mile east of Cranborne, it was included in the same grants as the manor of Cranborne; in the time of Elizabeth it belonged to the family of Molyneux: latterly, for many years, it was in the possession of the family of Bartlett, who resided here. It was sold by Thomas Bartlett Esq., of Wareham, to J. S. W. S. Erle Drax Esq., of Charborough Park, to whom it now belongs.

The lower mill at Hollwell is in the tything of West-worth, a farm in the parish of Edmonsham, and liberty of Bindon Abbey.

* Okeden's Report.

Hawis, Countess of Gloucester, gave to this abbey the mill of Cranborne, which Edmerus held with a moor. Richard Camerarius, or the chamberlain, gave also the whole land of Lindhull, from the east part of the water of Cranborne with a moor.†

Monkton Upwimborne.

A Hamlet, manor, and tything of its own hundred, two miles west of Cranborne. It is a small hundred, comprising the tythings of Chettle, Tarrant Monkton, Boveridge, Blagden, Verwood, Monkton Upwimborne, and lands in the parish of Wimborne Minster; all of which belonged to the abbey of Tewkesbury, and were united in a hundred, for the purpose of exempting the Abbot's tenants from suit and service at the court of the Earl of Gloucester, at Cranborne. Monkton anciently belonged to the Priory of Cranborne. In Domesday book it is stated, that the church of Cranborne holds Wimborne, (*i. e.* Monkton) &c. 20 Edward III. 1347, Hugh de Mohaunt held half a fee in Upwimborne of Lady de Burgh. The King held the fourth part of a fee which formerly belonged to John Tranchesoil, by forfeiture of John Matravers. 8 Henry IV. 1407, John

† Where is Lindhull ?

Plecy held lands here of Thomas Wake and Elizabeth his wife. 15 Henry VIII.—the Abbot and Convent of Tewkesbury demised to John Chafer, and to John and Simon his sons, for the term of his life and the survivor, the farm of the site of the manor of Upwimborne, with all houses, lands, meadows, feedings, and demesne pasture, and all estrays,* and all underwood growing in Oakley Wood, parcel of the said manor, and all oaks within the said Woods, and they should diligently keep the said Woods, and cause hedges to be made about every coppice within the said Wood, for the preservation of every coppice, at their own proper cost. They should not sell any oak without leave of the Lord, nor cut any coppice until sufficiently grown; they should have timber for repairs and fuel, and at their own cost should exonerate and acquit the Lord from all charges to the Ranger of the Chase of Cranborne, and all other things, by reason of the wood and underwood above mentioned. 37 Henry VIII. the manor and capital messuage of Upwimborne, and Oakley wood in Cranborne, parcel of the abbey of Tewkesbury were granted to Thomas Macham and his heirs for £321 14*s.* 2*d.* value £17 4*s.* 6*d.* who, 4

* Cattle found strawing within a Lordship and not claimed within a year and a day, after due proclamation, become forfeited to the Lord.

Edward VI. had license to alienate to John Hawles, Margaret his wife, and the heirs of John. It sometime subsequently, belonged to Humphrey Sturt Esq., of Critchell, by whom it was exchanged for the manor of Long Critchell, with the Earl of Shaftesbury.

Here was formerly one of the chapels belonging to Cranborne, demolished in 1742. A. D. 1550, the commissioners returned, in the chapel of Upwimborne, a chalice, a pair of vestments, a cope, and two bells in the tower. The family of Hawles was of great respectability. John, Son of Thomas Hawles, of Salisbury, resided here, who was an eminent lawyer, and in 1695 made solicitor general. He was one of the managers of Dr. Sacheverel's trial, and died in 1716. He published "remarks on the trial of Edward Fitz-Harris," 1690, and a reply to a pamphlet, called "the Magistracy and Government vindicated," 1689.

A bourne, or stream, dignified with the title of river

——" Cleere Allen in her race,
Which calmlie cometh downe from her deere mother chase
Of Cranburn that is call'd,"*——

rises here, and flows into the Stour at Wimborne Minster. The original name of this stream, would seem to have been Vin or Win, derived from the celtic word Gwent or Went,

* Drayton's Polyolbion.

Gwynne, Wynne, Win or Vin; signifying fair, white—*as winter,* the white season.

The ancient British town Vindogladia, or Ventogladia, (from Gwent or Vin, and Gladh, a vale or river,) was situated on the high ground about two miles south-west of Monkton, where there are many extensive earthworks † remaining; but we regret to add, that agriculture, the ruthless foe of antiquity, has seized upon the site of this remarkable, and classical remain; and each succeeding year, as it sees the golden grain waving over its banks, will more and more obliterate the record of its ancient state; so that the future antiquary will find a difficulty, in decyphering the language stamped on the treacherous soil, "hic fuit Ilium."

Verwood or Fairwood.

A Hamlet and tything in Upwimborne hundred, four miles east of Cranborne, consisting of two small manors, which probably belonged to the priory of Cranborne, and afterwards to the abbey of Tewkesbury. One of these manors called Cray's Farm, belongs to W. Fryer Esq. and the other called Potterne, anciently Wimborn Potterne, to Lady Bingham, the relict of General Sir George Bingham. The tithes

† See note on Vindogladia in Appendix.

of these manors were purchased by — Ford Esq. of the Marquess of Salisbury. The old chapel of Verwood was in ruins in 1666; a new one has been erected by subscription, on land given by W. Fryer Esq., endowed by the Marquess of Salisbury, and consecrated in 1829, where Divine Service is regularly performed by the Vicar of Cranborne, or his Curate, whose stipend chiefly depends on the bounty of the neighbouring gentry.

Verwood is situated on the border of an extensive tract of heathy land, of wild and desolate aspect. On that part of it belonging to the manor of Boveridge, is a spot surrounded by very irregular, hilly ground, called "Wild church bottom"—and the highest eminences around, have singular names attached to them, as "Mount Ararat, Stephen's Castle," &c. We cannot believe that a Christian Sanctuary ever reared its head on this lonely spot, but, if the worship of a people be traditionally recorded in the name, we would suppose that people to have been of a colony, the original inhabitants of this Country, and this spot, the site of a Druidical temple or altar. There is a quarry of sandstone there. That this bleak region was colonized by the ancient British population, we have no doubt, for they have left a tumulus, or barrow, on almost every hill: several of them have been opened; in one was found an urn of the rudest material and manufacture, and of very large size, inverted, filled with fragments of human bones, and covered by a large triangular slab of sandstone: in another were found three spear or arrow heads, beautifully shaped of flint. To some of these tumuli, the name of "Robin Hood's butts" is applied; probably, from the circumstance of their having been made the "butt" or mark, when archery was universally practised, and a matter of legislative enactment. We must also notice a large block of sandstone, called the "Wur-stone," (wur, being the provincial pronunciation of Hore or Hoar, boundary,) which was an ancient boundary stone.* The peasantry were accustomed to regard it with a sort of superstitious reverence, and told long tales about the impossibility of removing it; to which we may attribute the fact of its preservation for a long series of years. We therefore regret that some impious hand† has at length dissolved the spell, and buried the old landmark in its native earth,—"its place knoweth it no more." In a record of 8 Edward I. 1280, concerning the bounds of Cranborne Chase, "le Horestone, near the road leading to the great bridge of Ringwood," is

* See note on Hoar-stones in App.

† See Deut. c. XXVII. v. xvii.

set down as one of the points of boundary in this neighbourhood. What was it, and where, if not this stone?

Eastworth.

Is a farm and manor, adjoining Verwood, and the manor and farm called West-worth, which is in the parish of Edmonsham, and liberty of Bindon abbey. Both these manors seem to have been anciently comprehended under one title, Horsych, or Horsyth, now, Worth, or Wur, and belonged to the Newburgh family. Roger Newburgh, founded Bindon abbey, A. D. 1172. A. D. 1332, Robert Newburgh, had license to erect an oratory in his manor at Horsyth, in Cranborne parish.*—36 Henry VIII. 1521, certain lands and tenements in Worth, *alias* East-worth, were granted to John Bartlett, *alias* Hancock, and Robert Bartlett, and it is certified that, "Eastworth doth lye nigh none of the kyng's Majestie's houses, reserved by a keeper, and from his Highness' chase of Cranborne four miles."† 4 Edward VI. 1551, a tenement for the maintenance of a Camp here was granted to William Place.‡

* Hutchins' confounds these two manors, and places Eastworth in Ensham Parish.

† Record in the Augmentation office. ‡ Hutchins.

The manor belonged to the Hoopers, of Boveridge, and now to Richard Brouncker Esqr. whose uncle purchased it of Edward Hooper Esqr., of Hurn Court, Hants.

On the Origin and Progress of
Hunting in Britain, from the
Earliest Period to the
Reign of King John.

The universality of the law of nature that compels the isolated barbarian to depend upon his own resources for the preservation of his existence, is so obvious, that it might be justly deemed superfluous to adduce any argument in support of the opinion, that the original inhabitants of Britain applied themselves to the practice of hunting. It may not, however, be uninteresting just to glance at the proofs by which the opinion may be coroborated. And in the first place, we appeal to the examination of those ancient places of sepulture, the tumuli or barrows, which are so plentifully scattered over the surface of our Dorset and Wiltshire Downs. The spade of the antiquary has there revealed to us the secret things which the earth's mantle had enshrouded for twenty centuries or more,—the fragile Urn, containing a chieftain's ashes, with the remains of his stone, bronze, and iron weapons or implements, and the bones of various animals, particularly the fragments of the antlers of a large species of Deer, then a native of this land, which may be conjectured to have been deposited as sacrificial offerings, or as trophies of the skill and valour of the departed hero. To this ancient mode of interment the poet Ossian, beautifully alludes; and whether or not his poems be regarded as an authentic record of the habits and manners of the Celtic race, at any rate, the author is true to the analogy of savage life, as invariably representing his heroes as renowned hunters, "Ossian!" says the dying Oscar, "carry me to my hills! raise the stones of my renown! place the horn of a Deer, place my sword by my side.! The torrent hereafter may raise the earth, the hunter may find the steel, and say, this has been Oscar's sword, the pride of former years."*—About eighteen centuries have elapsed since the dawn of history first broke upon the dark and benighted shores of Britain; beneath its dim and distant light we proceed to gather the second series of our proofs. Cæsar, Strabo, Diodorus Siculus, and other writers of this æra, relate that, the ancient Britons lived, chiefly on animal food; were clothed in the skins of wild beasts; possessed a fine breed of dogs much esteemed on the Continent for their excellent hunting qualities; that, the Phœnicians traded with them for skins and

* Temora, Book I.

dogs for the chase; whence we infer that the Britons were well skilled in the practice of hunting, and followed it too on commercial principles. At this period, the soil of Britain was comparatively waste and uncultivated; its surface was darkened with extensive forests, swarming with wolves, boars, and foxes, whose predatory incursions on the flocks of sheep and herds of cattle, rendered this practice a necessary measure of security and protection. At a subsequent period, when under the Roman government, the cultivation of the soil was taught and encouraged, an exterminating warfare was hotly waged against those wild and ferocious denizens of the land, who were thus robbed of their native domains, and driven to take refuge in more limited and impracticable fastnesses. Hence the origin of separate tracts of woodland, which were afterwards denominated forests. As our enquiry proceeds we shall find, that this which was originally a result of necessity, in after times became converted into evil and formed the basis of a monstrous system of tyranny. It was the policy of the Roman government in Britain, to endeavour to reconcile the subjugated inhabitants to their yoke, by yielding to their tempers and prejudices and national habits, from the fear of endangering the stability of its conquest, by provoking a spirit of insubordination and resistance. This fact, coupled with the known principle of the Roman law, that every subject should enjoy an equal right to such things as nature had made a common property, satisfactorily explains the circumstance, that the Roman power laid no restriction on the killing of wild animals. The Britons were permitted to enjoy the undisputed license of hunting in their forest-lands, and were probably encouraged by the example of their civilizing conquerors.* This privilege however was soon taken from them, when the ruthless Saxon made himself master of their Country. Retaining more of savage nature in his rough and indomitable disposition, than the civilized Roman, he was accustomed to regard hunting, as an indispensable branch of education. In the chase he learned, like the Greek, (as Xenophon informs us) to use his weapons with dexterity: became habituated to deeds of daring courage; and tempered to the endurance of toil, fatigue, and privation, and thus was initiated to bear his part in conflicts of a sterner warfare. To this educational system, we may in some measure attribute the notable valour displayed in the battle field by the great Alfred; who as his historian Asser

* Roman mosaic pavements have been discovered in several parts of England, having pictorial representations of subjects pertaining to the Chase. At East Coker in Dorsetshire, one was discovered a few years ago, in which the figures of hounds pursuing Deer were beautifully depicted.

relates, excelled all others before he was twelve years old, in skill and success as a hunter. It were indeed an error to deny that the prevailing custom of hunting, was productive of any advantages and beneficial results; but alas! how lamentably neutralized they were by the ferocity of disposition, the barbarous state of society, and all the savage cruelties engendered in its train! Thus, was the poor broken spirited Briton debarred from the enjoyment of his ancient rights, and robbed of his patrimony by the implacable Saxon, who vested the forest-lands in himself, making them the sole prerogative of the crown, restricting the amusement of hunting to the privileged orders, and protecting them by the most arbitrary laws and sanguinary punishments. The law of Canute granted at Winchester A. D. 1016, which is the earliest on record relating to hunting in this country, gives us an insight into many curious particulars.—He appointed three orders of officers to superintend the affairs of the Forests, whose duties were somewhat analagous to those of verderers, regarders, and foresters as now constituted. He abolished the Ordalian law,* excepting in extraordinary cases. He commanded that all offences should be punished according to their degree, and the rank of the offender. Hunting or killing Deer, especially

* See note *d d* in App.

the Stag, which was deemed a "royal beast," subjected the offenders to heavy fines and imprisonment. Slaves if thus offending, were condemned to be flayed alive, outlawed or punished with death. Freemen were allowed to hunt and kill game, and to cut wood on their own land; but were enjoined not to make a Chase of their own, nor to trespass on the King's. Greyhounds were prohibited unless they were hamstrung,† and if they approached within ten miles of the Forest, were subject to forfeiture and fine.—Such are the outlines of Canute's enactments, tempered, we may observe, with the principles of mercy and justice, though deeply tinctured still with the barbarous spirit of the times. We may learn from them the wrongs and sufferings of a former age. One grand feature this law presents, is the distinction therein drawn between royal property and private property, which must have insured it a hearty welcome from those who had been accustomed to see their rights and liberties invaded and trampled on, at the monarch's sovereign will and pleasure. And this just distinction continued to be respected during the

† Genuscissio, dividing the sinews in the ham, called also hocksing or hocksinewing. The same purpose was effected by cutting off the three claws of the forefoot, called lawing or expeditating, a term derived from the true *dog*-latin verb expeditor, to make lame. This latter plan was introduced in King Henry II. reign.

stout restoration of the Saxon monarchy under Edward the Confessor, who, says William of Malmesbury, "took the greatest delight in following a pack of hounds in pursuit of game, cheering them with his voice," and it appears he was not selfish in his pleasures, for he confirmed the statute which gave to every freeman the liberty of hunting on his own lands; requiring however, that every one should abstain from hunting in the King's lands on pain of death. With the accession of the Norman dynasty, revived the dormant spirit of tyrannical oppression, marking the Conqueror's reign as one of merciless severity towards his prostrate subjects. Of William it is said, that "he often blamed Canute for his overmuch gentlenesse unto those he had conquered, whose steps he meant not to tread:*" true to this heartless resolution we find him depopulating villages, razing the altars of religion, and rapaciously seizing on their sites to form one extensive tract of forest-ground,† whereby he obtained the merited title of "the father of wild beasts." Nor does it appear that he held the lives of his subjects in any greater respect than their property, for he punished offences committed against his forest with death, and tortures worse than death itself: so that it did seem a manifestation of retributive justice, when two of his

* Speed. † The New Forest.

sons and a nephew were killed in the act of enjoying their unhallowed pastime in the very scenes of this iniquitous spoliation. The custom of hunting had now exceeded all bounds of moderation and legitimate enjoyment: its prevalence and effects are thus described by John of Salisbury, a writer of the twelfth Century.— "In our time," says he, "hunting and hawking are esteemed the most honorable employments and most excellent virtues by our nobility, and they think it the height of their worldly felicity to spend the whole of their time in these diversions; accordingly they prepare for them with more solicitude, expense, and parade than they do for war; and they pursue the wild beasts with greater fury than they do the enemies of their country: by constantly following this way of of life, they lose much of their humanity, and become as savage nearly as the very brutes they hunt." From this period the sole right of pursuing and taking all beasts of chase, and such as were accounted game, was centered in the monarch, or such only as were authorized by him; and this on the principle of the feudal law, that the King is the ultimate proprietor of all the lands in the kingdom, they being held of him as the chief Lord. Of William's successors we are informed, that they "greatly multiplied and extended the range of forests, by afforesting the lands of Earls, Barons, Noblemen, and Gentlemen, which were any where near to or adjoining the royal forests."* "Husbandmen with their harmless flocks and herds were driven from their well-cultivated fields, their meadows, and their pastures, that wild beasts may range in them without interruption."† And eventually in John's reign, "the greatest part of the realm was become a forest, to the great grief and sorrow of the best sort of inhabitants of the land, for by reason that the boundage of the forest was then so great and the laws so sharp and cruel, it was almost impossible for any man that was dwelling or abiding within the bounds of the forest, to live without danger thereof."‡ Oppression and cruelty had now reached the acmé of endurance. There is a point of moral suffering to which human nature may be strained with comparative impunity; force it beyond that point, and the energy and elasticity of feeling, if not utterly crushed and broken, will recoil against the power that unnaturally trifles with its sensibilities. In this manner was Magna Charta wrung by a suffering people, from a despotic monarch, and fixed for ever as a barrier between the throne and their private rights and liberties. To one section of the great Charter of liberties termed the Charta de Foresta, or Charter of

* Manswood's forest laws. † John of Salisbury.

‡ Manswood.

the liberties of the Forest, we shall find reference made in the succeeding pages of our history of Cranborne Chase, we will therefore transcribe it here, and so bring these introductory remarks to a conclusion.

Charter of the Forests.

1. All Forests which King Henry our Grandfather afforested and made, shall be viewed by good and lawful men, and if he have made Forest of any other wood more than of his own demesne whereby the owner of the wood hath hurt, WE WILL that forthwith it be disforested. And if he have made Forest of no men's wood but his own, then WE WILL that it remain Forest still, saving the common herbage, and other things in the same Forest, to them who were before accustomed to have the same.

2. Men that dwell out of the Forest from henceforth shall not come before the justices of our Forest, by no common summons, unless they be impleaded there, or be sureties for some other that were attached for the Forest.

3. All woods which have been made Forest by King Richard our Uncle, or by

King John our Father,* unto our first coronation, shall be forthwith disforested, unless it be our demesne wood.

4. All Arch-bishops, Bishops, Abbots, Priors, Earls, Barons, Knights, and other our freeholders, who have their woods in Forests, shall have their woods as they had them at the time of the first coronation of King Henry our Grandfather, so that they shall be quit for evermore of all purprestures, wasts, and assarts,† made in those woods after that time until the beginning of the second year of our coronation. And those who from henceforth do make purprestures, wasts, and assarts in the same, without our special license, shall answer for the same.

5. Our Regarders‡ shall go through the Forest to make their regard as it hath been accustomed at the time of the first corona-

* The Charter bears date 9 Henry III. A.D. 1225, it having then received the Royal sanction after many ineffectual attempts on the part of the King to get it annulled. It was more fully confirmed, 34 Edward I. and again, 1 Edward III.

† Purpresture,—encroachment on the Forest, by building on enclosing land. Wast,—felling wood and timber without license. Assart,—Destroying woods and converting them to arable land.

‡ Regarders,—The duty of these officers was to enquire into all offences of the Forest, and to superintend all the other officers in the execution of their duties, to enroll and make presentments to the courts. The office was sometimes granted by the King in fee for life.

tion of King Henry our Grandfather, and none otherwise.

6. The enquiry or view for lawing of dogs being within our Forest, shall be made from henceforth when the regard is made, that is to say, every three years, and then it shall be done by the view and testimony of honest men, and not otherwise. And he whose dog is not then found expeditated shall be amerced, and shall pay for the same three shillings. And from henceforth no ox shall be taken for lawing of dogs. And such lawing shall be done by the assize commonly used, *i. e.* that three claws of the forefoot shall be cut off by the skin. But from henceforth such lawing of dogs shall not be done but in places where it hath been accustomed from the time of the first coronation of the aforesaid King Henry our Grandfather.

7. No Forester or Beadle,* from henceforth shall make Scot-ale,† or gather garb‡ or oats, or any corn, or lamb, or pig; nor shall

* Forester,—his duty was to preserve the vert, *i. e.* every thing that bears a green leaf and venison of the forest; to attack offenders and make presentments at the courts. There were Foresters in fee made by the King under the Great Seal, who paid rent for the office; and others held it for life only. Beadle,—an inferior officer, whose duty it was to attend on the service of the courts.

† Scot-ale,—the keeping an alehouse within the Forest by an officer of the same, to induce persons to spend their money for fear of his displeasure.

‡ Garb,—wheatsheaf.

make any gathering but by the sight, and upon the oath of the twelve Regarders when they shall make their Regard. So many Foresters shall be assigned to the keeping of the Forests, as reasonably shall seem sufficient for the keeping of the same.

8. No Swainmote* from henceforth shall be kept within our realm but thrice in the year. First, the 15*th.* day before Michaelmas,‡ when that our Gistakers¶ of our woods come together to take agistment|| in our demesne woods; and about the feast of St. Martin in winter, when that our Gistakers shall receive our pannage.† And to these two Swainmotes shall come our Foresters, Verderers,§ Gistakers, and none other by distress. The third Swainmote shall be kept in the beginning of the fifteen days before the feast of John the Bap-

* Swainmote,—a court of freeholders, consisting of the officers of the Forest presided over by the Verderer. It is intermediate between the court of attachments and the high court of the Justice in Eyre. It tried by Jury, and had the power to convict, but not to sentence.

‡ Holyrood day.

¶ Gistakers,—Agisters, officers appointed to take in cattle to feed in the Forest.

|| Agistment,—The money paid for pasturage.

† Pannage,—The money paid for feeding swine on mast.

§ Verderers,—judicial officers elected by writ by the county. Their duty, to keep and maintain the assize of the Forest, to view, receive, and enroll the attachments and presentments of all manner of offences. There are generally four in every Forest, who ought to be Esquires. The office is like that of Coroner, to hold inquisition on bodies of the Deer.

tist,|| when that our Gistakers do meet to fawn our deer. And at this Swainmote shall meet our Foresters, Verderers, and none other by distress. Moreover, every forty days through the year, our Foresters and Verderers shall meet to see the attachments of the Forest,* as well for green hugh,§ as for hunting, by the presentment of our Foresters, and before them attached. And the said Swinmote shall not be kept but within the counties in which the same have been used to be kept.

9. Every freeman may take agistment in his own wood within our Forest at his pleasure, and shall take pannage. Also, we do Grant, that every freeman may drive his swine freely and without impediment through our demesne woods, to agist them in his own

|| St. Edmund's day,—from this day to the 15*th.*, day after Midsummer, St. Cyril's day was called the Fence month, when no cattle or beasts were permitted within the Forest, for fear of disturbing the Deer at the time of Fawning.

* The court of Attachment,—it did not pass judgment on any offences above the value of 4*d.* all above that sum were enrolled and presented to the Swainmote.—Attachments were made by goods, and chattels, by bail, and by body, to appear before the Swainmote.

§ The same as Vert,—Vert was of three, kinds, *viz.* over-vert, *i. e.* timber-wood; nether-vert, *i. e.* bushes, underwood, &c.; special-vert, *i. e.* every tree and bush bearing fruit to feed the deer. All trees and bushes in the King's demesne woods are special Vert. Hunting,—the same as venison,—all beasts of the Forest or chase were accounted venison. The beasts of the Forest, are the Hart, Hind, Hare, Boar, and Wolf. The beasts of Chase, the Buck, Doe, Fox, Martin and Roe.

woods, or elsewhere they will. And if their swine tarry one night and lie within our Forest, there shall no occasion be taken thereof whereby he may lose any of his own.

10. No man from henceforth shall lose either life, or member, for killing our Deer, but if any man be taken therewith and convicted for taking our venison, he shall make a grievous fine, if he have any thing whereof to make fine; and if he have nothing to lose, he shall be imprisoned a year and a day, and after that, if he can find sureties he shall be released, and if not he shall depart the realm.

11. Whatsoever Arch-bishop, Bishop, Earl, or Baron, coming to us at our command, passeth by our Forest, it shall be lawful for him to take or kill one or two of our Deer, by the view of the Forester, if he be present; or else he shall cause one to blow a horn for him, that he seem not to steal our Deer. And thus they shall do in returning home from us.

12. Every freeman from henceforth without danger shall make in his own wood, or land, or water, which he hath within our Forest, mills, springs, pools, marl-pits, dikes, or arable grounds, without enclosing the arable grounds again; so that it be not to the annoyance of his neighbours.

13. Every freeman shall have within his own woods, eyries of hawks, sparrow-hawks, falcons, eagles, and herons; and shall have also the honey that is found within his woods.

14. No Forester from henceforth, who is not a Forester in fee, paying to us rent for his bailiwick, shall take any cheminage* within his bailiwick. But a Forester in fee paying us rent for his bailiwick shall take cheminage, *i. e.* for carriage by cart, the half year two-pence, and for another half year two-pence; for a horse that beareth loads, for half a year one half-penny, and for another half year one half-penny; but of those only that come as merchants through his bailiwick by his license, to buy bushes, timber, bark, coal, and in another place to sell it again where they will at their pleasure. But for none other carriage by cart, cheminage or toll shall be taken; cheminage shall not be taken but in such places only where it hath been used to be taken. Those who bear upon their backs, bush, bark, or coal, to sell, though it be their living, shall pay no cheminage to our Foresters, except they take it within our demesne woods.

15. All that be outlawed of trespass within our Forest since the time of King

* Toll for passing through the Forest.

Henry our Grandfather, unto the first year of our coronation, shall come to our peace without let, and shall find to us sureties, that from henceforth they shall not trespass unto us within our Forest.

16. No Constable, Castellan, or Bailiff, shall hold plea of Forest, neither for green hugh nor hunting; but every Forester in fee shall make attachments for plea of the Forest, as well for green hugh as for hunting; and shall present them to the Verderers of the provinces; and when they be enrolled and enclosed under the seals of the Verderers, they shall be presented to our chief Justices of our Forest* when they shall come thither to hold pleas of the Forest, and before them they shall be determined.

* Chief Justice of the Forest,—Justice in Eyre, an officer appointed first by Henry II. A. D. 1184. He was a Peer of the realm, a member of the privy council, and appointed by special commission to decide on all offences committed within the Forest. His court might be held every third year by warrant to the Sheriff and chief Warden of the Forest; and all who held lands within the Forest were summoned to attend. This court is now disused: the last was held in the reign of Charles I.

Of Cranborne Chase.

The extensive tract of land situate principally in the north-east part of Dorsetshire, but extending also into the adjoining counties of Wilts and Hants, to which this title is applied, was originally one of the ancient Forests of this kingdom, and acquired in all probability the name of "Chase" in consequence of being granted by William Rufus to Robert Fitz Haymon; for Forests obtained this appellation on grant by the Sovereign to one of his subjects.* It always appertained to the honor of Gloucester, and was therefore intimately connected with the manor of Cranborne, which occasioned its having been termed the Chase of Cranborne from a very early period, even from the time of Henry III. as will appear in succeeding documents. It was an appendage of the hundred and manor, and generally included in the

* A Chase differs from a Forest in not being governed by any special laws, but by the common law; its only officers are Keepers and Woodwards: it differs from a Park, in not being enclosed. A subject may possess a Forest with all its laws and privileges, by special grant from the King; but if in that grant there is no power given to hold Forest Courts, then that Forest becomes a free Chase.—*Manswood.*

same grants at various times made by the Crown, until a final separation by sale took place in the reign of James I.

Thus 8 Edward II. A. D. 1315. The King granted to Richard Lovell, the manor of Cranborne with the chase and other its appurtenances in the county of Dorset, at the King's pleasure.

41 Edward III. A. D. 1368. The Earl claims to have in his manor of Cranborne free hundred and free chase belonging to the said manor, according to the perambulation formerly made, and warren in his demesne lands within the said hundred.*

35 Henry VIII. A. D. 1544. The King made a jointure upon Queen Catherine of the borough, the hundred, and the chase of Cranborne, and the Park of Blagden in the county of Dorset.†

4 Edward VI. A. D. 1551. The King granted to Sir. William Herbert, K. G. for twenty-one years, all the lordship and manor, hundred and chase of Cranborne,‡ with all their rights, liberties, members, and appurtenances, in the county of Dorset.||

* In the Tower.
† In the Augmentation office.
‡ The hundred and chase of Cranborne.
|| In the Augmentation office.

15 James I. A. D, 1618. The King granted to William, Earl of Salisbury, and to his lawful heirs—all the free chase and free warren of Cranborne, with all the privileges jurisdictions, liberties and hereditaments, called and known by the name of Cranborne Chase, in the counties of Dorset, Wilts, and Southampton, &c.

A. D. 1671. The Earl of Salisbury sold it to the Earl of Shaftesbury for £3500; having previously (8 Jac I.) alienated one of the principal walks or districts, called Fernditch, to the Earl of Pembroke.

A. D. 1692. The Earl of Shaftesbury surrendered his estate to his son, Anthony Lord Ashley, who reserving the manor of Berwick St. John, sold the chase and lodges to Thomas Freke, Esq. of Shroton, for £3500.* The latter gentleman dying in 1698, bequeathed the chase to Thomas Pile and Elizabeth Freke for their lives, with reversion to George Pitt, Jun. Esq., of Strathfieldsaye, Hants, afterwards Baron Rivers, to whom it devolved A. D. 1714, and remained in the possession of his successor until the period of its disfranchisement in 1828.†

* The manor of Berwick St. John was sold to the first Lord Rivers, it is said for £10,000.

† See Lord Rivers' title to the chase in App.

The territory of the chase was divided into two districts of unequal extent, the less being circumscribed by the greater, and distinguished by the inner or less, and the outer or large bounds. These boundaries are respectively set forth in a subsequent document of the 8 Edward I. A. D. 1280, and are therein referred back to the time of King John, when the history of the chase commences.* The outer bounds include an area whose diameter from east to west is from twenty to twenty-five miles; and from north to south from fifteen to twenty miles; in circuit about one hundred miles, containing seven or eight hundred thousand acres of land, comprising seventy-two parishes, and ten thousand of population, taking in some portion of the city and towns of Salisbury, Wilton, Shaftesbury, Blandford, Wimborne Minster, Ringwood, Fordingbridge, and Downton: the inner bounds include a district about ten miles in length from north to south, three or four miles in breadth, and about twenty-seven miles in circuit, consisting chiefly of woods and pasture land to the amount of about forty thousand acres. The whole was parcelled or subdivided into eight walks or districts, *viz.* Rushmore, Staplefoot, Cobley, Burseystool, Westwalk, Fernditch,

* See the Map and the document.

chiefly within the inner bounds, Alderholt and Chettered between the inner and the outer bounds. There were also in former time nine Parks for the preservation of Deer in the out-grounds, or, the district beyond the inner bounds, *viz.* Wardour, Wilton, Falston, in Wilts; Breamore, Burgate, Rockbourne, in Hants; Alderholt, Blagden, Gunville, in Dorset. It must not be thought that the whole of this extensive domain was ever the private property of one individual; it consisted in fact of numerous independent estates, an inconsiderable portion being the actual property of the owner or lord of the chase, whose rights and franchise lay in the exclusive liberty and privilege of feeding and preserving the Deer, on any part of the soil within the bounds of the chase; but the district included within the inner bounds, was the part mainly appropriated to the preservation of these animals, which were of the species called "Fallow Deer," and existed in great numbers. In the reign of James I. and his successor, the chase was estimated to contain two thousand head, in later periods the stock amounted to several thousands more, but it was difficult, if not impracticable, to ascertain their exact amount. In 1828 they were computed to amount to upwards of twelve thousand, but not to exceed twenty thousand; in very severe winters, when food became scarce, the mortality amongst them has been known to be excessive, and then their carcasses were eagerly sought after by agriculturists for the purpose of manure. The preservation of so large a stock of Deer, necessarily required a large establishment of keepers, which together with contingent expences, must have demanded a heavy expenditure. This may have induced the second Lord Rivers, and his father, to let off, as they did, some of the walks to gentlemen in the neighbourhood, who preserved the Deer therein at their own expence, and dealt with them in every respect as their own. In justice to those noblemen, we should express our belief, that the sentiments of kindness and liberality, and consideration for the feelings of others, equally if not more powerfully prompted them to this relinquishment of their rights; an act, which we are of opinion, was never so duly appreciated as it ought to have been. Rushmore and Staplefoot walks were always retained by the noble owners; but Burseystool was held by the Rev. W. Chafin, and others; West-walk by Lord Dorchester, Peter Beckford, Esq., &c.; Cobley-walk by the Earl of Shaftesbury; and Chettered by the Sturt family. Chettered appears to have been originally a separate chase,* afterwards united to and considered an integrant part of Cranborne Chase. It consists of several freeholds, chiefly woods and arable land, in the parishes of Tarrant Monkton, Launceston, Rushton, Keynston, Long Critchell, Gussage St. Michael, and Wichampton.

1 Edward VI. A. D. 1547. Chettered part of the Forest of Cranborne, with the liberties of the Forest and Chase, were granted to Edward Duke of Somerset.

Of the Officers belonging to the Chase.

In the earliest periods, namely when the chase was held by the Earls of Gloucester, the officials consisted of the Steward, the Foresters, and the Woodwards; whose duties were divided between the charge and preservation of the deer and the care and management of the woods. The Steward was the superior officer, presided at the courts, and had the general superintendence. In records of Edward I. the names of Geoffrey de Lukenore, Peter de Rissance, and Adam de Bekesgate, Stewards, occur. The Foresters were seven, one of whom was the chief or head Forester.

3 Edward I. A. D. 1275. William de Coveshall was head Forester.

* See the document.

16 Edward I. Gilbert de Cors. In records of the same date, the following names of Sub-foresters occur, *viz.* Samuel and Walter Brice, Walter de Pulton, John de la Sale, John de Cors, John le Archer, William le Bale, John Follyott, John de la Malverne, Robert le Stor, David de la Wodelond, William de la Hyde, and Nicholas de Mary's. The Foresters enjoyed certain privileges attached to their office. When the Abbey of Tewkesbury was valued, 26 Henry VIII. the Prior of Cranborne claimed before the Commissioners, and was allowed an outgoing, a reprise of thirty shillings annually from his possessions in Cranborne, *viz.* the fees of the Foresters of our Lady the Queen of his chase of Cranborne, to wit, in victuals every Tuesday and Friday, yearly thirty shillings. By a court roll of 1 Edward VI. the two Foresters of Alderholt walk used to receive this allowance. Also when the manor of Chettle, which belonged to the same Abbey, was valued, the Abbot claimed as a reprisal the worth of twelve bushels of wheat, 8*s.* eight bushels of barley, 4*s.*, and eight bushels of oats, 2*s.* 8*d.*; delivered to the Foresters of our Lady the Queen of her chase of Cranborne, one year with another 14*s.* 8*d.* Also when the manor of Woodyates, which belonged to the Monastery of Tarrant, was valued, the Abbot claimed the following deduction, *viz.* "the

charge of bread, ale, and fish, every Friday weekly, for five Foresters of the chase of Cranborne for their dinner at Woodyates; together with the victuals for their dogs at the same time." The office of head Forester was sometimes held by a person of distinction. In the time of Richard II. the Earl of March made his brother Edmund Mortimer, head Forester and Keeper of the chase of Cranborne, and chief superintendant of the Parks of Blagden and Alderholt, and of all the other woods of the Earl, parcel of the manor of Cranborne.* This officer was also called the Ranger, as 1 Edward IV. A. D. 1461. The King granted to Walter Harding for life, the office of Ranger of the chase of Cranborne in the county of Dorset. And 22 Edward IV. To Thomas Dakham "our Valet, the office of Ranger of our chase at Cranborne, and Keeper of Rushmore Lodge."†

12 Elizabeth, A. D. 1570. The Queen granted to the Earl of Pembroke the office of "Seneschal of our manor of Cranborne, the office of warden and keeper of our chase of Cranborne, in the county of Dorset, with all the rights, members, and liberties belonging thereto, and the office of ranger of the said

* In the Tower. 38 Henry VI. The Earl of Wiltshire held this office.

† These two records are in the Appendix.

chase, also the office of keeper of our Park of Blagden; and he was allowed £6. 1*s.* 8*d.* per annum for his office of warden and keeper of the chase, and for the rangership 60*s.* 10*d.* per annum, and the same sum for the office of keeper of Blagden Park."* The following names of Rangers and their deputies occur in records of the date of Elizabeth, James I., &c.

Rangers,

Sir Thomas Aylesbury, A. D. 1627, Thomas Hooper, Sir Thomas Gage, Sir Henry Ashley, Thomas Hawles, A. D. 1668.

Deputy Rangers,

Sir John Rogers, Richard Nicholas, John Stockman, Sir Matthew Arundel, Joseph Compton, Colonel Fitz-James, A. D. 1668.

George Chafin obt. 1766. was the last head Forester or Ranger.† In later periods the officials consisted of a ranger, a keeper to each walk, under-keepers, woodwards, and promoter. The last named officer was one of ancient appointment, whose duty it was to impound all sheep found straying in the woods, and all cattle found in such woods as had no rights of common pasturage, or that had entered the accustomed woods before the cus-

* In the Augmentation office. † Chafin's Chase.

tomary periods of admission; his fee was 8*d.* per hoof, and 2*s.* 6*d.* per score of sheep.

Of the Courts.

The Courts were held once and sometimes twice a year in the manor house of Cranborne, whilst the chase belonged to the Lords of the manor; afterwards at Wimborne St. Giles's, when the Earl of Shaftesbury held it; and latterly at Rushmore Lodge; the Lord's steward presided, and the keepers and woodwards attended to make presentments of any damage done to vert or venison from the holding of the last court to the present, and to make return on oath of the number of Deer killed, or found dead in their respective walks, in the same interval. All the keepers within the inner bounds were compelled to attend. The woodmen took an oath not to destroy the Deer, the vert, or the browze, and to conform themselves in making the fences, &c., agreeably to the laws and usages of the chase; new woodmen and keepers were also then appointed, and sworn to be true and faithful to the Lord; the keepers had no written appointment. By the court Rolls it appears that seven Foresters regularly attended and made presentments from the reign of Edward I.

8 Edward I. Gilbert, Earl of Gloucester claims a free court of the chase, with pleas of vert and venison, with attachments of men, and to take from such as were convicted, emendals in the same court. A free court was allowed to the Earl of Gloucester 8 and 9 Edward I. Many years ago the court exercised an authority not only of attaching the goods, but the bodies of offenders, and committing them to the chase prison, in the manor house at Cranborne; still it appears by the presentments that its powers were exercised with praiseworthy moderation. When persons were distrained to appear for an offence, and they denied it, a writ of *venire facias* was issued to the steward of the chase to summon twelve men in the vicinage, to try the matter in dispute: when the penal statutes against Deer stealers were enacted, this court fell into disuse.

Pleas and Perquisites of the Court.

In the 24 Edward I. A. D. 1296. they were valued at 60*s*. 27 Henry VI. A. D. 1449. £10. 11*s*. 6*d*. 27 Henry VIII. A. D. 1536. 26*s*. 8*d*. 28 Henry VIII. 39*s*. 2*d*. 31

Henry VIII. 6*s.* 6*d.* 32 Henry VIII. 16*s.* 1*d.* 38 Henry VIII. 9*s.* 2*d.* 1 Edward VI. 7*s.* 6*d.**

Of the Lodges, and Particularly of Rushmore Lodge.

Lodges were tenements appropriated for lodging the keepers, and other officers of the chase, and there was one in each of the eight walks, the chief or head lodge being that wherein the courts were usually held. By notes of evidence taken in a trial between the Earl of Salisbury, plaintiff, and Lord Arundel and others, defendants, 13*th.* March, 15 Jac. I. it appears that Robert, Earl of Salisbury rebuilt the four lodges of Cobley, Staplefoot, Burseystool, and Westwalk, and that the Earl had not any woods or coppices within the less bounds, unless about his new lodges; and that Rushmore Lodge was in ancient times a tenement rented of the Earl of Pembroke, and afterwards purchased by the Earl of Salisbury as part and parcel of the manor of Berwick St. John.† After this purchase, Lord Salisbury enclosed some of the waste lands around the lodge, and agreed to pay the

* See the Appendix.

† See the evidence in Appendix.

tenants of Berwick manor as a compensation for the loss of the pasture, a buck every summer, and a doe every winter; nevertheless, the agreement was much neglected, in consequence of which, the tenants and freeholders threatened to pull down the fences of the enclosure These differences however were amicably settled at a Court of the manor of Berwick, held in 1669, when a formal agreement to the above effect was entered upon the Rolls, and signed by William Constantial, seneschall, Edward Stillingfleet, deputy seneschall, and others present.* The earliest information concerning Rushmore Lodge, is contained in the following Records, which have been adduced as evidence, that it was not originally a Lodge of the chase, but a dwelling of the Abbess of Wilton's Wood-ward.

14 Edward III. A. D. 1354, At a court holden at Berwick, this year as appears by the Abbey book of Wilton, Robert Saleman, being attached for damage done in the wood of the Lady of Rushmore, and claiming pasture therein, recourse was had to the old charter, of the manor of Berwick, and it was found therein, that, Robert de Ryshmere, held by charter freely in fee half a yard-land, and paid yearly 2*s.* four-hundred eggs, and twenty-four hens, and ought (in feodo) to take care of the Lady's

* Hundred of Chalk,—Modern Wilts, by C. Bowles Esq.

wood. And he shall have as much pasture as he shall require for his own cattle, but not for other people's, and housebote and haybote.

48 Edward III. At another Court holden this year, John, son of Robert Saleman, appeared on the essoign day which he had, to shew what, how much, and by what services he claimed to hold of the Lady by descent from his father; who thereupon shewed that he held one messuage and half a yard-land freely with the appurtenances in Rushmore, to which holding belonged the office of Wood-ward of Rushmore, by yearly rent of 2*s.* twenty-four hens, and four-hundred eggs &c. At a subsequent Court held the same year, John Fallings, servant of John Cogk, upon the aforesaid land takes every Monday a full cart load of underwood in the wood of Rushmore, by delivery of the Wood-ward, as much as he can carry with one horse out of the wood of the Lady, yet because he caused that load to be carried with two horses he was attached &c.

34 Edward III. At a Court holden there the Jury present that Rogar Molshull required three cart loads of Underwood, from the Lady's wood, in the name of the Rector of Chalk in one week, which Rector hath truly right to require every Monday, one cart-load in the wood of the Lady called Cheotell, and on no other day of the year; and if the said

Rector be prevented by rainy weather or other reasonable cause, he may require two loads on the Monday following; and if further prevented, he may on the next Monday take two loads, but not more; and because the said Roger, took the said cart-loads contrary to the right of the Rector to the disinherison of the Lady and the Church, the said Roger is in mercy &c.

1 Henry V. A.D. 1413, Berwicke. At a Court holden there, it was commanded to distrain Robert Saleman, tenant of one messuage, and half a yard-land, freely in Rushmore, to make satisfaction to the Lady of 2*s.* rent, twenty-four hens, four hundred eggs, &c. And it was testified that sufficient distress was found.

22 Edward IV. Thos. Dukham, was appointed keeper of Rushmore Lodge.

37 Henry VIII. When the Chase belonged to Queen Catharine, the accountant was allowed 33*s.* 4*d.* "for repairs made upon the Lodge of Rushmore *within* the Chase of Cranborne by the Ranger there this year with the consent of the Queen's Counsellors."

The Lodge is a good substantial mansion, built by the first Lord Rivers about eighty years ago; part of the old building being still retained and converted into offices. In the Hall over the mantelpiece is the following inscription.

Cranborne Chase.

Orders and instructions for the management of the said Chase made and given at a Court held for the said Chase the 16*th.*, day of *December*, 1713.

Imprimis,—That the Ranger keep a pack of doggs at Rushmore Lodge, and the same do consist of seven couple at the least, and to be kept constantly in hunting.

Item,—That no keeper, underkeeper, or other person, presume to hunt otherwise than in company with the Ranger, or deputy Ranger, and then with the Ranger's doggs only.

Item,—That all warrants and orders for Deere directed to the said Ranger, or his deputy, be served by the said doggs, or immediately directed and sent by the Ranger or his deputy, to the severall keepers as formerly.

Item,—That no underkeeper presume to kill a Deere without directions in writing from the Ranger or his deputy, except in Chittered, and then not without direction of the Ranger or his deputy, or the masterkeeper.

Item,—That noe Buck be killed after Hollyrood-day, and noe Doe after Candlemas in each season.

Item,—That all these orders and instructions, be set up in the outward Roome at Rushmore Lodge, for all persons to take notice thereof, and that copies thereof be sent to the underkeepers of the severall Lodges.

There are many good paintings of horses, dogs, and other subjects connected with sporting, in the mansion, which has become a favourite residence of the Lord and Lady Rivers. It would indeed be no easy task to point out a spot combining similar advantages, where the pleasures of retirement may be enjoyed in the midst of a scene of great sylvan beauty, and at the same time the eye may delight itself in soaring over a wide expanse of country, chequered with the variety of wood, and wold, bounded in the misty distance by the shores of the British Channel.

Of Cheminage.

Cheminage is the toll due by custom for a way through a Forest. By the Charter of the Forest, it was limited to 2*d*. per cart, and half-penny per horse bearing loads, passing through the Royal Forests; but in Cranborne Chase, when the custom had obtained from the time of Henry .III. at least, the toll demanded was 4*d.* for every wagon or cart, and 2*d.* for every pack-horse.

In the 39 Henry III. A.·D. 1255, it was presented that the Earl's Bailiffs take Cheminage.

In the 3 Edward I. A. D. 1275, the hundredors of Chalk and Downton, and the men of the Borough of Wilton, complained of Cheminage being taken at Bulbridge, in Wilton, and at Ayleswade bridge, in Fisherton; and the hundredors of Candon, of its being taken every where within the metes.

In the 7 Edward I. the Knights upon their oath said that the Foresters of Chettle, (in the hundred of Chalk) and of the chase of Cranborne, took Cheminage at the bridge of Ayleswade, and at Bulbridge, and in other places where they ought not to take it, according to the tenor of the Charter.* Without enquiring now, into the justice of these complaints, we may observe that they prove at any rate the antiquity of the custom, which may be further traced through the succeeding reigns of Henry VI., VII., VIII. Edward VI., and Jac. I.† even unto the period of the disfranchisement of the chase rights. It appears to have been discontinued at Bulbridge, since that part of the chase, wherein it is situated, namely Verditch walk, was

* See Records. † See Appendix.

disposed of; but at Harnham bridge the custom was preserved to the latest period. During the fence month, that is, fifteen days before Midsummer and fifteen days after, from the 20*th.* of *June* to the 20*th. July,* buckhorns were put up at the bridge, and a chain extended across the road to intercept such as were liable to the toll. The authority for taking Cheminage was granted by warrant under the hand and seal of the Steward of the chase. Thus in 1710 a warrant granted by Dennis Bond, Esq. Steward, runs in this form;—
"These are to authorize and require John "Bailey, of Harnham, in the county of Wilts, "labourer, to receive of such person or per-"sons, that shall drive any wagon, or cart, or "other carriage over Harnham Bridge, in the "said county, at any time or times between "the 9*th.* of *June* and the 9*th.* of *July* next "ensuing the date hereof, the sum of 4*d.*, and "the further sum of 2*d.* for such horse which "shall pass the said bridge, between the above "mentioned times, according as the same hath "from time to time been constantly paid. "The same right belonging to the Lord and "Proprietor of Cranborne chase.
"*Given under my hand and seal,*
"*this* 6*th. day of June,* 1710."

3 Henry VI. The Ranger accounted for 6*s.* 8*d.* for Cheminage, at the bridge of Sarum

and Wilton.—27 Henry VI. 6*s.* 8*d.*—6 Henry VII. 11*s.* 4*d.* and it is stated that "the residue of the Cheminage pertains of ancient custom to the Ranger."—27 Henry VIII. to 1 Edward VI. 13*s.* 4*d.* for Cheminage.*

Free Warren.

The Proprietor of the chase always enjoyed the right of killing the small game found upon the lands within the inner bounds. Grants of free warren have been made by the King at various times, to the owners of estates lying between the inner and outer bounds. Thus, 35 Edward I. A. D. 1307, The King granted to John de Berwycke free warren in all his demesne lands, in Norrington, in the county of Wilts.

16 Jac. I. A. D. 1619, The free warren of the manor of Child Okeford was granted to Sir George Trenchard. In the time of James I. Sir Edmund Uvedale had free warren in Bridmore; Mr. Hannam in Blagden; Mr. Horsey in Ashcombe; the Earl of Devonshire in Badbury; Mr. Chafin in Chettle; the Earl of Pembroke in Verditch; and it appears that in more than one instance the owners pleaded the grant of this right in defence of

* See Appendix.

their practice of killing the Deer that were found on their estates. As when Mr. Chafin, then the high sheriff of Dorset, was summoned before the Justice in Eyre, for hunting and killing Deer in Littlewood, in his manor of Chettle, upon his stating his grant of free warren, the Justice replied, "he might then kill the Deer and spare not." Also, Thomas Gawen, Esq. of Norrington, was in the habit of hunting, killing, and carrying away Deer in Manwood, within his manor, without interruption from the keepers;* but there can be no doubt of the illegality of this practice, which was not warranted by the privilege, and contrary to the rights and liberties of the chase. Some-time after Lord Rivers had given up several Deer-walks to different gentlemen, he relinquished his right to the small game, with the exception of rabbits and woodcocks, which were always killed by his keepers, and considered their perquisites. It is said that Mr. Doddington, afterwards Lord Melcombe, who held Burseystool-walk, was the first who appointed a regular game keeper in the chase;† George Chafin shot the keeper's dogs, which occasioned a serious dispute between him and Mr. Doddington, and a challenge ensued, but the matter was amicably arranged. Mr. Julines Beckford, who held West-walk, took the liberty

* See "Evidence" in Appendix. † Chafin.

some years after to appoint a keeper, which Lord Rivers, then Mr. Pitt, did not oppose, being desirous of ingratiating himself with the County, and soon after that the appointment became general throughout the chase.

Customs and Usages.

Within the inner bounds, the chase comprised a great number of coppices, intersected by ridings or alleys, for the convenience of hunting; the borders are in general planted with holly-trees, whose leaves are a favorite food of the Deer, and were appropriated to their use during the winter season; these together with the ivy found in the woods, were every where claimed and reserved by the keepers for that purpose, and are called the vert. After fourteen, fifteen, or sixteen years' growth, the underwood, consisting principally of hazel, was deemed to have attained maturity, when it was felled and sold to dealers for firewood, fencing, the making of hurdles, spars for thatching, &c.; after which, the coppices were enclosed with wattled fences (no other kind of fence being allowed within the chase,) of such a height as a Deer would not leap over, unless hard pressed by hounds; the Deer therefore were debarred from feeding on the young wood, until such time as less injurious consequences would follow their admission into the coppices; their exclusion continued until the third years' growth of the wood, when it was customary to admit them to the feed by making leaps and creeps, that is, by lowering so much of the fences in certain places, and making spaces through them, as would permit the Deer to leap over with facility, and give entrance to the young and weakly. It has been averred that this custom was illegal, inasmuch as a Statute enacted in the 22 Edward IV. 1482, made it lawful for subjects having woods in forests or chases to enclose them for the space of seven years, for the better preservation of the young spring; whereas, previously to this time, no one could enclose his woods, after felling the timber, for more than three years, which by throwing them open at so early a period to beasts and cattle, was attended with great destruction. These animals, however, were never admitted into the coppices of the chase before the fourth year, and in some parts before the seventh year of their growth, when the fences were levelled, and the "black cattle, rother beasts, and runners,"* were permitted to rove therein at large, in the uninterrupted

* This is the term used in old leases, and signifies horses, horned beasts, colts, and calves.

enjoyment of the rights of common pasturage. On the 12*th.* of *May,* (old May-day) the fences were torn up, becoming the woodman's perquisite, and the cattle continued to feed in the woods until the 23*rd.* of *November* following, (Martinstide.) This ancient privilege, so valuable to the leaseholders, in many of the parishes adjoining the inner bounds, was threatened with extinction in the parish of Sixpenny Handley, shortly after the act for the disfranchisement of the chase had expired. At this period, the Marquess of Anglesey, who is the principal landowner in that part of the chase, adopted the ill-advised measure of enclosing his woods to the exclusion of the common feed. So hasty a proceeding was promptly resisted by several of the respectable inhabitants, who broke down the newly raised fences; whereupon, writs were served on several parties concerned in the transaction; but after the causes had been pending for some time, and trial as yet delayed, Dibben, one of the defendants, brought his action for damages sustained by the loss of his right of pasture, and the question being then submitted to reference, was tried before Mr. Serjeant Bompas and a special jury at Woodyates Inn, in *Sept.* 1834, and a verdict was given in favor of the inhabitants of Handley with costs. The woods afford a great means of support to numerous families, whose privileges it were unwise as well as ungenerous to abridge. The nutting season attracts large parties of the neighbouring peasantry, who bivouac for days together within the sylvan shades, pursuing their cheerful toil unmolested, and at length return to their homes bending beneath the burthen of their spoil! That useful animal the pig enjoys the privilege of a run in the woods, where great numbers may be seen in some seasons picking up a very profitably living on the fallen nuts and acorns, which they devour with great avidity.

The season for killing bucks commenced in the beginning of *July,* and it was customary to present the first of the season to the bench of Magistrates at the quarter sessions, then held in the summer at Shaftesbury. The last buck was always killed on the first day of Shroton Fair, *(Sept. 25th.)* which was the signal for the commencement of fox-hunting in the chase. The season for killing dry does began at Martinstide, and ended at Candlemas. The chase venison was ever held by competent judges in the highest estimation, for its unrivalled flavor and fine condition; many of my readers will doubtless remember the liberality with which this delicacy was dispensed, and the hospitable feelings and social intercourse thereby engendered and called into lively play. Buck hunting was a very favorite amusement with gentlemen of the last century; and the hounds always kept for this purpose by the Ranger of the chase, afforded them a good opportunity for the enjoyment of the sport. Early in the morning, or late in the afternoon, was deemed the most preferable time of the day, as the scent is then stronger, and the work both of horse and hound performed with less labor and fatigue than under the rays of a noontide sun. It was customary for regularly bred buck hunters, to meet every season on the 29*th*. of *May*, with oak boughs in their hats or caps, and to hunt young male deer, in order to enter the young hounds, and get the older into wind and exercise preparatory to the season of buck hunting: this was called *blooding the hounds*, and the young deer killed were called *blooding* deer.* The ancient sport of hawking, once so prevalent in this country, is still brought to mind by the term of *hawking downs*, which is applied to many large tracts of open ground in and near the chase; formerly covered with gorse and fern, and the resort of pheasants and partridges; the woodcock afforded great sport as he flew across the *plecks*, or glades, when disturbed in the surrounding wood† Fox-hunting has been long established in the chase; Thomas Townes, Esq. of Stapleton,

* Chafin.

† Chafin.

kept the first pack of fox-hounds in the year 1730.* The Rev. William Chafin, and more recently Thomas Grove, Esq. of Fern, were masters of the Cranborne chase hounds, which no longer exist as a distinct establishment.

The inhabitants of Tollard Royal formerly claimed the privilege of a general hunt there during the time when Lord Arundell's court was open, which was always held under the shade of a venerable wych-elm, called the Lavermere or Larmer tree, on the first Monday in *Sept.* In 1789 Lord Rivers contested this right and obtained a verdict, which put an end to the Tollard Hunt; but it was afterwards customary for the chase hounds to meet there on this annual occasion, and kill a brace of bucks, which were always presented to Lord Arundell without payment of the usual fee.

The inhabitants of Handley exercised a similar custom during the sitting of the court-leet of that manor, from time immemorial; but in 1817 the validity of the privilege was contested by an action of trespass brought by Lord Rivers against Hardiman, of Handley: the plaintiff contended that the court was not a court-leet, none of the business usually transacted at such a court having been done there after the jury were sworn, and as it

* Chafin.

appeared to be nothing more than a hunting court, which the law does not recognize, the judge (Abbot) directed the jury to find a verdict for the plaintiff, and thus terminated this annual diversion.

The lands within the inner bounds were subject to a special admeasurement, as in forests, *viz.* eighteen feet to the rod or lug, (as it is provincially called) which is sixteen and a half in other places. They never plashed any quick or made any ditches against the Deer, and it was strictly forbidden to destroy any gorse or furze, or to break up any waste land; since the disfranchisement, many acres of wood have been grubbed up, and the land converted to tillage, a plan which in all probability, will, in the process of time, be extensively adopted.

Deer Hunters and Deer Stealers.

The two classes of persons thus designated differed only in the grade or station of life to which they belonged, the opprobrious title having been conferred on that section which was unable to meet the demands of justice, with those pecuniary resources, which the other had ever at command. The author of the history of Selborne well remarks, "there is such an inherent spirit for hunting in human nature, as scarce any inhibitions can restrain. Hence towards the beginning of this Century, (1700,) all this county (Hants) was wild about Deer stealing; unless he were an hunter, as they affected to call themselves, no young person was allowed to be possessed of manhood or gallantry." We may remark, that these statements are equally applicable to Cranborne Chase. The Rev. W. Chafin in his "History" states that, he had an uncle much addicted to the sport, and was so often detected, and so many penalties paid, that his elder brother put a stop to his career in good time. He also relates the adventures of a gentleman with whom he was acquainted in the early part of his life, who was the leader of a band of Deer hunters. In the frontispiece to his work, this gentleman is represented in the costume of the craft; which consisted of a kind of helmet, or cap, in structure and materials similar to a bee-hive, and somewhat resembling it in form, well padded inside, and a coat, called the jack, made of the thickest canvass, well quilted with wool; this was his armour. His weapons, a short sword, called a hanger; and a quarter staff: dogs and nets were the staple of his art; the chase keepers continued to be accoutred in this fashion down to the latest period. By the 3 and 4

William and Mary, thirty pounds was the penalty annexed to the offence of killing a Deer, which entirely failed as a preventive, with such as had an inclination for the sport, and money at their disposal, but when by the 10 George II. the second offence of Deer stealing was made felony, and all ranks of offenders assimilated in the punishment of seven years transportation, then Deer stealing soon ceased to be a gentlemanlike amusement, appeared in its true colours, and engaged the exclusive attention of the vulgar and the desperate. The chase was continually infested with those nocturnal depredators, who frequently united themselves in a body, and attacked the keepers in fierce and fatal conflicts. They were generally armed with guns, pistols, and a formidable weapon like a flail, with the striking part made of iron, called a swingel: they often wore the straw-cap. In the attack the keepers rushed upon them with their hangers, guarding themselves with the quarter-staff, a tough stick about four feet long, which they held in the middle with the left hand. A serious affray of this kind, occurred on the night of the 16*th.*, of *Dec.*, 1780, on Chettle common, between a party of seven Deer hunters, and five keepers. The ringleader, who was a trumpet-major of a regiment of dragoons, then quartered at Blandford, and whose name was Blandford, lost one of his hands in the battle, severed from the arm by the keeper's hanger. Severe wounds and bruises were received on both sides, and one of the keepers eventually died of his injuries; but the gang were all captured, tried at Dorchester, convicted, and sentenced to seven years transportation; but in consideration of the wounds they had received, the sentence was commuted to imprisonment for an indefinite period.* In 1791 a most desperate battle occurred at Rushmore Lodge, between ten Deer hunters, and the same number of keepers; one of the poachers was unfortunately killed from the blow of a quarter-staff, and both parties were severely wounded, but victory declared in favor of the keepers, and the whole gang were tried at Salisbury, convicted, and transported for life. The last engagement took place on the night of the *7th., of Dec.,* 1816. Four persons of Donhead, impressed with the idea that Lord Rivers had no Chase rights in Wiltshire, and that the Deer might be killed with impunity, entered the Chase with fire-arms, and were met at Burseystool walk by two of the keepers, who rushed upon them with their hangers and captured one of them, who impeached his companions; two of them were apprehended and committed with their companion for trial at Dorchester, where they were convicted, and

* Chafin.

sentenced to seven years transportation.* There are several spots in the chase, traditionally reported to have been the scenes of similar engagements, as Bloody Shard Gate, and Bloodway Coppice in Gunville parish. The mode of taking the deer pursued by these gentry, was that of hanging nets and nooses, in the paths frequented by the animals in their way from the woods to the feeding grounds, and then driving them with dogs into the snares. When one was captured, he was immediately slaughtered and left concealed, in order to be carried away when the risk of detection was supposed to be less imminent. The habit of deer stealing led, undoubtedly, to the occasional perpetration of crimes still more atrocious, and marked with the deepest shades of guilt. About the year 1738, a keeper of West-walk returning from Fontmel Church on Easter-day, was waylaid and murdered. The murderer was never discovered. Another murder was committed on a keeper of Fernditch walk, for which a man of the name of Wheeler, was executed and hung in chains on the spot; but the gibbet was soon cut down, and the body found some time afterwards in a deep well.†

In the 28 Henry VIII. Anthony Gilbert, Knt., Edward Willoughby, Knt., John Horsey, Esq., and Henry Ashley, were appointed Com-

* Chafin. † Chafin.

missioners "for the view and numbering of the wild beasts in the chase of Cranborne, and for the enquiry of hunters and malefactors, to be ascertained by them in the chase aforesaid, whereby their transgressions might be brought to light, that the truth and certainty of their default, might be most faithfully certified to the council of the said Lady the Queen." (Queen Catherine.)

Records and Transactions Relating to the Chase.

17 John, A. D. 1216. John, by the Grace of God, &c. to Hugo Neville, greeting:—We command you to make perambulation without delay, by trusty men of the neighbourhood of Romesham and Brustelton,* of the woods (de Bruillis) of those villages, to ascertain what is our chase there, and what is the chase of Geoffrey de Mandeville, *viz.* the chase which William, earl of Gloucester, father of Isabella the wife of Geoffrey, held. Likewise, perambulation of the Forest of Craneburn and of Chetterden, which is between our chase† and the chase which William Earl of Gloucester

* These places are not known.

† Probably Holt chase is here meant.

held. And such perambulation being made, let Geoffrey de Mandeville, without delay, have those Chases which William, earl of Gloucester, held. *Given at Runyngmede, 23rd day of June, in the 17th year of our Reign.**

34 Henry III. A. D. 1250. The Abbess of Wilton complains against Richard, earl of Gloucester, of a plea that he suffered her to take reasonable Estover† in her own woods of Fernditch and Chetell,‡ which are within the percursus§ of the said Earl's chase of Cranborne, and why he permitteth not the people of the said Abbess to take housebote and haybote, in the said woods without the view of the keepers of the said chase as they were wont, and ought to take as in the time of the predecessors of the said Earl, they were accustomed to take. And the Earl came not, and the Sheriff declared that he has no land in his county where he can take him, and farther it is testified that he hath land in the county of Dorset, and therefore the Sheriff of Dorset is commanded to take him, so that he appear on the octave of Saint Michael &c.

34 Henry III. The Abbess of Tarrant by her Attorney complains of Richard Earl of

* In the Tower.

† Allowance of wood for repairs, fuel, &c.

‡ These parts of the chase are in Wiltshire.

§ Percursus,—the right of free chase, which extended over the lands of other persons.

Gloucester, of a plea why he exacts fealty of the keepers of the said Abbess's woods of Chetell, which are within the precursus of the said chase of Cranborne, which never was accustomed to be required from them; and why he doth not permit her people to take housebote and haybote in the said woods without the view of the Foresters, as they ought and were accustomed to take, and as in the time of his ancestors, they were used to take.—And the Earl came not, and it was adjudged that he be attached to appear in fifteen days, from the day of Saint Hilary.

34 Henry III. The Abbess of Shaston, preferred a similar complaint in respect to her woods of Chetell.*

35 Henry III. An agreement was entered into between Richard de Clare, Earl of Gloucester and Hertford, and Agnes, Abbess of Saint Edward, Shaston, for composing certain differences that had subsisted between them, concerning her woods within the Chace of Cranborne, and the hundred suit which he required of her; whereby the said Abbess granted for herself and her successors that the Woodwards of her woods of Handley, Iwerne, and Fontmell, should without evasion come to the Earl's Court of Cranborne, and there swear to behave themselves faithfully, respecting the veni-

* These Records are in the Chapter-House Westminster.

son of the said Earl within the said chase, and give notice concerning offenders therein.—And the Earl in consideration thereof granted to the Abbess and her successors, that she and her men, freemen as well as villeins, should have every kind of Estover for her Abbey in her manors in the county of Dorset and Wilts, through the whole of the woods of the said Abbess within the chase aforesaid, so that she did not give or sell without leave of the Earl; and that it should be lawful for the keepers to attach offenders in the same woods, without the claims of the Abbess, but should not attach her or her men unless they were found with venison. Also, that the Abbess might enclose and cultivate a place at Handley, called Garston, so that the Deer by that enclosure were not impeded, but might go in and out. And that she and her successors should be henceforth free of every kind of suit at his Hundreds of Pimperne, Wareham, and Roughbergh. And the said Abbess gave for the Grant sixty marks.*

39 Hen. III., A. D. 1255. An Inquisition made before Roger de Thurkelby, and Robert de Shotenden, at Wilton, in the county of Wilts.

* In the Augmentation Office.

Hundred of Cadworth.

The Jury present that Richard de Clare, Earl of Gloucester, holds the manor of Cranborne, when he has free Chase, and, from the said Chase in the county of Dorset, he hath his course into the county of Wilts, where he hath no tenement, but only his percursus unto the banks of the Nodder, and unto the bridge of Ayleswade on the Avon, wherefore they say that by reason of his outward percursus (forinseci) he makes the whole county a forest, and his bailiffs take cheminage and distress of men in the county of Wilts, in the Hundred of Cadworth, and carry them to Cranborne, in the county of Dorset, contrary to the liberties of our Lord the King; and they take from certain men 20 marks and more at their pleasure, and this they have done for two years and a half past.*

3rd Edw. I., A. D. 1275. Inquisitions made before William de Braybef, and William Gerebert, the Justices in Eyre appointed to enquire on the oath of twelve Jurors, how many and what demesne manors, the King hath in the several counties, as well of the ancient

* In the Chapter House.

demesne of the crown, as escheats and purchases; also, what manors used to be in the hands of the King; who now hold them, by what warrant, from what time, and in what manner they are holden: also, of the fees of our Lord the King, and of the tenants who now hold them of him in chief, &c.; also of those who have appropriated to themselves free Chases or warrens without warrant, and likewise those who of old have had such Chases or warrens from the Royal Grant, and have unduly enlarged their metes and bounds, and from what times, &c.

Hundred of Chalk.

The Jurors say, that the Abbess of Wilton holds the Manor of Chalke, Berwicke, and Semelegh, with other Manors without the said Hundred of the King in Capite, belonging to his Barony, for five knights fees, &c., and that Richard, earl of Gloucester, father of the Earl who now is, did afforest to himself the woods of Chetell and Fernditch, and the whole country towards the borough of Shaston, north unto the bridge of Ayleswade as the Nodder extends itself along and as the bounds did extend by the perambulation made between the bounds of Wilts and Dorset, to the head of the Nodder, by placing there seven Foresters to attach men for Vert and Venison, throughout the aforesaid bounds in the county of Wilts, to come to Craneburn, in the county of Dorset, and there they amerce them at the will of the steward of the said Earl to the grievance of all the country: they take Cheminage and permit not any one within the bounds aforesaid, to take of his own woods without the view and license of the said Foresters, who grievously amerce them at Cranborne, in the county of Dorset. And if any one enclose his own wood within the bounds in Wilts, without the license of the Foresters, at Cranborne, in the county of Dorset, they are grievously emerced by the Earl's steward. And the Foresters impose unjustly at their will upon the men dwelling within the metes and bounds in Wilts, when they are malefactors of the venison of the said Earl, and them they force to come to Cranborne in the county of Dorset, and there grievously amerce them at their will, without the detection of any offender; and the same Foresters collect sheaves during harvest, within the metes and bounds in Wilts, and after harvest, extort by fear from people dwelling within the chase, wheat for their Feasts, and compel them to come to their ale shops: and they collect fowls against Christmas, lambs and their fleeces, to the great grievance of the whole country.*

Hundred of Dunworth.

The Jurors say, that the Earl of Gloucester hath a certain liberty granted by the King of having a certain free chase in the county of Dorset; and the same Earl and his bailiffs of Craneburn use the aforesaid liberty otherwise than they ought, by attaching the bodies and cattle of men dwelling in the hundred of Doneworth in the county of Wilts, and keeping them until those men have paid a fine at the pleasure of the Earl and his bailiffs. And they say, that whereas the said Earl hath free chases in his manor of Cranborne in the county of Dorset, he exceeds the metes and bounds of his liberty, by appropriating by his power to his said chase, the lands and woods as well of knights as of free tenants in the county of Wilts, by making attachments of Vert and Venison to the banks of the Nodder, and he holds the fence-month and pleas of Vert contrary to the assize of the Forest, since he hath neither Verderers nor Regarders.

* All this is contrary to the Charter of the Forest. See S. 7, page 110.

Hundred of Downton.

The Jurors say, that the Bishop o Winchester holds the manor of Dunton anc Bishopstone of the King in chief, &c., and hatl warren in his demesne lands in the said hun dred, from the time of Peter Bishop of Win chester, and of Henry father of the now King And that the Earl of Gloucester, who now is hath afforested by his force and power, all th county, the lands, vills, woods and pastures which are from the vill of Scefton (Shaston to the bridge of Ayleswade by the banks of th Nodder, and whatsoever is in the county o Wilts, from the bounds of the county of Dor set, unto the bank of the Nodder. And he claim this to be his Forest, by placing there hi seven foresters to attach of Vert and Veniso in the county of Wilts, to come to Cranborn in the county of Dorset, contrary to the law and custom of the realm and of the assize o the Forest, since he hath neither Verderer nor Regarders. He takes Cheminage also, every where within the aforesaid metes and bounds; doing all this, contrary to a perambulation o Forests made by the Bishops of Salisbury and Bath, William Longespie, Earl of Salisbury, and

William Bruyere, in the fourth year of the reign of Henry III.,* and hath done this, contrary to the dignity of our Lord the King, not permitting any one to take of his own woods, in the places aforesaid, without the view and license of his Foresters, whereas he hath neither Verderers nor Regarders, and so by right, he ought not to have any Foresters. Also, the Earl hath no fee or free tenement within the bounds aforesaid, by pretext of which he may claim Forest; nor is there any one within the said bounds, who holds or claims to hold of the said Earl; but each holds by Barony of the Lord the King in chief, as freely as the Earl holds his manor of Craneburn, and each holds by the mesne Lord, as is set forth. And the Foresters of the said Earl, enter upon the liberty of our Lord the Bishop of Winchester at Dunton, and exceed the metes and bounds otherwise than they ought, receiving gifts and making grievous attachments. And

* 4 Hen. III. A commission was issued to the sheriffs of Wilts, Dorset, Somerset, and other counties, reciting that the King had empowered the Bishop of Sarum and others, to see what Forests had been afforested in the Royal bailwicks, by King John and King Henry II. And the Inquisition thereof being made and shewn to Henry de Burgh, the King's Justiciar, and the King's Council, if that Inquisition should satisfy them, such Forests were to be disforested. (In the Tower) —*But no return to this commission, nor order, or instrument of disforestation, (of Cranborne Chase) have ever been found in any of the public offices for the custody of records.*

the Foresters of Craneburn take toll of the men of the said Bishop and of others of the county, of their carriages, and of their wood bought at Salisbury; also of men going to market, at the bridge of Ayleswade; of heath and timber, and of many other things, coming from the New Forest and elsewhere; and thus they exceed the metes and bounds of the said chase by ten miles, (leucas) to the greatest damage of the whole country. They say that the Foresters of Cranborne, to wit, Saverie and John Tuss, by their power took a cart-load of thorns of the parson of Bishopstone with their horses; and also a certain sumpter horse with a boy going towards the water, in the middle of the highway in the town of Bishopstone, and led them into Hamberstone, maliciously charging the said parson with stealing the said thorns in the Forest of the Earl, until the said parson gave them half a mark for the sake of peace.

Hundred of Damerham.

The Jurors say that the earl of Gloucester who now is, hath afforested by his own force and power the whole country, all the vills, woods, and pastures, which are from the vill of Shaston, &c., (as in the preceding). And that one Samaricus and Walter Brice, foresters by order of Geoffrey de Lenknore, steward of the said Earl, and other foresters take men within the said bounds in the county of Wilts for felony, and other offences, and by force bring them to Craneburn, in the county of Dorset, and condemn them there, and then enquire concerning their goods in Wilts, and cause them to be brought to Craneburn. And they attach men of offences in the liberties of other Lords holding of the King in chief, and bring them to Craneburn, and amerce them there at their will. And the said Foresters impose upon men dwelling within the bounds in Wilts, as being malefactors of venison of the said Earl, and cause them to come to Craneburn, and amerce them there at their will. And if any one have enclosed his wood, or part of his wood, without license of the said Foresters, they are attached to come from the county of Wilts, to Craneburn, in the county of Dorset, to make amends for their offences there at the will of the said steward. And the Foresters of the said Earl, viz. Samaricus and Walter Brice, came to Mertone (Martin), in the county of Wilts, by order of the said Geoffrey de Lenknore, steward of the said Earl, to the house of one John le Bor, and there, by force, took a certain man of Forton, maliciously accusing him of felony, and carried him to Craneburn, and there hung him without any reason at their will, and after that they went to Bridmere in the county of Wilts, and there took his goods, *viz.*, two oxen, of the oxen of Peter de Skidmere, saying that they were the goods of him they had hung, and took them to Cranborne by force and at their will, where they are detained. And the said foresters came by order of the said steward to Damerham, in the county of Wilts, to the house of Richard Martin, and there took a certain horse belonging to the man that was hung, value 10*s.*, and led it to Cranborne where it is detained. And they found in the coffer (loculo) of him that was hung a mark of silver, and a silver (firmaculum ?) value 8*d.* They also say, that John de la Hyde, had seizen of a certain tenement at La Hyde, by the escheat of one Adam Barringe who died without heirs, who held it of himself. One William de Coveshall, and other Foresters of the said Earl of Gloucester, by order of the said Steward, Geoffrey de Lenknore, came to La Hide, at the Feast of St. Michael, in the first year of Edward I., and ejected the said John from the seizin of his tenement, contrary to common justice, and in subversion of the Royal power, and delivered up the said tenement to Nicholas de Scorditch, who sold the same to the prior of Craneburn.

Hundred of Candon.

The Jurors say, &c., (in the same terms as in the preceding document relative to the Hundred of Downton.) And that the Foresters of the Earl of Gloucester came to Britford on the 1*st* of *August,* (ad gulam Augusti,)* with arms, and impeded the fair (nundinas) very much, and took toll of men, of their beasts and carriages, where toll was never accustomed to be given.

Hundred of Cadworth.

The Jurors say, &c., (as in the preceding.) And that Severicus, a forester of the Earl of Gloucester, and other foresters, by order of Golfrid de Lenknore, steward of the said Earl, came about the Feast of St. Michael, this year, to the plain of Fofunte, (Fovant,) and there took ten oxen, of the Abbess of Wilton, and drove them out of the county of Wilts, to

* Gula Augusti, the first of August; the day of St. Peter, ad vincula; called the *gule,* from *gula,* a throat, because on that day, the daughter of a Tribune at Rome, by kissing the chains of St. Peter, was thereby cured of a complaint in her throat. But *gule,* is more probably derived from the British *gwyl,* a feast or festival,—it was Lammas or lamb-mas day.

the manor of the said Earl, at Craneburn, in the county of Dorset, and detained them there against all pledge and surety, until the said Abbess gave the said Earl five marks for the sake of peace (de pace habenda.)

Borough of Wilton.

The Jurors say, that the Bailiffs of the Earl of Gloucester, of Craneburn, make attachments of Vert, even to the bridge of Bulbridge, without Wilton, upon those entering the said Borough with brushwood, by reason of his free Chase which he claims to have in his manor of Craneburn, in the county of Dorset.

Hundred of Loosebarrow,

County of Dorset.

The Jurors say, that the Earl of Gloucester, who now is, hath exceeded the metes and bounds of his Chase of Craneburn, between the way from Shaftesbury and Blandford, and the bank of the Stour, and makes attachments where they were never accustomed to be made.

Hundred of Gillingham.

The Jurors say, that in the reign of King Henry, father of the present King, Richard Earl of Gloucester, father of Gilbert who now is, exceeded the metes and bounds of his Chase of Craneburn, *viz.*, between the way of Shaston and Blandford to the bank of the Stour, and made there attachments, where they neither were accustomed nor ought to be made, and so it continues.*

Temp. Edward I. Gilbert de Clare claims to have in his manor of Craneburn, free Hundred and free Chase appertaining to the said manor, according to a perambulation formerly made, and warren in his demesne lands within his said hundred, return of writs, market, fair, view of frank-pledge, &c. The Jury say, that he hath not free hundred and free chase by the bounds underwritten, because, when Earl Richard, father of the Earl who now is, came first to the Estate, then these were the bounds, *viz.* from Chetell (Cheteles,) to Grimsditch, to the church of Handley (Henlegh), from that church to Deane (La Dene), from Deane to Gussich St. Andrew, from Gussich to La Ormdene to the head of Steppington (Stubhamp-

* The preceding Inquisitions are in the Chapter House.

ton), from Stubhampton to the head of Rutherseden, to the royal way which leads to Blaneford, to Shafton, and by that road to Tenersditch, from Tenersditch to Westwood, from the head of Westwood to Ridgeway, which leads towards Sarum to the bounds of Wilts, which lie between Ashmore and Ashgrove (Assemere and Essegrave), to Standen, from Standen to Mortresgore, from Mortresgore to Stythynghoc, from Stythynghoc by the road to Sandput, from Sandput to the head of Longcroft, and thence to Larmer (Lavermere), from Lavermere to Langden, from Langden by the bounds which divide Dorset and Wilts to Chettleshead.

Afterwards that, Peter de Rissans and Adam de Bekesgate, were stewards of the said Richard, who made attachments beyond the aforesaid bounds, *viz.* from Kingsettle to Sleybrondesgate, from Sleybrondesgate to the church of St. Rombald, from that church to Goldenoak (Gildenehok), to the head of Sturkel, and by that water to the bank of the Stour, and by the bank of the Stour to the bridge of Hayford, and from Hayford to the bridge of Blandford, and from that bridge to the bridge of Crawford, and from Crawford to Aldwynsbridge, from Aldwynsbridge by the water of Wimborn to Watford, by Watford to Stanbridge, from Stanbridge to La Langehaye, from

La Langehaye to Milesditch, and to Kings, from Kings by the way which leads to Lestford, from Lestford by the Craneburn water to La Horewythege, from La Horewythege to Aldelak, from Aldelak to Horestone to the bounds of Hants; and these bounds he used, but they know not by what warrant. They also say that he hath a warren in his demesne lands of Craneburn, and chase, and warren, in all his demesne lands and woods. Also they say, that he hath free hundred, a market, &c., from the time for which memory doth not exist. They also say that the said Earl claims to have a free court of his Chase at Cranborne, and pleas of vert and venison, with attachments of men, to to attach in the fact, or on suspicion, and to take emendals from such as are convicted in the said Court. They also say, that he holds a Court for vert and venison, and of all attachments made in any time of the year, and he takes fines and emercements from all those who are attached of vert or venison, and permits not any to course with dogs, the hares, foxes, cubs, &c.*

7 Edward I., A. D. 1279. A commission was issued to William Scammel, Dean of Sarum, and M. de Colombaire, directing them to choose twelve discreet and lawful men, knights

* This record is in the Exchequer. There was no Judgement upon it.

as well as others, that by their view a right perambulation be made (in Wilts, Dorset, and other counties), of that which had been made in the reign of King Henry III. and that the other articles in the Charter be fulfilled. The knights say, that the woods of Chetell, to wit, whatever is contained in Wilts, and that the grove of Fernditch, and all the hill country which is in Wilts, to the Avon, ought to be disforested of vert and venison, because certain woods among these woods were afforested in the time of the said King Henry, and some in the time of King John, and therefore ought to be disforested. And the said knights also say that the Foresters of Chetell, and Chase of Cranborne, take cheminage at the bridge of Aleswade, and at Bulbridge, and at other places where they ought not, according to the tenor of the charter: and did make attachments on the men of Wilts, and grievously amerce them in the county of Dorset, to the damage of the King, and the grievance of the whole country.*

8 Edward I., A. D. 1280. In the 6th, Edward I. A statute called the statute of Gloucester was passed for the inquiry into claims of franchises, in pursuance whereof the Earl of Gloucester made the following claim.

* In the Tower.—This perambulation was confirmed in Parliament, 1 Edward III.

Pleas before John de Ryegate, and his fellow Justices, itinerant at Sherborne, in the county of Dorset. The said Earl claims to hold in his manor of Cranborne, free hundred and free Chase, belonging to the said manor, according to a perambulation formerly made, and warren in his demesne lands within the said hundred, the return of writs &c., saving the liberties which any other within the same hundred claimed to have. Also, he claimed a free court of his Chase, and in the same pleas of vert and venison, with attachments of men, to attach them in the fact, or on suspicion, and to take from such as were convicted in the said Court full satisfaction. And that his Ancestors have used all the aforesaid liberties from the time whereof the memory of man is not to the contrary, and neither he, nor his ancestors have made any usurpation upon our Lord the King, or his ancestors, and prays it may be enquired of by the country. The knights for this purpose chosen, say upon oath, that the said Earl and his Ancestors have used the aforesaid liberties from the time whereof memory does not exist; and thereupon the said Earl went thence without day, saving always to our sovereign Lord the King, and his heirs, his actions when he shall be willing to speak thereupon.*

* In the Chapter House.

Hundred of Badbury.

8 Edward I. Pleas of the Crown before John de Reygate and his companions, Justices itinerant, at Shireburn, in the county of Dorset, in the octave of St. Hiliary, in the eighth year of the reign of Edward the King, son of King Henry. The Jurors say, that William le Forester, William Impelot, John Folyoch, Russel le Mouner, of Craneburn, Robert le Bur, William Cole, of Wylton, foresters of the Earl of Gloucester, came upon the fee of the Earl of Lincoln, within the said hundred, and took twenty-four oxen, or the same, for certain offences of which they accused men of the said Earl of Lincoln, whereas they had never transgressed in any demesne or bailwick of the Earl of Gloucester; and those oxen they drove away to Craneburn, out of the said fee, and detained them there a year and nineteen weeks; and they say that this was done before the Statute.* Also they present that a certain deer came wounded (Sagittatus), into the vill of Kyngeton (Kingston), on to the land of Hereward de Marreys, five miles (leucatas) beyond the Chase of the said

* The State of Marlbridge,—Marlborough.

Earl of Gloucester, and the Deer being weak his villeins and women took it, which Geoffrey de Lenknore, Steward of the said Earl, seeing, he sent there William de Conceshalle, William Impelot, and William the Forester to distrain the said Hereward for the said Deer; and they took there a thousand two teeth sheep (bidentes), and drove them to Pymperne, to the fee of the said Earl of Gloucester, and kept them there until the said Hereward paid a fine of twenty marks to the use of the said Earl of Gloucester.

From Gilbert, Earl of Gloucester and Hertford, twenty marks, which he had taken from Hereward de Marreys, for a certain Deer taken without his fee and his Chase.*

8 Edward I. Pleas of Jurates and Assize, before Salomon de Ross and his associates Justices itinerant at Wynton, in the county of Southampton, in the octave of St. Martin, in the 8th and beginning of the 9th year of the reign of King Edward. Gilbert de Clare, Earl of Gloucester and Hertford, was summoned before the Justices in Eyre, at Sherborn, in the county of Dorset, to shew by what warrant he appointed to himself free Chase from the royal way which leads between Shaston and Blandford, on the hill, on the western side of the said way unto the

* In the Chapter House.

water of the Stour from the bridge of Blandford, ascending by the Stour to the water of Sturkel, and by the water of Sturkel to Shaston; within the precinct of which appropriation, are contained the villages of Melbury (Melleber), Compton, Fontmel, Iwern Minster, Hanford, Chylde Hanford, Iwerne Curteney, Ranston, (Randulneston), Steepleton, Lazerton, Ash (Assch), Stourpain, Notford Lock, and Blandford; and thereupon William de Giselham, who prosecutes for the King, says, that when the said Earl had his Chase by certain metes and bounds, *viz.*, from Chetell's head to Grimsditch, and from Grimsditch to Handley, from Handley to Deane, from Deane to Gussich St. Andrew, to Brandone (Barendown), from Brandone to the head of Stubhampton, and by the middle of the vill of Stubhampton to the head of Rithersdene (Roger Hay's lane), from Rithersdene to the royal way that leads from Blandford to Shaston, and from that way to Thenerden (Tennersditch), and from Thenerden to the head of Westwood by the way called Rugwyk (Ridgway), which leads towards Salisbury to the bounds of Wilts, which lie between Ashmore and Ashgrove, and so to Stanton, and from Stanton to Mortegresmore, and from Mortegresmore to Singoak, and from Singoak to Sandpit, from Sandpit to the head of Longcrofts, and so to Warmer (Larmer), from Warmer to Buckden, from Buckden by the metes and bounds which divide Dorset and Wilts, to Chetell's head; the Earl appropriated to his Chase beyond those metes and bounds the said villages of Melbury, Compton, Fontmel, Iwerne Minster, Chylde Hanford, Iwerne Cortenay, Ranston, Steepleton, Lazerton, Ash, Stourpain, Notford Lock, and Blandford, which are out of his Chase, making in them attachments of vert and venison, in prejudice of our Lord the King and his dignity, &c. And the Earl came and said that there was a perambulation of the metes and divisions of his Chase of Craneburn, made in the time when King John was Earl of Gloucester, and that afterwards, in the time of King Henry, the father of the king who now is, there was made a certain Inquisition by Geoffrey de Langley and Richard de Worthing, the Justices appointed for the metes, divisions, and perambulation aforesaid, who took the said inquisition at New Sarum, in the 29th year of the same king. (Henry III.,) on the oath of the underwritten (here follow the names of the Jurors), who unanimously said, that these are the metes and divisions by which perambulation was made of the Chase of Richard, Earl of Gloucester and Hertford; *viz.*, from Bulbridge, in Wilton, to Hurdecote, (Hurcot), by the water of Nodder to the mill of Dyninton to the mill of Tyssebyr, (Tisbury), from the mill of Tyssebyr to Wycham (Wyke), from Wycham by the water of Nodder to where Semene (Sem), falls into Nodder, and so by the water of Semene to Semenehened (Semley), from Semenehened to Kingesethe (Kingsettle), near Shaston, from Kingesethe to Shaftesbury, namely to Sleybrondesgate, from Sleybrondesgate to the church of St. Rombald, from the church of St. Rombald to Gildenhoc, (Golden oak), from La Gildenhoc to the water of Sturkel, and from the water of Sturkel to the bank of Stour, and by the bank of Stour, to the bridge of Hayford, and from the bridge of Hayford to the bridge of Blaneford, and from the bridge of Blaneford to the bridge of Cranford, and from the bridge of Cranford to Aldwynesbrigg (Julian bridge), under Wimborn, and from Aldwynesbrig by the water of Wimborne to Waldeford (Watford), from Waldeford to Wichampton, from Wichampton to Pontem Petre (Stanbridge), from Pontem Petre to Longam Hayam, which leads to Muledich, from Muledich to Kings, from Kings by the way which leads from Lesteford through the middle of Estwood,*

* There is a difficulty in determining the line of boundary from Stanbridge to Horeston, several of the names being lost. Longam Hagam, means probably the long hedge or enclosure which leads to Muleditch or Milsditch, these and Kings we cannot indentify; Lesteford, the same probably with Letisford mentioned in Domesday survey, cannot be now ascertained; Estwood, the present Estworth.

from Lesteford by the Cranborne water to La Horewithie (or Horewyethe—Hoarwithy),* and from La Horewithie to Albelake (Eblake), to Le Horeston,† from Le Horeston by the way to the great bridge of Ringwood, from the great bridge of Ringwood to the bridge of Ford (Fordingbridge), from the bridge of Ford to the bridge of Dinton (Downton), from the bridge of Dinton to Aylwardesbrigg (Ayleward's bridge, in Fisherton), from Aylwardesbrigg to the aforesaid bridge of Bulbridge, in Wilton. And says, that the aforesaid villages which he ought to appropriate to his said Chase, are contained within the metes and divisions aforesaid; wherefore he says, he hath appropriated nothing to his said Chase of Cranborne, beyond the metes and divisions of the perambulation formerly made, and of the Inquisitions formerly made by the aforesaid Justices. And that the perambulation was made by the metes and divisions aforesaid, and in like manner the inquisition thereupon taken in manner aforesaid; and the Inquisition returned into Chancery by the Justices, was called thence to warrant the Inquisition aforesaid, which is in the King's Treasury. Therefore it was commanded the

* Hoarwithy,—see Note in Appendix, "Hoarstones." It is probably the spot now called "Crooked Willow," at Marrington near Horton.

† See page 96, and the same Note in Appendix.

Treasurer and Barons of the Exchequer, to certify to the Justices last in Eyre in Somerset, on the morrow of the Holy Trinity, upon the Inquisition aforesaid, and the metes, bounds, and divisions contained in it. Afterwards on that day, the Treasurer and Barons of the Exchequer did order a transcript of the said Inquisition under the Exchequer seal, in these words:—This is the Inquisition made by command of the Lord King Henry, the son of the Lord King John, on Thursday next, after the Feast of St. Dionisius, before Geoffrey de Langley and Richard de Worthing, appointed for this purpose at New Sarum, in the 29*th* year of the said King Henry, (III.,) on the oath of (here follow the names of the Jurors, and the bounds of the Chase as before specified). Afterwards, a day was given him in three weeks from the day of St. Michael, at Westminster, at the Parliament, &c. And then a day was given him at Wynton, in the octave of St. Martin, at which day the said Earl appeared, and prayed record and judgement, &c. And because it is manifest by the said Inquisition, that the said perambulation of the said Chase was made when King John was Earl of Gloucester, by the metes and divisions by which the said Earl now holds the same; and in like manner, the aforesaid Inquisition was taken by the said Geoffrey and Richard, by command of the Lord King Henry, father of the King who now is: THE LORD THE KING granted to the said Earl, that he should hold his said Chase by the metes, bounds, and divisions contained in the aforesaid inquisition, saving always the right of the King and of others, when they will to say otherwise (cum alias inde loqui voluerint). And the Sheriff of Dorset, is commanded to permit the said Earl to hold his Chase of Cranebnrn by the metes, bounds, and divisions contained in the aforesaid Inquisition.*

9 Edward, I. A. D. 1281. It is agreed between Gilbert de Clare, Earl of Gloucester and Hertford and John Abbot, of Glastonbury, that the said Earl hath granted for himself and his heirs, unto the Abbot, his heirs and successors, to make of his wood of Haywood, in his manor of Domerham, which he holds of the King in chief, such advantages as they please, without any attachment or impediment by the said Earl, his Bailiffs and Foresters. And that the Abbot and his successors, might enclose and ditch all their lands within their Manor of Domerham against the Deer of the Earl and his heirs; and if it happen that the deer should come on those lands, it is allowed the Abbot and his successors to drive them out

* In the Chapter House. This *quo warranto* was exemplified in Chancery under the Great Seal, on the application of Elizabeth de Burgh, 25 Edward III. A. D. 1352.

from thence, either themselves, or others, or with dogs. Moreover, a forester of Blakedon, on foot, appointed by the Earl, should take care of his deer without making any attachment, except of malefactors of venison taken in the fact. But if any be found in the said manor against whom there is a strong suspicion of the offence of venison, (transgressionis venationis,) the said forester should go to the court of the Abbot of Domerham, and should make known the suspicion to the bailiffs or other officers, of the Abbot, and one bailiff or other officer should go with the said forester to the suspected place and there make search, and if any venison be found in the house of the suspected person, or elsewhere in his custody or power, then he should take the person suspected and bring him before the presence of the Abbot of Domerham, and there keep him until he make sufficient amends to the said Earl for his offence, according to the custom of the Realm. And if no venison be found, then should no attachment be made. Moreover, it should be allowed to the head forester of the Earl, to ride with one groom (garcione) only, and look over the custody of the deer of the Earl with the said forester on foot. Also, that none of them have any thing of the Abbot, and his successors, or heirs, by custom or right, either in meat or drink, nor require or receive any except at their free will. From henceforth no distress, on attachment except for the fact of venison should be made by the said Earl, his bailiffs, foresters, or other officers, within the bounds of the said manor, or in the liberty of the said manor. No cheminage should be required or taken from henceforth of the said Abbot, his successors and heirs, by any of the bailiffs, or foresters of the said Earl or his heirs. And if it should happen that the manor of Domerham be dischased by any in future times, this agreement between the said Earl and Abbot shall in no wise prejudice the Abbot, or his successors, or the Monastery of Glastonbury.*

16 Edward I. A. D. 1288. Pleas of the Crown, before John de Metingham, John de Cobeham, Nicholas de Stapleton, and Elias de Bekyngham, the Justices in Eyre, at Sherborne, in the county of Dorset, in the octave of the Holy Trinity, 16 Edward I.

Hundred of Badbury.

De novis consuetud, &c. The Jurors say that Gilbert de Cors, head forester of the Earl of Gloucester, in his free chase of Blake-

* Harl. M. S. 1240. British Museum. Liber niger de Wigmore.

don and Chettell, and these his sub-foresters, *viz.*, Walter de Pulton, John de la Sale, John de Cors, son of the wife of Gilbert de Cors, John, son of Gilbert de Cors, John le Archer, William le Balc, John Folyot, John de Malverne, Robert le Stor, Henry, the companion of John Folyot, Philip, the forester, David de la Wodelonde, Geoffrey, the forester, William de la Hyde de Waldes, and Nicholas de Mareys, levied a new custom, by attaching all the carriages passing through within the limits of the said Chase with vert and deadwood, boards, and other things; and in like manner, to attach the empty carriages coming from the wood of freemen of the country, as well in the highway as elsewhere, and bring them to Cranborne, and extort amercements from those to whom they belong, before they can have them, at the will of the said foresters. And they do not permit freemen of the country, either to give, sell, or take, anything from their own woods for their use, except by license of the said foresters, and by their giving. They also take the dogs of free men of the country, running after hares, and foxes, and bring them to distant parts, and this they do in every place where they were accustomed to hunt. And they collect sheaves in autumn among poor men of the county who fear their malice and dare not contradict them. And they brew ale (faciunt braciare) once a year, and sell at their will, and so extort from men of the country pence by the power of the bailiff.* And they take from men having wood within the said Chase, for each acre 12*d.*; and likewise for every load of wood sold in their own woods passing by the road, they take 12*d,* or attach their carriages, to the oppression of all the people, and heavy loss, &c. Therefore it is ordered by the Sheriff, that he cause them to come, &c. Afterwards the said Walter de Pulton John de la Sale, William le Balc, John Folyot, Robert le Stor, Henry the companion of John Folyot and Philip the forester, came, and say that they have levied no new custom in their time, nor have committed any offence whereof they are accused, and throw themselves upon their country, &c. And the Jury say, on oath, that the said William le Balc made attachments of this kind now for one year, as a forester, whereas he is not a forester, nor accounted such by the Earl or his bailiffs, therefore let him be sent to gaol, &c. And they say that the said John de la Sale, John Folyot, Robert le Stor, Henry, and Philip, take the carriages of all passing through, and bring them to Cranborne, and make fine at their will; and take the dogs of free men in the Earl's Chase where they were always accustomed to hunt

* This was contrary to the assize of beer.

hares and foxes: and permit not free men to fell trees or cut branches in their own woods, and make attachments in the highway of dead wood and vert, &c., therefore let them be put in custody. Afterwards they made a fine of 20*s.* to Henry de Govyz, and Nicholas Malmeynes, &c. Of the said Walter de Pulton, they say he is not guilty of the said offence, and is therefore acquitted, &c.*

17 Edward I. Pleas of the Crown, before Solomon de Ross and his associates, Justices Itinerant, at Wilton, in the county of Wilts, on the morrow of St. Hilary. An R. Edward fil. Henry XVII.

Hundred of Altaworth.

The Earl of Gloucester claims to have view of frank-pledge, an assize of bread and beer, in North Mershton, which belongs to the honor of Gloucester.

Hundred of Sterkel.

The Earl of Gloucester, claims by his attorney, the same liberties here, from time which does not exist in memory.

* In the Chapter House.

Hundred of Kinwardeston.

The Jury present that Gilbert de Clare, Earl of Gloucester, holds this manor with the manors of Weycumbe and Bedewgude, of the king at a rent of £32 and in the said hundred and manors he claims to have return of writs, pleas of distress and gallows, view of free-pledge, assize of bread and beer, waifs, &c.*

18 Edward I. The Earl of Gloucester, surrendered to the king the manor of Cranborne with its Chase in the county of Dorset, by the metes and bounds in the time of the Justices in Eyre hitherto made, and the manor of Pimperne and Tarrant Gundeville within the county of Dorset.

And the King re-granted to the Earl and the King's daughter, Joan, his wife, and to the heirs of their bodies, the said Chase, to hold to the Earl, and Joan, his wife, and their heirs as entirely as the Earl held them on the day when he surrendered the same.†

24 Edward I. Inquisition post mortem of Gilbert de Clare, taken at Cranborne.

* In the Exchequer,—This record has been adduced to shew that the Earl of Gloucester did not claim any liberty of Chase, amongst his other claims, in these Hundreds which are within the large bounds in Wilts.

† In the Tower.

The Jury say, (inter alia,) that there are 1433 acres of wood where the pasture is worth yearly 100*s.* but it cannot be sold on account of the deer (propter bestias). And they say that the perquisites and pleas of the Chase are worth yearly 60*s.**

35 Edward I. An Inquisition post mortem, taken at Dorchester, of the lands, &c., of Gilbert de Clare, Earl of Gloucester and Hertford. The Jury found that the Earl held at his death the manor of Cranborne, and there was (inter alia) a certain Chase, which was worth nothing per annum beyond the sustenance of the beasts (ferarum).†

Grants of Free Warren.

22 Edward I. The King granted to the Abbess and Convent of Shaston and their successors, free warren in all their demesne lands of Donhead, Tisbury and Bradford, in the county of Wilts, provided the land were not within the King's Chase, &c.

31 Edward I. The King granted to John Husce (Hussey), and his heirs for ever, a weekly market and free warren in all his

* In the Tower,—This record is given at length in our account of the manor.

† In the Tower,—This record is given at length in our account of the manor.

demesne lands of Bridmere, in the county of Wilts, provided the land were not within the bounds of the King's Forest, &c.

35 Edward I. The King granted to John de Berwycke, and his heirs, free warren in all his demesne lands of Northyngton (Norrington), in the county of Wilts, provided the lands were not within the bounds of the King's Forest, &c.*

6 Edward II., A. D. 1313. John de Berwycke died seized of the manor of Northyngton, in the county of Wilts. It contained a mansion, with a garden worth yearly 4*s.*: two acres of meadow land, worth yearly 3*s.*: one hundred and forty acres of arable land, worth yearly 35*s.*: and a certain wood, containing five acres, worth 5*s.*: but there was no several feed or pasture there (nulla est ibi separatis pastura).†

13 Edward II. The Sheriff of Dorset was ordered to enquire on the oath of good and lawful men, whether it would be to the

* In the Tower. These records have been adduced to shew that the places therein named were not accounted within the Chase. It may be replied, that the peculiar terms of the grants were a mere legal form. The Chase, in point of fact, did not belong to the King, it was the Earl of Gloucester's. Norrington is in the parish of Alvediston,—Hundred of Chalk.

† This latter expression is singular, and signifies that it lay within the Chase, and consequently the feed and pasture belonged to the owner of the Chase for his beasts, as well as to the owner of the Manor of Norrington.

loss or prejudice of the King, or others, if he granted to his trusty and beloved Roger Damory* to enclose his wood of Blakedon, within the Chase of Cranborne, and to make a park of it, and that he and his heirs should hold the same. And if it be to the loss or damage, &c., then what damage, and whose: and how much the said wood contains, and what distance it is from our Forest. And Inquisition being made under your seal, send it to me, at Goseforde, in Northumberland, the 10*th* day of *August*. An. R. 13.

14 Edward II. Inquisition was taken at Cranborne, before the Sheriff of Dorset, on Friday, the 10*th* day after the Feast of St. Edward. An. reg. 14. And the Jury say, that it would not be to the loss or prejudice of the King, or others; and that the wood contains 500 acres, and is distant from the Forest of the Lord the King, of Gillingham, twelve miles (leucas) and more, and from the Forest of Clarendon, ten miles; from the New Forest, ten miles.†

16 Edward III., A. D. 1343. Elizabeth de Burgh applied to have the claim and allow-

* Roger Damory was the third husband of Elizabeth de Burgh, who was first married to William de Burgh, Earl of Ulster, and secondly, to Theobald de Perden. She inherited the Manor of Cranborne, &c.

† These records are in the Lib. nig. de Wigmore. M.S. Bibl. Harl., 1240. British Museum.

ance of Free Chase, a Free Court to the Earl of Gloucester, in the 8th Edward I., inspected and exemplified, and the same was done under the Great Seal, in the 25th Edward III.

32 Edward III. In the King's Bench it was adjudged by the Jury, between Elizabeth de Burgh, plaintiff, and John de Upton, of Berwick, defendant, that the said John, in the twentieth year of the then King, with force and arms entered the Free Chase of Elizabeth, at Cranborne, Pentridge, Ashmore, Gussage, Chettle, and Tarrant Gunville, and therein, without license, hunted the wild beasts, *viz.*, ten Bucks, and took and carried them away: and had repeated the offence for the last eleven years, against the peace of the King, and to the damage of the said Elizabeth, of forty marks. Therefore it was adjudged, that she should recover of the said John, her damages, and he being present in Court, was committed to the custody of the Marshall. In the next year the damages were paid and he was discharged.*

* In the Chapter House. It has been objected to this record, which is *conclusive* of the rights of Chase, beyond the inner bounds, that the places therein mentioned were the demesne of Elizabeth de Burgh, and consequently she might make Chase of them if she pleased: for demesne lands were excepted in the provisions of the Charter of the Forest. But, by an Inquisition, taken at the death of Elizabeth de Burgh, she died seized of the Manors of Cranborne, Tarrant Gunville, and others; and neither Pentridge, Ashmore, Gussage, nor Chettle, are mentioned.

41 Edward III. The King commanded his Treasurer and Chamberlain to certify into his Chancery, under the Exchequer seal, the claim of liberties of the Earl of Gloucester and Hertford, of Free Chase, &c., and the same was done accordingly. The Earl of Gloucester claimed to have in his manor of Cranborne, Free Hundred and Free Chase belonging to the said manor according to the perambulation formerly made.*

22 Richard II., A. D. 1399. By an Inquisition, post mortem, of the lands, &c., of Roger Mortimer, Earl of March, it was found that he had appointed his brother Edmund, for the term of his life, chief Forester and Keeper of the Chase of Cranborne, and chief warden of the Parks of Blakedon and Alderholt, and all other wood of the Lordship of Cranborne, which were parcel of the manor of Cranborne.†

6 Henry IV., A. D. 1405. An extent and customary of the manor of John Savage, of Tollard Govitz, on the oath of divers tenants of Tollard, Tarrant Gunville, and Stubhampton, who say that there is one Park there, separated by equal measure by metes and bounds, encompassed with a ditch from the Park, called Lucy's Park, which Park so separated

* In the Tower. † In the Tower.

contains by estimate four acres, which is a separate demesne at all times of the year, whose pasture is worth beyond all reprisals *26s. 8d.**

1 Edward IV., A. D. 1461. The King granted to Walter Harding, the office of Ranger of the Chase of Cranborne, in the county of Dorset.†

2 Edward IV. By an Inquisition taken at Cranborne, it was found that within the Lordship of Cranborne, there were a capital messuage and sundry fields, and the king had there a park with wild beast, called Blakedon Park, and a wood called Alderhold Park, and a wood called Bowerwood, and Castlewood, and a wood called Pitacre, and a free chase called Cranborne Chase, with many beasts as appears by a perambulation lately made: in which chase the king hath a court called Woodcourt, as appears in divers rolls. And he hath a Hundred there, called the Hundred of Cranborne and a Court, and hath an Honor called the Honor of Cranborne; that Richard, Duke of York, the King's father was seized of the manor of Wyclekesworth (Keysworth), as parcel of the manor of Cranborne, and Castlefield.

* This record has been cited to prove that Tollard Park, between the inner and outer bounds, was an ancient Park.

† In the Tower.

22 Edward IV. The king granted to Thomas Dakham, valet of the Crown the office of Ranger of the Chase of Cranborne, and keeper of Rushmore Lodge, vacant by the death of Walter Harding.

30 Henry VIII., A. D. 1539. The King granted to Sir Giles Strangways, Knight, the office of Steward of our Lordship or Manor of Cranborne, in the county of Dorset, with its members and appurtenances, and the office of Warden and Master Ranger and Keeper of our Chase of Cranborne, in our county of Dorset, *and in our county of Wilts,* and of all wild beasts in the said Chase being and to be, and also the office of Master of the Drift of the wild beasts of the said Chase, with all ways, &c., to the said offices, and every of them anciently belonging, to hold for life. And for the office of Steward, his fee was annually 66*s.* 8*d.* For the officc of Warden, Master, and Keeper, annually 100*s.*; and for the office of Ranger, annually £6 1*s.* 8*d.*

35 Henry VIII., A. D. 1544. The King made a Jointure upon Queen Catherine of the manor and lordships of Pimperne, Gussich, Tarrent Gunville, Knoll, Steple, Wyke, Portland, Holwell, Marshwood vale, the boroughs of Wareham and Cranborne, and the hundreds of Pimperne and Cranborne, and the forests and chases of Gillingham, and Cranborne, and the Parks of

Gillingham, Marshwood, Cricklade, and Blackdon, in the county of Dorset, and the office of Feodary of Cranborne.*

36 Henry VIII. In a particular of lands and possessions granted to Sir John Rogers, is contained a requisition by him to purchase of the King, by virtue of the King's commission, for sale, the premises specified which are thus described, *viz.*,

"As to parcel of the dissolved Monastery "of the blessed Mary, at Winton, in St. Mary, "Blandford, in the county of Dorset, and as "to parcel of the possessions of the suppressed "Monastery or Priory of Bremmer, in the "Manor of Pimperne, in the county of Dorset," —the auditor's certificate states that "the said "premises lyeth nigh none of the King's "Majestie's Manors or houses whereunto his "Grace hath accesse or repayre. That the "lands in St. Mary, Blandford, and Charleton, "be in distance from the Chase of Cranborne, "eight miles."

36 Henry VIII. In a Particular of lands &c., granted to Henry Longford, *viz.*, the manor of Woodyatts and Gussage St. Andrew, in the county of Dorset, with the Parsonage of Woodyatts, &c., it is certified that "they be manors of themselves, and lyeth within two miles of Queen's Grace's Park of Cranborne." Of a te-

* An Officer of the Court of Wards.

nement in Handley—it is a Guylett and parcel of no manor, also it lyeth within a mile of the Queen's Chase, Cranborne.

36 Henry VIII. Of lands granted to George Rolle, Esq., and George Haydon, Gent., in the Parish of Shapwicke, it is stated, that they are "from anye off the Kyng's Majestie's Houses whereunto his Highnes hathe anye accesse or repeyre tenne miles, and from anye of his Grace's Parks, Forests, and Chases, ten miles." Of lands granted to John Bartlett, *alias* Hancock, and Robert Bartlett, in Worth, *alias* Eastworth, in the county of Dorset, it is certified that "Estworth doth lye nigh none of the Kyng's Majestie's Houses reserved by a keeper and from his Highnes' Chase of Cranborne four miles." Of lands in Tarrant Antyocheston (Antioch) it is certified, that "Park, Forest, Chase, or any house of the King's grace reserved or kept for the accesse of his Highnes their is none adjoining." Of the City of New Sarum it is certified "lyen nigh none of his Grace's Forests, Parks, or Chases."

37 Henry VIII. Of lands, &c., granted to Thomas Macham, *viz.* the Manor of Upwimborn, within the parish of Cranborne, in the county of Dorset, parcel of the hundred of Upwimborne, and of the dissolved Monastery of Tewkesbury,. it is certified, that "it is a manor of itself, nevertheless parcel of the

hundred of Upwimborn, and lyeth also three or four miles from the Queen's Chase of Cranborne, and not nygh any of the King's houses reserved with a Keeper for the access of his Highness."

Of lands, &c., granted to Sir Thomas Arundell, *viz.*, the Manor of Fontmell, with the Hundred of Sexpen, parcel of the dissolved Monastery of Shaston—it is certified that, "the said manor and hundred lyeth nere none of of the Kyng's Grace's Parks, Forest Chases, or Mansion Places, whereunto his Highnes hath accesse at any time."

Of the manor of Barton, near Shaftesbury, it is certified that, "it is parcel of no other manor, park, forest, chase, or any house of the Kyng's Grace, there ys none adjoining."

Of the Manors of Burdeshurst (Bridzor, near Wardour) it is certified that, "it lyeth from any of the King's hede houses which ben kept by a keeper for the accesse and repayre of his Majestie, and also from any of his Forests, Parks, or Chaces, the distance of of six miles."

Of the Manors of Donhead St. Mary, and Donhead St. Andrew, Charlton, and Combe, in the county of Wilts, it is certified that "they be manors of themselves, and not adjoining or nighe any of the King's Majestie's Houses, Forests, Parks, or Chases, which his

Grace hath accesse, or repayre to at any time, saving the Park of Wardour."

Of the Manors of Melbury and Compton, in Dorset, it is certified, that "it is parcel of no other Manor, Park, Forest, Chase, or any House of the King's Grace, there is none adjoining."

38 Henry VIII. Of Lands, &c., granted to George Strangways and Richard Savage, parcel of the dissolved Monastery of Tewkesbury, consisting of the Rectory of Tarrant, (which?) it is certified that "the said Rectorye is intyre of itself, and lyeth nigh none of the King's Majestie's Houses, whereunto his Grace hath any accesse or repayre, ne nigh any of hys Highnes' Forests, or Chases, to the knowledge of the auditor."

Of Lands, &c., granted to John Bellow and John Broxholm, *viz.*, a farm called Lopeshall or Damerham, in the county of Wilts, it is certified, that "it lyeth nere none of the King's Majestye's Houses, Parks, Forests, or Chases."

7 Edward VI. A.D. 1553. Of Lands, &c., to be granted to John Cohk and Henry Bodenhome, *viz.*, a farm in Ebbesborne Wake, and Girardeston, in the county of Wilts, it is certified that they "lye nighe none of the King his Majestie's houses reserved by a keeper, but in distance from his Grace's Chase of Craneborne one or two miles."

Of Lands, &c., granted to Lord Wriothesley, consisting of the town and borough of Shaston, it is certified that they lie not "nygh any of the Parks, Forests, or Chases or Mansion Place, reserved or kept for the accesse or repayre of his Highness."

3 Elizabeth, A. D. 1561. Of lands, &c., granted to Edmund Twynhion, *viz.*, the manor of Tarrant Monkton, it is certified that it "lyeth not nere any of the Queen's Majestie's houses of accesse, but a two myles from the Queen's Majestie's Chase of Cranborne."*

1 Edward VI., A. D. 1547. The King, by letters patent, granted to Edward, Duke of Somerset, all that part and parcel of our Forest of Cranborne called Chettered, in our county of Dorset, as Queen Katherine hath held the same, and all those our woods called Queen's Coppice in Chettered, also the land and soil of those woods, and in the liberty of our Forest and Chase in Chettered, Michael Gussage, Keyneston, Rushton, Munckton, Tarrant Lanston, and Long Critchell, in the county of Dorset.†

* The preceding records, from the 36 Henry VIII. to 3 Elizabeth, inclusive, have been cited to shew that the places therein mentioned were not at that time deemed to be within the Chase, although they are all between the inner and outer, or upon the outer bounds. Their respective distances from the inner bounds, are pretty accurately stated in the Auditor's Certificates. They are in the Augmentation Office.

† In the Rolls.

4 Edward VI. The King did deliver, grant, and to favour let, unto Sir William Herbert, K. G., for twenty one years (inter alia). all his Manor and Lordship of Cranborne, the Hundred of Cranborne, and the Chase of Cranborne, with all their rights, liberties, members, and appurtenances, in the county of Dorset, and which were formerly part of the jointure of Queen Katherine.

— Edward VI. The King granted to the Earl of Pembroke, the Chase of Cranborne, with all the rights, members, liberties, and appurtenances in the county of Dorset.

12 Elizabeth, A. D. 1570. The Queen granted to Henry, Earl of Pembroke, the office of head Steward of her manor of Cranborne, and of Warden and Keeper of her Chase of Cranborne, in the county of Dorset, and Keeper of Blakedon Park, in the Manor of Cranborne, and the office of Bailiff of the Manor and Hundred of Cranborne, and the office of Bailiff of Cranborne, which offices, William, late Earl of Pembroke, father of Henry, lately had, and enjoyed for the term of his life.

22 Elizabeth. Pleas at Westminster, before Jacob Dyer, Knight, and his associates, Justices of the Lady the Queen. An. Reg. 22.

Wilts.

William Weare, late of Woodcotes, in the county of Dorset, Yeoman, was attached to answer to the plea of Thomas Topp, why he entered by force and arms his Close at Bridmere, and trod down and destroyed his corn, with certain cattle, cows, pigs, and sheep, to the value of 100*s.*, and committed other offences to the damage of the said Thomas Topp, and against the peace of the Lady the Queen, on 5*th* day of *May*, in the 19*th* year of the Queen's reign. And the aforesaid William, by John Budden, his attorney, defends and says he is in no wise guilty of the said trespass, for there is one acre of land called Blackacre, in Bridmore, which was the soil and free holding of him, the said William, and he had a right to tread down and destroy the corn there with his cattle if he pleased. And the said Thomas replied, that the trespass was committed in a close called Bridmorefield, containing by estimate, sixty acres of arable land, to which the acre, called Blackacre (in Barra) belongs, and therefore seeks Judgment and Damages, &c. And the said William says, that before and at the time the alledged trespass was committed, the Queen was seized of the Chase of Cranborne, which extends as well into the county of Wilts, as in the county of Dorset, in her demesne and fee in right of the Crown, within which Chase there then were, and had been from time of which the memory does not exist, bucks and does, and other beasts, and Keepers in the said Chase, to keep, govern, and hunt the deer; and that the close called Bridmore field, has been from all the time aforesaid, within the metes and bounds of the said Chase. And further, the said William saith, that at the time of the trespass he was one of the Keepers of the Chase, and as one of the Keepers, drove the stray (divisos) deer in the said close, to the other deer within the Chase, and in so doing they eat, and trod down, and destroyed, the corn in that place, and that he might go into the said close for that purpose as he pleased, which is the same trespass as the other, wherefore he asks Judgment whether the said Thomas should bring an action against him. And the said Thomas replied, that he is ignorant of the defendant's plea, and says, that the close called Bridmore field, is not within the metes and bounds of the Chase, and asks that it be enquired of by the country. Therefore it is commanded the Sheriff to cause twelve men to come here on the morrow of the Holy Trinity to try the issue, &c., on which day the said Thomas and William appeared by their attornies. And it was adjudged that the said Thomas, do recover of the said William, his damages, on account of the trespass: whereupon the said Thomas gratuitously pays into this Court, whatever damages are adjudged to the said William, therefore the said William is quit of his damages, and he may take them, &c.*

23 Elizabeth. Thomas, Earl of Sussex, chief Justice in Eyre, certified, that among the Rolls of the Queen's Chace of Cranborne, it appeared that John Swane, of Blandford, had been summoned before him and charged to have used his Purlieu† within his manor of Tarrant-Gunville, and the demesnes of Ranston, next adjoining the Chase of Cranborne, in the county of Dorset, contrary to the laws and ordinan-

* In the Common Pleas Treasury.

† Purlieu.—Lands adjoining a Forest which were afforested by Henry II., Richard I., or John, and afterwards disforested by virtue of the Charter of the Forests. It signifies, perambulation, insomuch as King Edward I. ordered perambulation to be made of Forests, with the view of carrying into effect the provisions of the Charter. The owners of lands and woods within the Purlieu had power to cut down timber, and convert meadow and pasture into arable land, and they might hunt the beasts of the Forest, towards the Forest, but not follow them into it, nor forestall them in their return thither. The King appointed an officer called a Ranger to rechase them back into the Forest. *Memwood.*

Purlieu was obviously a misnomer, as applied to the lands adjoining the Chase. The afforestations cannot be proved.

ces of the forest, *viz.*, in not permitting the keepers to rechase the Deer in his Purlieu into the Chase, as the keeper's had used and of right ought to do; and also in forestalling the Deer, and killing of unseasonable Deer, contrary to the laws of the forest; and also for cutting and enclosing his coppices by the space of seven years to the prejudice of her Majesty's game within the Chase, as appeared by a bill exhibited for the Earl of Pembroke, Lieut. of the said Chase. Forasmuch as it appeared to the Lord Chief Justice by confession, as well the plaintiff as of the defendant, that the said John Swaine, had time out of mind had a Park and Purlieu within the manor of Gunville, and the demesne of Randleneston (Ranston), in the county of Dorset. IT WAS ORDERED, by the assent of the parties, that the said John Swayne, might at his will and pleasure cut down and enclose all such his woods and coppices being within the Purlieu of Gunville, and which had commonly heretofore been known and used as Purlieu within the manor of Gunville and the demesne of Ranston, without suing or having license for the same. AND ORDERED, that the said John Swayne should suffer the Keepers and Underkeepers of the Chase to hunt and rechase the game out of his said purlieu within the Manor of Gunville, and demesne of Ranston, without disturbance as heretofore, the keepers had used and of right might by the laws of the forest, and the said John Swayne and Robert Swayne, shall thenceforth without disturbance of the keeper's use hunt, and of the said Purlieu as by the laws of the forest and *customs of the said Chase* they ought to do and in no other sort. And that it should be lawful to the said John Swayne, to inclose his Park of Gunville, only so that the Deer of the Chase should not come into the same, provided that the said John Swayne, should not make any Deer leaps out of the said Chase into his Park of Gunville, whereby he might let any of the Deer into his Purlieu.

The Argument Deduced from the Preceding Records.

Let us review the facts contained in the preceding Records, and impartially consider whether the evidence they afford be or be not conclusive in respect to the rights, which where ever claimed and exercised by the owners of the chase, although disputed and contested on many occasions, by the proprietors of lands over which these rights extended.—Their opposition to them was mainly based upon a construction which they attached to the earliest transaction recorded in the history of the Chase, *viz.*, the perambulation made by King John, whilst Earl of Gloucester, of its metes and bounds; assuming it to have been the definition of certain extensive afforestations made either by himself, or by his brother Richard, or by his father Henry II., and consequently the definition of a right, which was subsequently abrogated by the Charter of Liberties, but strangely and perversely upheld in defiance of the laws and constitution of the country. The obscurity in which that ancient transaction is veiled permits the free exercise of conjecture; before however we admit the correctness of an hypothesis involving an improbability, let us proceed to enquire whether the subject may not bear a simpler and more rational solution. In the statement of the Earl of Gloucester's claims, in the 8 Edward I., the perambulation made by John is incidentally mentioned as having been recognized as the boundary of the chase, in an Inquisition taken in the 29 Henry III., and the Earl was thereupon permitted to hold his Chase by the metes and bounds of that inquisition. Now, this Inquisition was taken just twenty years after the grant and confirmation of the Charter of the Forests, but as it does not appear to have been intended for the purpose of carrying out the provisions of the Charter, in respect to recent afforestations within the circuit of its perambulation, it becomes desirable to ascertain what other explanation can be suggested to account for the circumstance of the Inquisition being taken, and the following has been proposed, with every semblance of truth. The honor of Gloucester with the free Chase of Cranborne, was, during the minority of Gilbert, first Earl of Gloucester and Hertford, in the wardship of Henry III. nineteen years, and after that fifteen years during the minority of his son Richard, as appears more fully from the following record. "County of

Kent, 5 Edward I. the Earl (Gilbert de Clare) by his attorney says, that Gilbert de Clare, Earl of Gloucester and Hertford, his grandfather, was in wardship of the Lord King Henry, father of the now Lord the King, nineteen years and more, and after his death, Richard de Clare, Earl of Gloucester and Hertford, son and heir of the aforesaid Earl Gilbert, and father of the same Gilbert the now Earl, was in like manner in wardship of the aforesaid King Henry, for fifteen years or more, which same King had the custody of the lands and tenements of either during the whole time aforesaid, whereby their lands and tenements were exceedingly and diversely destroyed. And when the aforesaid Earl came of age, having seizin of his lands, he accosted the aforesaid King Henry, and shewed to him that their lands and tenements whilst he and his father Earl Gilbert, were in his wardship, throughout divers places in England, were so destroyed to his disinheritance, and therefore he sought for remedy; whereupon the King Henry assigned Robert Walbrond, and certain other his justices to enquire thereupon more fully the truth, and *Inquisitions* having been thereupon made throughout divers parts of England, it was found that the towns of Ditton &c., &c." Gilbert the first Earl of Gloucester and Hertford died in 1230, now if we add to this date the fifteen years his son Richard was in wardship, 1245 is given as the time when he came of age and made complaint of the destruction of his property, a time which very nearly coincides with the Inquisition.

29 Henry III., (1246,) whence we infer that during these long minorities of thirty-four years, the rights and privileges of the Chase, had been neglected and infringed, in common with his other property, and that the intent of this Inquisition was, to restore him to the possession of the Chase, as freely and fully as it had been held by John. Hence the Inquisition may be correctly deemed to have been a transaction of a private nature, and in no way connected with the public affairs of the Forests. In like manner, the Perambulation made by John, whilst Earl of Gloucester, may be strictly viewed not as a record of his own afforestations, but as the definition of an Ancient Right that ever had appertained to the Honor of Gloucester, and was enjoyed by him as the Lord of that Honor. It is quite certain that John, as King, made no encroachments within this disputed territory, because his perambulation was made in the reign of Richard I. (he did indeed make encroachments within the adjoining Forest of Blackmoor, which were dealt with according to the provisions of the Charter in the 7 Edward I.):

nor is there any evidence to shew that either Richard I. or Henry II. afforested any of the lands contained within the bounds of his perambulation, we therefore infer that the metes and bounds therein set forth were established at an antecedent period of which we have no record, and probably originated in the Saxon æra.

In the deed of Gift (noticed in a former part of this work) made to the Church of Cranborne, by Fitz-Hamon, in the reign of William Rufus, and confirmed by William, Earl of Gloucester, in the reign of Henry I., the existence of a Forest or Chase in connexion with the Manor of Cranborne, is distinctly implied, although its bounds are not specified. In the writ of the 17 John, "the Forest of Cranborne, Chetterden, and the Chase of Geoffrey de Mandeville, which William, Earl of Gloucester, held" are particularized as distinct tracts of forest land, all of them being contained within the bounds of his former perambulation, whence we infer that the King retained those parts of the Chase termed the Forest of Cranborne, and Chetterden, after the marriage of his divorced wife Isabella, with Geoffrey de Mandeville, and that the divided territory was afterwards reunited on the accession of Gilbert de Clare, to the Honor of Gloucester, and from that period continued to be designated the Chase of Cranborne.

The Inquisition, 29 Henry III., is confirmed by the writs of the Abbesses of Shaston and Wilton, 34 Henry III.; by the agreement with the Abbess of Shaston, 35 Henry III.; and by the Inquisition of Cadworth, 39 Henry III.

But the Presentments of the 3 and 7 Edward I., seem strongly contradictory of the Earl of Gloucester's claims and practices, which are said therein to be contrary to a Perambulation made in the 4 Henry III. Now, this Perambulation was made, it is presumed, in pursuance of a Commission, issued to the Sheriffs of Dorset and Wilts, in common with those of other counties, to enquire what Forests ought to be disforested according to the intentions of the Forest Charters, but no return to this Commission, nor instrument of disforestation (of any part of the Chase) has ever been found in any of the public offices for the custody of records, which may be deemed tantamount to the non-existence of any such important document. May we not, indeed, regard these Presentments as the complaints of interested individuals, actuated by ignorance or prejudice, or stimulated, perhaps, by a vague sentiment of public justice? In estimating the motives of men living in that remote period, we must bear in mind that a great political measure had then been recently introduced, for the purpose of ameliorating the civil condition of the people whom we may imagine as growing more jealous of their liberties, and in a state to be more under the influence of their feelings and passions, than of the calm dictates of their judgment, when those liberties were menaced with fresh invasion. Truly there was a spirit of tyranny and injustice breathing in the body of the Forest laws, even under their mildest and most restrained administration, which made any pretext for relieving themselves from their yoke, most welcome to those who were groaning under its oppression. They would not, we may be sure, respect an Ancient Right, or be scrupulous about enquiring into its validity, when the exercise of its privileges was primâ faciê opposed to the enjoyment and security of their own rightful property. Hence then, the origin of these Presentments, and we will go farther, and admit in justification, or the supposition of the probability that the Earl of Gloucester may have revived some dormant custom, established some long neglected claim, or in one way or another appeared to exceed the bounds of his authority, with the express design of substantiating his title to an Ancient Right, which he knew would be looked upon in that awakening age, with feelings of jealousy and distrust.

This we maintain is at least a fair supposition, but we must altogether dissent from the opinion, that the Earls of Gloucester, to whom these presentments refer, who, be it remembered were first and foremost amongst a powerful aristocracy, combined to wrest the confirmation of the great Charters from the vacillating, unprincipled Monarch,—that these noblemen, we say, were either guilty of the dishonesty of wilfully holding at the same time the possession of property to which they were not lawfully entitled, or so nobly disinterested as to be regardless of the certainty of becoming the victims of that patriotism whose altars they were striving to raise! we therefore adopt the conclusion that the Juries of the 3 and 7 Edward I. laboured under an erroneous or prejudicial impression when they presented that "the Earl of Gloucester had afforested all the county, from Shaston to Ayleswade-bridge, by the river Nodder, and what was in the county of Wilts, from the county of Dorset to the river Nodder," and "that it ought to be disforested," because they ought to have been aware if they really did not know that the Inquisition 29 Henry III., taken thirty years before, had established the Earl's claim to the metes and bounds of the perambulation of John, within which that district of the Chase is included. The question, however, was brought to an issue by the enquiry and trial upon these Presentments, in the 8 Edward

I.; but previously to this we find a record of a claim of franchise made by the Earl of Gloucester, wherein it is stated, that "the Earl claimed to hold, in his manor of Cranborne, free Chase, according to a perambulation formerly made, a free Court of his Chase, pleas of vert and venison, with attachments of men, &c. And the Knights upon oath say, that the Earl and his ancestors have used the same liberties from the time whereof the memory does not exist," thereby establishing a prescriptive title to the Chase. Upon the subsequent trial the Earl pleaded the Inquisition 29 Henry III., founded on the Perambulation of John, and "the King granted that the Earl should hold his Chase by the metes and bounds and divisions aforesaid. "This transaction is recorded in a document of very great importance, called the quo warranto, 8 Edward I., which, notwithstanding the subtleties of forensic ingenuity, is, in the plainness of truth and reason, the allowance of liberties to the full and free extent of the claim then made by the Earl of Gloucester, and ever afterwards insisted on by the proprietors of the Chase.* The Judgment

* It has been objected, 1st., that this was not a Judgment, because the terms used are "Rex dominus concessit, salvo semper jure Domini regis, &c., and was merely a Grant, which the King could not make. 2ndly, that the terms "salvo semper jure &c." are inconsistent with a Judgment. 3rdly, that it binds no man although no saving had been made. 4thly, that

was subsequently ratified by the surrender and re-grant of the Chase, 18 Edward I. The usage of the outer bounds is proved by the Inquisition, 13 Edward II., and by the Judgment 32 Edward III. In the 41 Edward III. the Earl's claim was rescinded in the Courts of Chancery and Exchequer.

In the face of this evidence it has been contested that the lands contained between the inner and outer bounds have been afforested since the æra of Henry II., consequently that the Judgment on the quo warranto is of no effect, because by the 42 Edward III. every Act of Parliament made against the provisions of the Charter of the Forests is rendered null and void. The county of Wilts has been the principal arena of these disputes, an objection having been raised to the validity of the exercise of the Chase rights over property in that county. In support of this view, the Presentments 3 and 7 Edward I. have been appealed to; the Grants, 22, 31, and 35, Edward I., have been adduced; the records relating to Rushmore Lodge; the Grants, 1 and 22 Edward IV., 4 Edward VI., 12 Elizabeth, which seem to restrict the Chase to the county of Dorset: the Grants of Henry VIII.,

the Earl put himself on the record, and not on the country: and 5thly, that the execution is directed to the Sheriff of Dorset, who could have no jurisdiction in Wilts.

Edward VI., and Elizabeth, which seem to restrict it to the inner bounds: these have been met on the other side by Presentments made at the Chase courts from Henry VI. to Charles II.,* the custom of levying chimenage in Wiltshire, from the reign of Edward I., and by the evidence contained in the preceding documents. With regard to the apparent restrictions and limitations of the Chase, there is reason to conclude, that after the demise of the Clare family, and when the property belonged to the Crown, its rights and privileges were not enforced with that strictness which had been previously obtained; the reassertion of those neglected liberties proved the fertile source of litigation, with the history of which, we are now about to proceed.

* In Appendix.

Legal Proceedings, etc.

9 James I., A. D. 1612. The King granted to Robert, Earl of Salisbury, "all that our hundred of Cramborne, otherwise Cranborne, with all its rights, members and appurtenances, in our counties of Dorset, Wilts, and Southampton, or in either or any of them; and all that our Lordship and Manor of Cranborne, and all the Manor and Lordship of Cranborne, Holwell, otherwise Halliwall, with all its rights, &c., and all the Chase, free-chase and free-warren of Cranborne, and all the privileges, jurisdictions, liberties, and hereditaments, called or known by the name or names of Cramborne Chase, otherwise Cranborne Chase, in the counties of Dorset, Wilts, and Southampton, or in either or any of them; and all and singular messuages, lands, &c., as well in the said county of Dorset, as in the counties of Wilts and Southampton, or in either or any of them, to the aforesaid hundred and manor of Cramborne, or Cranborne, or to the Chase of Cramborne or Cranborne, in anywise soever belonging or appertaining, or as being member, parts, or parcels, of the said Hundred, Manor, Lordship, or Chase of Cramborne or Cranborne, heretofore had known accepted, demised, leased, used, occupied, or

reputed; and all the Chimenage, Chinage, and Chivage, of our said Lordship, Manor, and Chase of Cramborne, or Cranborne, aforesaid, and all those our rents, lands, and tenements, in Damerham, in the aforesaid counties of Dorset, Southampton, and Wilts, or in either or any of them, to hold to the said Earl in fee."

14 James I., A. D. 1616. Edward Wood, a tenant of Lord Arundell's at Tollard Royal, brought an Action against William Budden, one of Lord Salisbury's keepers, for a trespass in breaking his close and hedges at Tollard Royal. Defendant pleaded that William, Earl of Salisbury, was seized of a certain great and ancient Chase, called Cranborne Chase, which extended in and through the pasture in question, as in and through the whole of the Town of Tollard Royal, and that the keepers had been accustomed to view, drive, and chase, the wild beasts in the said pasture; that the Plaintiff had obstructed the passage of the keepers, by erecting hedges, which the defendant broke down for the view and safe custody and chasing of the deer of the Chase aforesaid, in the same straying levant of couchant. The Plaintiff denied that the keepers of the Chase used to enter the pasture, or that the Chase extended in and through it, or in and through the whole residue of the Town of Tollard-Royal. The Jurors upon their oath say, that as to any trespass in the aforesaid

pasture, and breaking the hedges, the defendant is not guilty; and farther say that the Chase did not extend itself in and through the aforesaid pasture, as well as the residue of the Town of Tollard Royal, as the Plaintiff in his replication alleged; and they assess the damages of the Plaintiff, by occasion of the tresspass, in the second issue to 12*d.*, and for costs, 6*d.*, therefore it is considered that the Plaintiff recovered against the said defendant his damages assessed, and also £19 18*s.* 6*d.* to him at his request for his costs, &c., by the Court of Increase adjudged which said damages amount in the whole to £20, therefore, &c. In consequence of this decision the Earl surrendered up his Grant to the King.

14 James I. Indenture of Surrender from William, Earl of Salisbury, to the King, in consideration of a certain sum of money to him paid by his Majesty, of all that the Chase, free Chase, and free Warren of Cramborne, and all privileges, jurisdictions, liberties, and hereditaments, called or known by the name of Cramborne or Cranborne Chase, in the counties of Dorset, Wilts, and Southampton, &c., to hold to the King, his heirs and successors,—same year a re-grant was made to the Earl and his heirs of all the Chase, &c., and the court of Cranborne, and all jurisdictions, liberties, franchises, commodities, advan-

tages, emoluments, and hereditaments, with all their appurtenances of what kind, nature, or sort soever they be, or by what names soever they are known, deemed, called, or acknowleged, situated, lying, and being, issuing, growing, renewing, or arising within the aforesaid counties of Dorset, Wilts, and Southampton, or elsewhere, wheresoever to the aforesaid Chase or Warren of Cranborne, in any wise howsoever belonging, appertaining, incident, appendant, or incumbent, or as being member, parts or parcels of the said Chase and Warren, were heretofore, had known, accepted, occupied, used, or reputed,— to hold to the said William, Earl of Salisbury, and the heirs of his body lawfully begotten for ever yielding for the same yearly to us, our heirs and successors, 20*s.* of lawful money of England, at the receipt of our Exchequer at Westminster.*

15 James I. The Earl of Salisbury, filed his bill in the court of Exchequer, against William, Earl of Pembroke, Thomas, Lord Arundel, Edward Wood, Thomas Gawen, Robert Topp, and others, stating the King was lawfully seized in fee in right of his crown, of one great and ancient Chase, commonly called Cranborne Chase, extending itself by the limits,

* It has been observed that by thus creating a remainder to the Crown, the Earl opened an access to the Court of Exchequer, where he expected to obtain a decision in his favour.

liberties, and bounds thereof, in the counties of Dorset, Wilts, and Southampton, (then follows the specification of the out bounds,) and that by virtue of the last mentioned Grant, Plaintiff became entitled to the said Chase according to the bounds set forth, and complained that he had been interrupted by the Defendants in the enjoyment thereof, within the limits and bounds of a certain walk of the said Chase extending into the county of Wilts, called Burseystoole Walk, *viz.* in Tollard Green, Tollard Park, Honey Bags, Wiltshire, and Park Coppices. He also charged Robert Topp, with interruptions in Bridmore, and Thomas and Catherine Gawen, with interruptions in Norrington and Manwood, to the disinherison of the Plaintiff, of his Estate tail, and his Highness of the reversion. Lord Arundell, and Edward Wood, his tenant, filed their demurrer to the bill, and stated that before the Letters Patent to the Plaintiff from King James, the Plaintiff had endeavoured to use Tollard, as parcel of his Chase, whereupon the said Edward Wood, had brought an action of trespass at Common Law, against the Plaintiff's Keeper, and issue was joined whether Tollard were a Chase or no Chase, which was tried at the Common Pleas bar, and the Verdict passed for Wood, and found to be no Chase. That the Plaintiff did also, before the said Trial, exhibit his Bill in Chancery, where all the matters in question were examined and were still undetermined. That the Plaintiff after the Judgment and Verdict at Common Pleas bar, upon pretence of money paid him, (when in truth none was,) did grant the Chase to the King, and take it back in tail, reserving 20*s*. rent to his Majesty, which was done of purpose, and by the policy of the Plaintiff, to molest the Defendants under the privilege of the King's reversion; and for that the Suit still depended in Chancery, and a Verdict at Common Law before this Bill preferred; and for that the Plaintiff at his own charge had procured both the Grant to the King, and from the King, under a small rent after a Verdict: and for that the matters of this Bill were properly to be tried at the Common Law, therefore the Defendants demurred in Law, and demanded Judgment, whether they should answer or not, and if they must the Lord Arundell said that he was seized in tail of the lands in Tollard, and the same did lie without the Chase, and that the owners of those grounds had used to hunt and kill Deer at their pleasure, and preserve them as they list. By reason whereof the said Edward Wood, had prohibited the keepers of the Chase to come there, and had preserved the Deer there as he thought fit, and they denied that the grounds did lie in the Chase, or that the keepers of the Chase had used without interruption to walk the grounds of the said Lord Arundell.

The Defendants the Gawens, by their answer denied the bounds of the Chase to be so large as stated in the Bill,—said that their lands of Norrington did lie without the bounds of the Chase, that they had Free-warren in all their lands, and had used to make hedges and fences, to keep out the Deer of the Chase from coming there, and they denied that the keepers had used to walk there, but by permission only, to shake off the hounds and fetch in the Deer which had fed out of the Chase.

The Defendant Robert Topp, by his answer said that Bridmore did lie without the bounds of Cranborne Chase, and that the owners of Bridmore had used to make hedges and fences, and to hunt and kill the Deer at their pleasure, and had appointed keepers there, and had kept out the keepers of the Chase, and brought actions against them for coming there.

In this cause the Plaintiff and Defendant produced a mass of evidence, the principal part of which is before stated; *viz.*

The Record of the Court of Common Pleas, in 34 and 35 Henry III. The Inquisition 29 Henry III. The agreement with the Abbess of Shaftesbury 35 Henry III. The

Quo Warranto 8 Edward I. The allowance of the Earl of Gloucester's claim, at Sherborne 8 Edward I. The judgment of the Court of King's Bench 32 Edward III. Court Rolls—Presentments of Offences committed in the Defendants lands—and examined witnesses.

On the part of the Defendants the following Records were proved. The Rolls of Wilton 17 Edward I. containing the Earl of Gloucester's claim of Liberties in the hundred of Altaworth, Sterkell, and Kynwardeston, at an Eyre holden for the county of Wilts, to shew that no liberty of Chase was claimed.—The Commission of Perambulation 4 Henry III. The Presentments for the hundreds of Donworth, Dunton, Domerham, Candon, Cadworth, Chalke, Gillingham, and Louseburgh, and the Borough of Wilton 3 Edward I. The Perambulation 7 Edward I. The Confirmation 1 Edward III. The Verdict upon the Trial at Sherborne in the reign of Edward I.—The two Grants 18 Edward I.—The Grant 12 Elizabeth.—The three Grants of Free-warren in the reign of Edward I.—The Extent and Customary 6 Henry IV.—Five Records in the Abbey-book of Wilton respecting Rushmore-Lodge of 14 and 48 Edward III. 34 Edward and 1 Henry V.—The Judgment of the Court o

Common Pleas 22 Elizabeth, and the same 14 Jac. I.

A great number of witnesses were examined on both sides. On the part of the Plaintiff it was deposed, that the Chase was reputed to extend into the county of Wilts; that Deer depastured, and that the keepers had walked, hunted, and killed in Tollard, Ebbesborne, Berwick-St.-John, Bridmore, Norrington, Broadchalk, Burchalk, Stoke, Knighton, Chettlehead, Wichampton, Rushton, Tarrant-Monkton, Langton, Long-Critchell, Rawston, &c., all which places are without the inner bounds, and that they were reputed parts of the Chase—that the Lords of Tollard were only used to hunt there once a year at their annual Court—that Rushmore-walk was part of the Chase, and the owners of Coppices there gave notice to the Ranger of felling their coppices,—that persons had been taken for hunting in the Wiltshire Woods and been obliged to make their peace,—that fee-wood had been taken by the officers of the Chase in Bridmore, Norrington, and Ebbesborne, &c. On the part of the Defendants, many witnesses were also examined, who deposed that the inner bounds were reputed the proper bounds of the Chase,—that the owners of Norrington and Manwood coppice had used to hunt and kill Deer at their pleasure, and that these places were accounted to lie without the inner bounds, and the keepers did use to ask permission to re-chase the Deer,—that Tollard had always been reputed to be without the Chase, and the Lords and Tenants had hunted and killed Deer there at their pleasure,*—that the owners and tenants of of Bridmore had hunted and killed Deer and forbidden the keepers to come there, and that it was accounted to be without the bounds of the Chase, and that Sir Henry Ashly being Ranger of the Chase took a lease of the Lord of Bridmore, of free-warren, and liberty to hunt there,—that all the owners and Inhabitants of all the Villages and Towns next adjoining, without the inner bounds, and within the larger bounds, in Dorset and in Wilts, had ever used to hunt and kill Deer coming without the inner bounds, without interruption although the keepers looked on,† and that the keepers did not use to make their walks into any of the villages or lands lying without the inner bounds.

* Thomas Bower, of Donhead St. Andrew, æt 92, deposed the killing of Deer in Tollard Fields so frequently that he became "weary of venyson for they did often eat the same boyled with bakon."

† John Swayne of Gunville, deposed that he together with Mr. Chafin, Lord of the manor of Chettle, and High Sheriff of the county of Dorset, had hunted and killed a Deer, within Littlewood Coppice in the manor of Chettle, and were summoned to appear for the same before the Justice in Eyre, upon Mr. Chafin's proving his right of free-warren, the Justice said he might kill the Deer there and spare not.

17 James I. Upon the hearing of this Cause in the Exchequer Chamber before Sir Tulk Greville, Kight, Chancellor and under Treasurer of the Exchequer; Sir Lawrence Tanfield, Knight, Lord Chief Baron; Sir Edward Cremlie, Knight, and Sir John Denham, Knight, Barons, and which hearing lasted eight days, the following Decree was pronounced; that the Earl of Salisbury should have liberty for feeding and preserving the Deer of the Chase, within the pasture grounds, wood-grounds, and coppices, called Tollard-Green, Tollard-Park, Honey-bags, Wiltshire, and Park Coppices, in Manwood Coppice and in the Wood-grounds, and Coppices lying within the manor of Norrington.

Pending this suit a commission was issued, dated *25th June*, 16 James I. directed to Sir Francis Popham, Sir John Daunsey, Sir Thos. Hungerford, and Thos. Hinton Esq. which recites the pendency of the suit, and because it seemed to the Treasurer, Chancellor, and Barons to be highly necessary for hearing and determining the suit, that the bounds of the Chase should be distinctly expressed and explained to their view, the Commissioners empowered the persons therein named, to make Map, or Plot of the whole Chase, containing as well the large bounds claimed by the Plaintiff, as the short bounds set up by the

Defendants, and appointed two surveyors skilled in the business, to attend the Commissioners *viz.*, Thomas Aldwell, named on the part of the Plaintiff, and Robert Corbett, for the Defendants, which Commission was to be returned in one Month from the Michaelmas following.

16 James I. *Oct.* 13*th* 1618. The return of the Commission is dated from Marlborough and certifies that the Commissioners had met at New Sarum, when there were present, Mr. Sherfield, Attorney General, counsel for the Plaintiff, and Lord Arundell himself, with Mr. Wood, two of the Defendants, in whose presence the Commissioners had given orders to the two Surveyors to go forthwith in and with the drawing of a Plot of the Chase, exactly describing the larger as well as the straighter bounds, according to the several pretences of the Plaintiff, and Defendants; but for that the Commissioners thought it not meet that the Map should be charged with any particular description more than such as might be pertinent to make the bounds the more evident to the view, the counsel for the Plaintiff would not assent that his surveyor should join in the work, whereupon the Commissioners had given the best instructions they could to the other surveyor to proceed therein alone, who had accordingly made a Map of the Chase describing the bounds according to the pre-

tences of either side, which was affixed to the Commission.*

17 James I. After the verdict of the Common Pleas, and Lord Salisbury's filing his Bill in the Exchequer, the inhabitants of Tisbury, Wilts, petitioned the King that "he would signify to the Court of Exchequer his Royal pleasure that his name should not be used to the hinderance and prejudice of Justice, and that his pleasure be that the bounds of the Chase should be tried in some of the Courts of Justice, at the Common Law, where boundaries ought to be determined, and not in the Exchequer chamber, which is a Court of equity only."

18 James I. A Petition was presented to the House of Commons, setting forth the grievances that fell upon twenty thousand inhabitants within seventy parishes in the counties of Dorset, Wilts and Hants, and praying for leave to exhibit a bill for reversing the decree of the Exchequer.

19 James I. A bill was filed by the Earl of Salisbury, against Robert, John, and Richard Swayne, for interrupting his keepers in the walk of the Chase called the West-walk,

* The Map is preserved in the Exchequer. An attested copy was taken by Walter Harding, of Blandford, in 1618, from which the Map in this work has been reduced and engraved.

* No proceedings in this cause have been found.

in grounds pretended to be called park, woods, underwoods, pasture, and coppices, within the said walk, and the limits, liberties, and bounds of the said Chase, in the county of Dorset.*

7 Charles I. 1632. The Earl of Salisbury filed his Bill in Exchequer against John Cole, owner of the manor of Witchampton, in Chettered walk, for interrupting his Lordship in the enjoyment of his Chase, in the grounds of the Defendant. The Defendant by his answer insisted that Chettered Walk lay five miles out of the bounds of the Chase, and he claimed a free warren and free chase in his grounds there.

The Decree states, that after hearing many ancient Court Rolls, of the said Chase of Cranborne read, it appeared that in the times of Henry VI. Edward IV. and Henry VIII. divers presentments had been made against several persons for offences committed against vert and venison within the said Walk called Chettered Walk, and particularly within the manor of Witchampton, for which the offenders had been punished, and for that it appeared by the depositions of divers ancient witnesses that the keepers of Chettered Walk, did use to walk over the grounds called Dean's-leaze, Witchampton-Park, and Sley-gates without any contradiction, and the said grounds

* No proceedings in this cause have been found.

have been always taken as part of Chettered Walk, and that the Deer of the Walk did also feed there, being within the limits of the Walk, and that Chettered Walk was one of the six Walks of the Chase, it was therefore, this 19*th* day of *Nov.*, 8 Charles I., ordered, adjudged, and decreed by the Right Hon. Sir Humphrey Davenport, Knt., Lord Chief Baron; Sir John Denham, Knt.; Sir Thos. Trivor, Knt.; and Sir James Weston, Knt., the Barons of that Court in the presence of the parties, and of their counsel, that the Plaintiff and the heirs of his body, and in default of such issue, the King's Majesty, his heirs and successors, and all others that should or might thereafter become owners or proprietors of the Chase of Cranborne, might and should have liberty for feeding and preserving the Deer of the said Chase, within the grounds called Dean's-leaze, Witchampton Park, and Sleygates, without the let, hindrance or interruption of the Defendant, John Cole, or his heirs, or any claiming by or from him, or them any interest in the said grounds; and it was further decreed, that the keepers of Chettered Walk should have liberty to walk in the said grounds, without let, hindrance, or interruption; and that if the said John Cole, should at any time disobey that decree, he should pay such costs for the present suit as upon a

Bill to be made for that purpose, should be taxed by one of the Barons of that Court: and it was lastly ordered, that the Injunction formerly granted for staying the said John Cole's proceedings at Common Law against the Plaintiff Hicks, the underkeeper be continued.

When Lord Shaftesbury enjoyed the Chase, he never, it is stated, pretended to any other right beyond the small bounds in Dorset, than for his keepers to re-chase the Deer, particularly out of woods belonging to Mr. Fownes, in Stepleton; Mr. Ryves's, woods in Ranston; Mr. Swayre's, in Gunville; and the woods formerly called Preston's, now Bower's; and the liberty of pursuing the Deer there when hunting. The owners killed Deer at their pleasure, and the people killed strayed Deer without prosecution. Mr. Freke, who purchased the Chase of Lord Shaftesbury, desired that the owners of these woods would neither themselves kill his Deer, nor encourage the country people to do so. And on this condition, he offered them as much venison as they desired to have, and promised that his keepers should re-chase the Deer, and keep them as much as possible from trespassing. All the owners acquiesced excepting Mr. Ryves, who declined to give his consent, lest it might afford occasion for disputes in after times. This agreement subsisted for a few years without any dispute, until the keepers attempted to convict some persons for killing Deer on some of these Gentlemen's Estates, the latter deemed it prudent to screen the offenders lest their convictions might thereafter be made evidence against their Estates. They accordingly opposed the convictions, and upon asking the keepers whether they would swear that the grounds and woods where the Deer had been killed, were within the bounds of Cranborne Chase, and they refusing to do so, the Justices acquitted the men. Several instances of this kind occurred, and the Gentlemen exerted their right by killing Deer, and forbidding the keepers to hunt on their Estates. A reconciliation however took place, and the former agreement was again entered into by all, except Mr. Ryves, who continued all his life to exercise the right of killing Deer, lest his acquiescence should become a precedent against his successors. When the Chase came to Mr. Pyle, and Mrs. Freke, upon the death of Mr. Freke, these disputes became more frequent and one lasted seven or eight years, during which time the Gentlemen killed the Deer, forbid the keepers coming on their Estates, and threatened actions against them. At length in 1703, some of the keepers having been caught hunting on the Estate of Mr. Fownes, he brought an action of trespass against them.

3 Anne, A. D. 1704. Pleas before our Lady the Queen, at Westminster.—Fownes, *v.* Maurice Michel, Sen., ditto, Jun., Matthew Michel, and Richard Andrews. The Plaintiff complains that they on the 20*th* of *April,* 3 Anne, entered with force and arms an enclosed ground belonging to Richard Fownes, called Broadleaze, at Stepleton, without leave, and there hunted, killed and carried away forty does, twenty hares, two hundred rabbits, ten pheasants, and fifty partridges ; and trod down and destroyed the herbage there, to the value of £5, and pulled down fences lately made to the extent of forty lug, and committed other enormities against the peace, &c. The Court directed the Sheriff, (Harry Chafin,) to inquire into the damages by the oaths of twelve men, who having made the enquiry at Sherborne, on the 18*th* day of *April,* 4 Anne, and returned the same into Court, it was adjudged that the Defendants should pay £11 damages to the Plaintiff.

After this, matters went on quietly until Mr. Freke's death, and afterward when the Chase had come into Mr. Pitt's possession.—It is stated that intimacy and good feeling existed between him and the neighbouring Gentry. They had venison given them as often as they pleased, and frequently hunted together on their Estates. The keepers were allowed to re-chase the Deer, and when they were remiss, the Gentlemen would send messages to the keepers expressing their determination to kill, if the Deer were not re-chased, which was accordingly done without delay.—In the year 1726, however, the keepers took William Harvey, and Thomas Watts, killing a Deer on the Estate of Mr. Ryves, and in 1727, detected Thomas Stone, in a similar offence on Mr. Bower's Estate, and got them convicted, but the Gentlemen interfered, removed the convictions, and got them quashed. These proceedings which shewed the disposition of the owner of the Chase to extend his rights beyond the inner bounds, alarmed the neighbouring Gentry, who filed Bills in Chancery, to perpetuate the testimony of ancient witnesses in support of the inner bounds, to which Mr. Pitt replied, and insisted on the larger or outer bounds.

A. D. 1731. Mr. Pitt, brought an action of trespass against Mr. Fownes, Mr. Bower, and others, for hunting and killing Deer on New Down, and Collier's Heath, part of Mr. Bower's Estate, and on Broadleaze, part of Mr. Fownes's, Estate, the same ground for a trespass on which Mr. Fownes had obtained a verdict against Mrs. Freke's keepers. The Jury to the surprise of all present, it is said, brought in a verdict for the Plaintiff. The

Judge however, reserved a case which was never argued, whether an action of trespass could be maintained against a person for entering a Chase, and killing a Deer, the soil being in the Defendants possession. The evidence in this trial, on the part of Mr. Pitt, went to prove, that his keepers had walked, hunted, and ranged the Defendants woods, for killing and preserving the Deer, as they did in other parts of Cranborne Chase. After this verdict, in 1736, Lord Arundell, Mr. Fownes, Mr. Ryves, Mr. Harbin, Mr. Bower, and others determining to try the question of the larger bounds, with Mr. Pitt, filed a Bill in Chancery, but before the cause was brought to issue, Mr. Bower, to whom being a Barrister the management of the cause was entrusted, died; and no further proceedings were taken.

A. D. 1728. John Wyndham, filed a Bill in Chancery, to perpetuate testimony against George Pitt, Jun., Esq., stating that he had been seized in fee for fourteen years of a certain coppice, called Manwood, containing fifty acres, and of a certain Down, called Trow Down, containing about three hundred acres, in the parish of Alvediston, Wilts.— That the coppice, and Down, abutted upon Cranborne Chase, which was anciently a forest belonging to the Kings of England, and they had been from time immemorial a purlieu belonging to the Chase but were no part of it, being divided therefrom by a ditch, or some other well known boundary. That John Wyndham, and his ancestors had an immemorial right to the said purlieu, and had been used to appoint a ranger or keeper, and had a lodge for him within the same. The Bill prays that commissions may issue for examining witnesses.—The Defendants, George Pitt, Jun., and his sons, by their answer admit that John Wyndham, was seized in fee of the said Coppice and Down, and believe that the Chase, though formerly in the hands of the crown, was never a Forest, and deny that Manwood and Trow Down, are purlieu, and that John Wyndham, has appointed keepers, or that there was ever a lodge there. It appears by certain papers, that William Jay, and Thomas Keene, received a commission out of Chancery, for examining witnesses in this cause on the part of the Plaintiff, but no depositions were taken.

1728. John Wyndham, brought an action of Trespass in the King's Bench, against Richard Ashford, one of Mr. Pitt's keepers, for entering his close called Manwood, and killing his dog there. Ashford pleaded in justification that Manwood, had been immemorially within the bounds of the Chase, that he was looking after the Deer, and the dog was hunting there. The Plaintiff replied by traversing that the Chase did not extend in, by, and through the Close called Manwood. After a trial of fourteen hours, in which the parties went through all their evidence, and just before the Jury were returning with their verdict, Mr. Wyndham, was nonsuited, in consequence as it is said, of an error in the pleadings, the Plaintiff being unable to prove that the Defendant ever trespassed on Manwood, the fact being that he stood on Norrington Down, adjoining to, and not on Manwood, and shot the dog on the Down. From this period it does not appear that any other suits occurred relative to the bounds of the Chase, until 1749, when Lord Rivers's keepers, Ogden, and Bailey, having pulled down some fences belonging to Mr. Harbin, at Gunville Park, he commenced an action against them, which was brought down for trial at Dorchester Assizes, but Lord Rivers, having it is said, retained all the counsel on the Circuit, the Plaintiff was unable to proceed. The Plaintiff, it is said, re-erected his fences, and kept Deer in his park, at Gunville, without further interruption from Lord Rivers, and consequently did not think it necessary to proceed with his action.

Subsequently to this, Lord Rivers, commenced actions against some of Lord Arundell's tenants, at Tollard Royal, who claimed and exercised a right to hunt and kill Deer there, during the time his Lordship's Court was open. Lord Arundell defended the actions, but his attorney not being prepared at the Assizes, the trial was deferred on condition that the Defendants should undertake that Lord Arundell's tenants should not hunt at the next Court, which was acceeded to. At the following Court, however, some persons, against his Lordship's express orders, hunted and killed some Deer at Tollard, whereupon Lord Rivers's agent entered up judgment, and carried down a writ of enquiry to assess damages.—Soon after this, other tenants of Lord Arundell, also claimed and exercised the same right of hunting and killing Deer there, whilst the Court was open, against whom Lord Rivers brought his action and obtained verdicts. In *Oct.* 1791, Longman, White, Dunsford, Brinton, and Kiddle, five of Lord Rivers's keepers, having drawn the covers of several coppices at Ashcombe, Wilts, belonging to Lord Arundell, and having trespassed on his fields there, and trod down his corn &c., his Lordship brought an action against them in Michaelmas term 1794. Defendants pleaded the general issue &c. that Lord Rivers was seized of Cranborne Chase, lying as well in the county aforesaid, as in divers other counties, and that the closes in which the trespasses were committed, were within the bounds of the Chase; that his keepers had lawfully entered the said closes to look after his Deer, and did thereby unavoidably tread down the grass &c. Plaintiff replied, that the Defendants of their own wrong broke and entered the said close &c. And traversed that they were within the bounds of the Chase. This cause was to have been tried at the Salisbury Lent Assizes, in 1794, but the opinions of counsel given in consultation being unfavourable to the Plaintiffs' case, it was abandoned.

In the King's Bench, 55 George III. Wiltshire to wit, Lord Rivers, Plaintiff. Thomas King, William Want, and William Bradley, Defendants. Tried before Judge Holroyd, and a special Jury at Salisbury Lent Assizes, 1816.

The Plaintiff complains that the Defendant, did on the 12*th* day of *January*, 1814, with force and arms break and enter the Chase of the Plaintiff, in a certain part thereof called Trow Down, in Alvediston, in the county of Wilts, and did then and there with certain dogs, to wit, greyhounds, lurchers, and other dogs, without the leave or license of the said Lord Rivers, unlawfully chase, hunt, wound, kill, take, and carry away the bucks, does, and fawns, to wit, twenty bucks, twenty does, and twenty fawns, to the value of £50. there then found, and being, and converted, and disposed thereof to their own use. The second count of the indictment specified the driving, chasing, and hunting, the bucks, &c.,

of the Plaintiff. The third count was similar to the first, except stating the trespass to have been committed in Goscombe Coppice, instead of Trow Down. The fourth count similar to the second, substituting Goscombe Coppice, for Trow Down. The fifth count, that they seized, took, and carried away the bucks &c. Wherefore the said Lord Rivers says he is injured and has sustained damage to the amount of £500. and therefore he brings this suit &c. The Defendants pleaded, that the bucks &c., mentioned in the first and second count were one and the same, and that the Defendant Thomas King, was possessed of a certain parcel of land called Trow Down, and because the said Bucks &c., were wrongfully eating and depasturing the grass and herbage of the said Thomas and doing damage there, he, in his own right, and the other Defendants, his servants, by his command, with the said dogs, which were proper for the purpose gently drove, chased, and hunted, the said bucks &c., out of the said piece of land, doing no unnecessary damage to the said bucks &c. Wherefore they pray Judgment of the said Lord Rivers, ought to have or maintain his action thereof against them &c. And as to the third and fourth counts, they say that the bucks &c., therein mentioned are one and the same, and that the said Thomas was lawfully possessed of a certain close or parcel of land called Goscombe Field, and because the said bucks &c., were wrongfully eating and depasturing there &c., the said Defendants gently drove, chased, and hunted the said bucks &c., out of the said close into Goscombe Coppice, and were there chased, and hunted, and a little bitten by the dogs against the will and consent of the Defendants, therefore they pray &c. And as to the fifth count they say, that a certain Deer was pursued and driven against their will and consent, into a yard or enclosed place, in Alvediston, whereupon they for the preservation of the said Deer, from hurt or injury, gently laid their hands upon him, and detained him there, and gave the said Lord Rivers notice thereof. Wherefore &c. Lord Rivers replied, that the Defendant, Thomas King, was not lawfully possessed of Trow Down, and that he, the Plaintiff, is seized in his demesne as of fee, of and in the Chase called Cranborne Chase, in the said first and second counts mentioned; and that the said Chase was, and from time whereof the memory of man is not to the contrary, hath been, and still is, a Chase for the keeping and feeding bucks, &c., therein, and that the parcel of land called Trow Down, is within and part of the said Chase, and that the said bucks, &c., were lawfully in the said parcel of land, eating and depasturing the grass and herbage, until the said Defendants committed the trespasses mentioned, and this the Plaintiff prays may be enquired of by the country &c. The Plaintiff also replied that the parcels of land called Goscombe Field, and Goscombe Coppice, where within and parts of the said Chase, and that they committed the said trespasses in the form and manner as complained against them. Therefore to try this issue let a Jury &c. At the trial the Plaintiffs' evidence proved the grant of the Chase to the Earl of Salisbury, by James I. that the keepers had been accustomed to hunt and kill the Deer, uninterruptedly on Trow Down &c. He adduced the same evidence respecting his rights of Chase, as had been formerly brought forward to support the Bill, filed in the court of Exchequer, 15 James I. against the Earl of Pembroke, Lord Arundell and others, for killing Deer in the parish of Alvediston and Tollard, and proved the decree of the Chancellor and Barons in that cause, that the Earl of Salisbury and his successors were to have liberty to feed and preserve Deer in Manwood Coppice, and other woods in the manor of Norrington &c. He produced ancient Court Rolls of the manor of Cranborne and presentments,* from which it appeared that persons had been fined for killing and hunting Deer within the large bounds, which

* See Appendix.

fines had been paid. The Defendants pursued the same line of defence as in the above mentioned proceedings, 15 James I. and proved that cheminage money when refused had not been enforced; that Deer had been killed uninterruptedly on the road from Shaftesbury to Downton within the large boundary, and no prosecutions instituted although known to the keepers, and that the lands and coppices within the manor of Norrington, were not deemed to be within the bounds of the Chase, until after the decision on the Bill, 15 James I. The Jury returned a verdict for the Defendants, thereby denying the Plaintiffs' claim to liberties of free chase, within the county of Wilts, which was the point mainly contended for, in the action, a verdict therefore subversive of Lord Rivers's ancient rights. The Defendant, Mr. King, was the owner and occupier of Alvedistone Farm, and tenant of the Farm of Northington, or Norrington, belonging to Mr. Wyndham, in which the places in question are situated.—The other Defendants were his shepherds, who acting under his orders, drove away with greyhounds and other dogs the Deer, that came to feed on Mr. King's turnips. The keepers shot two of the dogs, which was made the subject of two separate actions; but they were set at rest by the unexpected issue of this final and memorable trial.

The Disfranchisement.

A negotiation for the disfranchisement of the Chase, was set on foot in 1787, the proposal having been previously intimated to Lord Rivers, by Lord Temple, afterwards, Marquis of Buckingham, and a committee of proprietors was appointed, of which Anthony Chapman Esq. of Gunville, was chairman, who proposed the terms of £200. per annum, to Lord Rivers, which however was indignantly refused, and an intimation conveyed that no less a sum than £1000. per annum, and a park round Rushmore Lodge, would be deemed an equivalent for relinquishing his rights of Chase. This, on the side of the proprietors, was deemed an exorbitant demand, and thus the negotiation for the present terminated.—An "authentic account" of the transaction was published by Lord Rivers, in 1791, containing the correspondence with remarks, and we confess we cannot rise from its perusal, without a deep sense of the honorable and straightforward line of conduct pursued by the noble owner of the Chase, as contrasted with the opposite party, who, through their organ the chairman appear to have been actuated not so much by the principle of fair and equitable dealing, between man and man, as by the assumption of this preconceived theorem, "the Chase is a great public mischief, as well as private injury, and ought therefore not to exist,"—a theorem, whose fallacy and injustice were triumphantly exposed in the "observations" of Lord Rivers. To this the chairman replied in "a letter to the Noblemen, Gentlemen, and Proprietors &c." At a meeting of the committee, held at Woodyates Inn, *Nov.* 29*th*, 1790, it was resolved that "the Proprietors unite for the defence of their property from any encroachment that may be made thereon, and appoint a Committee for that purpose; and that the Marquis of Buckingham, the Marquis of Bath, the Earl of Shaftesbury, the Earl of Uxbridge, Lord Arundell, Lord Camelford, the Hon. James Everard Arundell, Governor Parry, George Jackson, Thomas Grove, Peter William Baker, Edward Buckley Batson, John Elliot, Esqrs., together with the chairman, or any three of them, be requested to form the said committee, to take such legal and constitutional steps as they shall judge expedient for the said purpose." In 1803, the negotiation was renewed, when Lord Rivers, repeated his demand of £1000 per annum, with a park of the value of £250 per annum, but as he had purchased some woods near

Rushmore, he offered to accept a park near West Lodge. The committee of Proprietors consented to treat on these terms, but on account of the difficulty of procuring the lands required the agreement was not effected.* At length an Act of Parliament, 9 Geo. IV., was obtained for the disfranchisement of the Chase, by which it was provided that Lord Rivers, and his heirs, were to receive from Michaelmas, 1829, the clear annual rent of £1,800 per annum; to dispose of twenty thousand head of Deer, to retain free the Lodges of Rushmore, West Lodge, and Bussystool.† The Act expired *Oct.* 10*th*, 1830, and thus was the final disfranchisement of Cranborne Chase accomplished.‡

Conclusion.

The disfranchisement of the Chase was entirely a voluntary concession on the part of its noble proprietor, who was doubtlessly induced to accede to their proposal, from the conviction of the instability of his rights, which the last decision of a Jury had invalidated,—a decision arrived at, we hesitate not to affirm,

* West's History of Chase.

† Hundred of Chalk, (Modern Wilts) by Charles Bowles Esq.

‡ Act for disfranchisement in App.

in opposition to the clearest testimony in support of an ancient right, that was ever produced before a court of Justice. It was not however, enough to prove the prescriptive nature of that right, or its actual enjoyment for a period of more than six hundred years ; it was not enough to substantiate its title by documents of unimpeachable authority, for there was a pre-existent bias in the minds of those who sat in judgment upon them, there was a secret prejudice against the possession of a power and a privilege, which some had even the boldness to assert were too princely and extensive to be safely entrusted in the hands of any subject. It is obvious from what we have related, that for the last two centuries, the disposition on the part of interested individuals, to dispute the tenure of the Chase, and to curtail its privileges, had assumed a most determined front; each partial success was lauded as a triumph; each instance of defeat proved the stimulus to renewed exertion; but it was an unequal contest, wherein one unsupported individual had to sustain the brunt of a perpetual warfare waged by a combination of enemies, and it therefore became an act of prudence to resign on favourable terms, the possession of a right that was already threatened with extinction. We would not defend the principle of the Forest law, but on the contrary, freely admit it to have been the offspring of an unenlightened age, the remnant of the dark and byegone days of barbarism, a strange inconsistency in a land of light and freedom; nevertheless we do maintain that Lord Rivers's rights were clearly and convincingly expressed, and that their tenure ought to have been deemed as sacred and inviolable as that of any other description of property. And with what justice were those rights assailed, insomuch as the property of the assailants was originally granted, or purchased as subject to the exercise of those rights?

We are constrained however, to admit, that there were circumstances which rendered the disfranchisement a measure of public utility and benefit. Loud and general were the complaints of agriculturists, whose lands bordered on the Chase Woods, respecting the devastation of their crops by the Deer, and the expences contingent on the protection of their property; to this important class of individuals the extermination of the Deer has proved an effectual and permanent relief. But what shall we say of its effects upon the labouring class? With strong temptations to the commission of crime, and feeble powers of moral resistance, no wonder that the Chase exerted a baneful influence on the condition of the humble ranks of life; we do not indeed write unadvisedly when we state, that it proved to them a nursery of idleness and vice, and a source of misery in numerous instances that might be pointed to amongst the families of the neighbouring peasantry. The temptation has been done away, and though the evils to which it has given rise have not yet been wholly eradicated, we do still confidently anticipate that in process of time the moral infection will have entirely exhausted itself, and become inert. Amongst the upper class of society too, a demoralizing agency was at work, evidencing its existence in the frequent outbreaks of litigation, and keeping up a feeling of animosity and ill-will, where friendship and kindness ought to have prevailed. Every one, then, of reflecting mind, and philanthropic sentiments, cannot lament that evils of sad extension and vital nature, have received their death-blow in the extinction of the cause from which they originated; and none but the disappointed gourmand, or the foe of those mutual bonds which knit together the framework of society, will deny the benefit of annihilating the principles of disunion, or will remember with serious regret the disfranchisement of Cranborne Chase.

FINIS.

Notes.

Note *a* page 10.

The Crane, (grus cinerea) though at the present time an occasional and very rare visitant to this country, was formerly much more frequent. Dr. Turner states that he often saw young birds in our marshes. Sir Thomas Browne, of Norwich, who wrote in the time of Charles II. says in his works, " Cranes are often seen here, in hard winters, especially about the champaign and fieldy parts. It seems they have been more plentiful, for in a bill of fare when the mayor entertained the Duke of Norfolk, I met with Cranes in a dish." In the Norfolk Household book they are noticed, and in Dugdale's Origines Juridiciales, the price of a Crane in London is 10*s*. Leland in his "Collectanea" says in the bills of fare at the feast of Archbishop Neville, two-hundred and four Cranes are mentioned, and according to Sir David Lindsay, they formed a part of the bill of fare at the grand hunting entertainment given by the Earl of Athol to James V. of Scotland, and to the Queen's mother on the banks of the Loghaine, in Glen Tilt. At a Sergeants' dinner given at Ely House, A.D. 1555 *Oct.* 16*th* before the King, Queen, Judges &c., there were seven dishes of Cranes and three of Bustards. There are only five or six instances on record of its having been killed in this country during the last fifty years. With regard to the Bustard, which was formerly so abundant that a flight of twenty-five was seen by Mr. Chafin, on Salisbury Plain in 1751, it is now exceedingly rare. A female Bustard was shot on Colden Common near Winchester, in January 1839. *Yarrell's Birds &c.*

Appendix.

Appendix.

Court Rolls.

1 Edward VI. *October* 6*th*.—At a Court then holden, William Herbert, Knt., chief Steward and chief Keeper, present.

1. The Keeper of the west part of the Chase appeared by his deputy, and having been sworn, presented nothing, but that all is well.

2. The Keeper of the east part of the Chase appeared and having been sworn &c.

3. The Riding Forester appeared &c.

4. West Buckden.—The Foresters appear, and having been sworn, present that Walter Frye, of Guncoyte, several times in the last summer, agisted with three hundred sheep, within the Chase of our Lady the Queen, in the coppice under Burchhill, in consumption of the herbage and destruction of the shoot, in prejudice of the Lady and the Deer. Therefore let him be distrained before the next Court. And that Margery Bernard, of Chettle, widow, hath withdrawn an ancient due payable from time beyond memory, *viz.*, yearly, one quarter of wheat, one quarter of barley, and one of oats, and certain hens, from the Ranger and Foresters, to the great detriment of the officers, and prejudice of our Lady the Queen, therefore let her be distrained.

5. East Buckden.—The Foresters appear and present that John Swayne, of Woodcotes, in the fence-month last past, broke and entered the coppice called Lorden-Hall, and led

therefrom one plough colt, which had been distrained by the Forester, contrary to the custom of the Chase &c., therefore let him be distrained. And that Henry Langford, of Woodyates, hath this year withdrawn certain grain due of old time, payable yearly to the Foresters, *viz.*, six bushels of wheat, and on every Friday, weekly, refreshment for the Ranger and four persons, to the great prejudice of our Lady the Queen, and the great detriment of the officers of the Chase. Therefore let him be distrained &c.

6. CHITTERED.—The Foresters appear and having been sworn, present nothing, but that all is well.

7. ALDERHOLT.—The Foresters appear and having been sworn present, that for these eight years hath been withdrawn an ancient yearly due, payable out of the house of the late Nuns of Shaftesbury, of 3*s.* 6*d.* and out of the cell of Cranborne, on Wednesday and Friday, weekly, refreshment for the two foresters together and for their horses and dogs, to the prejudice of our Lady the Queen, and the great detriment of the said Foresters, therefore distresses &c.

8. BLAKEDON.—The keeper of the Park appeared, and having been sworn, had nothing to present, but that all is well.

9. BURCHALKE.—The Woodward appeared, and having been sworn, presented nothing.

10. ASHEMERE.—The Woodward appeared &c. At this day came Roger Staynour, of Barwick, and William Hill, of Fontmell, and put themselves in the mercy of the Court, for trespasses by them made as in the preceding Court appears, and their fines are taxed that they may not again offend as appears upon their heads, and they are at this time dismissed from the Court.

At this Court it is presented on the oath of the Ranger, that Walter Whitmarsh, of Stooke; Katherine Weres, of Handley, widow; William Horsey, of Alveston, Esq.; John Staynismore, of Barwyke; Edmund Bowre, of Donet Marye; William Bowre, of Donet; Robert Topp, of Bridmore; Richard Benbury, of Gunville; Robert Ingram, of Wademanton;

Christopher Swetnam, of Shroton; William Syverwast, of Tollard; and Walter Frye, of Gunville; being lawfully summoned to answer to the Lady the Queen, at this Court, for divers trespasses by them committed, as in the preceding Court appeared, came not, therefore every one of them is in the mercy of the Court, as upon their heads.

The amount of this Court 3*s.* 2*d.*

2 Edward VI. *July 24th.*—At a Court holden at Cranborne, the Keeper of the west part of the Chase appeared by his deputy, and being sworn presented nothing, but that all is well.

The Keeper of the east part, &c.

The riding Forester appeared, and being sworn, presented that Thomas Morgan of Wodecote, about the Feast of the Invention of the Holy Cross last past, disturbed the Deer of the Lady the Queen, within her Chase at Tinkly with three greyhounds, to her great prejudice, therefore let him be distrained. And that there happened a murrain among the Deer of the Lady in the last summer, to the number of fifty.

West Buckden.—The Foresters appeared, and present that Walter Frye of Gundeville, hath sold, since the last Chase Court, one coppice called Groves, without license of the chief keeper being applied for and obtained, contrary to the custom of the Chase, and to the prejudice of the Lady the Queen, therefore let him be distrained. And that William Skymere, of Fountmyll, hath since the last Court, commonly depastured his sheep in Fountmyll's wood, and under Fountmyll's wood, under Herd's coppice next Wossooke's Pitts. And that John Mounke, of the parish of Fountmyll, for a like trespass with his sheep, at the same time and place. And William Still, of the same place, for a like trespass with his sheep, at the same time and place, to the number of sheep belonging to the said William and John, of three hundred, to the prejudice &c., therefore let them be distrained. And that William Morgan, of Ashemere, since the last Court, hath entered and perambulated the Chase of the Lady the Queen in West Buckden, with a bow and arrows, contrary to the custom of the Chase, therefore &c., And that Thomas

Pamyngton, of the same, for the like trespass at another time in the West Buckden, within the said Chase, &c., therefore &c. And that Walter Frye, of Gundeville, in the last summer with his dogs, killed one buck within the Chase, therefore &c. And that the said Walter Frye, since the Feast of the birth of Christ, entered the Chase at Bures, and there with his dogs killed one Deer, to the prejudice of the Lady and diminution of the Deer, therefore &c. And that John Style, of Fount myll, since the last Court, hath entered the Chase of the Lady the Queen next Wrabbeshaw, and there with his dog killed one doe, to the prejudice of the Lady and destruction of the Deer, therefore &c.

East Buckden.—The Foresters then appeared, and having been sworn, present that Thomas Morgan, of Wodecote, in the month of December last, entered the Chase of the Lady the Queen at Shavedown with his greyhounds, and killed one fawn, to the prejudice &c., therefore &c. And that Richard Vincent, of Ebbesborne, because he hath not sufficiently amended the hedges of his coppice called Rugge coppice within the Chase, by reason whereof, the shoots of the same coppice are destroyed, therefore &c. And that the said Richard Vincent, before the time accustomed, broke and carried away the hedges of the coppice called Earl of Shrovesbery's coppice, by which breaking, the shoot is destroyed, to the prejudice &c., therefore &c. And that Walter Kerley, of Penterigg, hath permitted the hedges of the coppices towards Hinoks and Bere to be uninclosed, by which the shoots of the said coppice is destroyed, therefore &c. And further they present, that there happened in the last summer time a murrain to the Deer of the Lady, to the number of fifty.

Chittered.—The foresters appeared, and having been sworn present nothing, but that all is well.

Alderholt.—The foresters appeared, and having been sworn, present that their ancient due as in the Court is as yet witheld, therefore it is referred to the Council of our Lady the Queen.

Blakedon.—The keeper of the Park there appeared and having been sworn had nothing to present at this day, other than all is well.

BURCHALKE.—The Woodward there appeared and having been sworn, had nothing to present at this Court.

ASHMERE.—The Woodward there appeared and having been sworn, had nothing to present, but that all is well.

At this day came William Bowre, of Donet, and Christopher Swetnam, of Shroton; William Horsey, of Alveston, gent.; Richard Benbury, of Gundeville, and every one of them puts himself in mercy of the Court, for their trespasses, and their fines are taxed that they should no more offend as upon their heads, and so far those trespasses they are dismissed this Court.

At this Court it is presented on the oath of the Ranger, that John Staynesmore, of Barwick; Edmund Bowre, of Donet; Robert Topp, of Bridmore; Walter Frye, of Gundeville; Robert Ingram, of Wodemanton; William Syverwest, of Tollard; Walter Whitmarsh, of Stooke; John Swayne, of Wodecotes; and Catherine Were, of Handley, widow; being lawfully summoned to be here in Court to answer to the Lady the Queen, the Lady of this Chase, for divers trespasses by them committed, as in the preceding more fully appears, came not, therefore every one of them is in the mercy of the Court as upon their heads.

The amount of the Court 9*s*.

24 Charles II. 1672. *Oct.* 16*th*.—At the Court of the Right Hon. Anthony Earl of Shaftesbury, of the Chase, holden at Wimborne-St.-Giles, by Samuel Eyre, Steward there, the Keeper of the east part Henry Butler, Esq. Keeper or Ranger of the east part of the Chase aforesaid, and the chief Foresters and Keepers of the Deer of Rushmore-walk now appeared.

RUSHMORE.—William Morgan, gent.; W. Still; Richard Grove; underkeepers, being sworn, present as follows.—

Imprimis,—they present one young Deer, killed by their own dogs; also, four Deer killed which were divided among persons residing near to the Chase; also, one young Deer called a Sorell, killed by the dogs, but by whose they know not; also, one Deer killed and allowed for the use of the Ranger;

also, one Deer killed and allowed to be given to the tenants of Berwicke-St.-John; also, one Deer, and two Fawns found dead.

COBLEY.—William Morgan, gent.; Francis Thorne; William Foyle; underkeepers, being sworn, present as follows.—

Imprimis,—they present one Deer killed and allowed for the use of Lord Arundell; also, one Deer hunted and killed by William Portman, Knt., with the assent of the chief Forester; also, one Deer killed for the use of Mr. Meredith, residing near to the Chase; also, one Deer killed and allowed for the use of the chief Forester; also, one Deer killed and allowed for the use of the Steward; also, one Deer killed and allowed for the use of Mr. John Bennett: also, two young Deer killed by their own dogs, for the use of the chief Foresters and underkeepers; also two Deer killed which were divided among persons residing near to the Chase; also, one Deer and one young Deer killed; a Sorell dead, from what causes they know not; also that Robert Bond, Nicholas Nott, Thomas Dibben, and William Dibben, since the last Court, have erected a certain house of habitation, or a place called Lowsplecke, within the limits of the Chase, to the nuisance &c. And it is ordered, that the aforesaid house shall be prostrated, pulled down by the parties aforesaid, before the Feast of St. Thomas the Apostle next coming, under the pain of £20.

The Keeper of the west part, Thomas Freke, Esq., Keeper or Ranger of the west part of the Chase, and the chief Foresters or Keepers of Westwalk, now appeared.

WESTWALK.—Edward Meggs, Thomas Dawkins, underkeepers, being sworn, present as follows.—

Imprimis,—they present one Deer killed and allowed by the warrant of the Lord of the Chase; also, one Deer customary killed and allowed to the tenants of Ashmore; also, seven Deer killed, which were divided amongst persons residing near to the Chase; also, two young Deer killed by their own dogs, which were divided among persons residing near to the Chase; also, one Deer killed and allowed for the use of John Bennett, gent.; also, one Deer killed and allowed for the use of the Ranger; also, one Deer called a fawn, killed and allowed for the use of the

Ranger; also, three fawns killed by the dogs of William Budden, of Ashmore; also, one Deer found dead, but how, they know not; also, that William Goddard cut down his wood within the Chase without the assent of the Foresters, to the injury of the Deer; also that William Goddard depastured his oxen in a certain wood called Downend coppice within the limits of the Chase, which said wood is of the age of three years and not more, contrary to the custom of the Chase and to the destruction of the Vert. And the said William came into Court, and acknowledged himself guilty of the several offences aforesaid, and put himself on the mercy of the Court, therefore he is in mercy 6*d.* only, which is paid into the Court; also, they present that Christopher Morey, depastured two hundred sheep in a certain wood called Gunville wood, within the limits of the Chase, from the 1*st* day of *June* last past, unto this same day, contrary to the custom of the Chase and to the destruction of the Deer, therefore he is in mercy 2*s.* 6*d.* and it is ordered that in future distress shall be made, if &c.; also, they present that Henry Barrett, of Sutton, depastured his sheep in his woods within the limits of the Chase, from the 27*th* day of *June* last past, unto this same day, contrary to the custom &c.,—therefore he is in mercy 5*s.*, and it is ordered &c.; also they present that the hedges of a certain wood called Puddleway coppice within the limits of the Chase are in want of reparation, by reason whereof beasts do depasture there, to the destruction of the Vert and to the injury of the Deer, and that Benjamin Symes is the verderer there, and ought to repair the hedges aforesaid,—therefore he is in mercy 6*d.*, and it is paid into Court, and it is ordered that the hedges shall be amended before the next Court, under pain of £2.

STAPLEFOOT.—Ralph Banks, Knt., chief Forester, and the keepers of the Deer of Staplefoot-walk, essoined (excused) by favor of the Court. The underkeepers Thomas Clarke, John Foyle, being sworn present as follows.—

Imprimis,—they present one Deer killed by their own dogs, which was divided among persons residing near to the chase; also, one Deer killed and allowed by warrant of the

Lord of the Chase ; also, two Deer killed and allowed for the use of the chief Forester ; also, one young Deer called a Prickett, hunted and killed by Thos. Leigh, Knt., with the assent of the Forester ; also, two Deer killed and divided amongst persons residing near to the Chase ; also, two young Deer killed by the dogs, but by whose dogs they know not ; also, one young Deer wounded and the leg broken ; also two buckstalls, one iron head-piece, one hat, one jack, one sword, and one staff, taken from the hunters unknown, and it it is ordered that they shall be brought into Court ; also that on the 1*st* day of *Sept.* last past, in the morning were found the marks of one Deer killed in Staplefoot-walk, and of one Deer or more killed in the highway between Cobley and Staplefoot-walk, and of divers men, dogs and nets, and that the footsteps of the aforesaid men were towards Broadchalk ; and further they present that in the evening of the said day, eight quarters of venison were taken in the custody of Henry Randall, of Broadchalk. It is ordered that complaint shall be made before the next justices of the peace &c.

BURSEYSTOOLE.—John Ryves Esq., chief Forester and keeper of the Deer of Burseystoole-walk, now appeared.—The underkeepers Thomas Soper, John Harding, being sworn, present as follows.—

Imprimis,—they present one Deer customary killed and allowed for the tenants of Ashmore ; also, one Deer killed by John Bennett, gent., Steward for Lord Arundell, at the Court Baron, holden at Tollard Royal ; also, four Deer killed which were divided among persons residing near to the Chase ; also, that John Frye, of Burseys, gent., continues a certain high hedge formerly set up by which the Deer cannot enter certain woods, called How-grove, Boston-grove, and Fluds-grove, which woods are of the growth of nine years at the least, and are within the limits of the Chase. And because the said John Frye, hath not shewn cause at this Court wherefore the same should not be pulled down, according to the order made at the last Court, therefore it is ordered that the aforesaid high hedge, shall be pulled down by both the underkeepers aforesaid.

CHITTERED.—Anthony Lord Ashley, chief Forester and Keeper of the Deer of Chittered-walk, now appeared. The underkeeper Richard Hughes, being sworn, presented as follows.

Imprimis.—He presented that Gerrard Napper, Bart., made a Park within the limits of the Chase to the nuisance &c., and it is ordered that the aforesaid Gerard shall shew cause at the next Court why the same should not be pulled down.

PENTRIDGE, WOODYATTS, CHALK.—William Herrington, Nicholas Tanner, Verderers there appeared and were sworn.

BARWICK.—Christopher Lambert, Verderer &c.

FUNTMYLL.—Edward Meggs, Verderer &c.

ASHMORE.—Stephen and Robert Kerley, Verderers &c.

GUNVILLE.—Benjamin Symes, Richard Hiscocke, Mark Stayner, Verderers &c.

WOODHOUSE.—John Durnford, Verderer &c.

SUTTON.—Edward Mitchell, &c.

HANLEY.—W. Lawrence, William Oake, Verderers &c.

FARNHAM.—William Feltham, Verderer &c.

WEST-WOODYATES.—John Barber, William Bench *alias* Agull, Verderers &c.

Affeered by John Fitz-James, gent.; Edward Meggs.

Memorandum,—that license was given under the seal of the Lord of the Chase to the aforesaid Gerard Napper, Bart., to enclose his Park in these words following; Anthony Earl of Shaftesbury; Baron Ashley, of Wimborne-St.-Giles, and Lord Cowper, of Pawlett, Lord High Chancellor of England, and one of his Majesty's most Hon. Privy Council, to whom these presents shall come sendeth greeting,—KNOW YE, that I, the said Earl of Shaftesbury, have given license unto Sir Gerard Napper, of More Critchell, in the County of Dorset, Knt., and Bart., and his heirs and assigns, to hold enclosed certain parcel of ground containing by estimation thirty acres or thereabouts lying and being in the parish of More-Critchell, and within the bounds and limits of my Chase of Deer, called Cranborne Chase, as the same is now set out and enclosed for the preservation of a stock of Deer, for the sole use and benefit of him the said Gerard Napper, his heirs and assigns, from henceforth for and during the natural lives of him the said Gerard Napper, Sir Nathaniel Napper, son and heir apparent of the aforesaid Gerard Napper, and Wyndham Napper, grandson of the said Sir Gerard Napper, and the life of the longest liver of them, yielding and paying therefore yearly unto me the said Earl, my heirs and assigns of the said Chase, the sum of 6*d.* at the Court of the said Chase, to be holden after the feast of the Holy Cross, provided that he the said Gerard Napper, his heirs and assigns, keep the said parcel of ground so well and sufficiently fenced with pales or otherwise, during all the said term that the Deer of the said Earl, his heirs and assigns, within the said Chase, may not leap over or enter the same.

Given under my hand and Seal this day of February, in the five and twentieth year of the reign of our Sovereign Lord Charles II. by the grace &c. Anno Domini, 1672.

The preceding Court Rolls are in the Exchequer. The Rolls in general, have been very irregularly preserved; there is one of Edward III., three of Henry VI., three of Edward IV., one of Henry VII., three of Henry VIII., some of Elizabeth, James I., Charles I., and II. Many are so obliterated, as to be illegible. A Distringas Roll, containing the names of persons fined at different Courts, or to be distrained upon from the period of issuing the last Roll, used to be made out annually, or every two years.

The style of the Court observed on the early Rolls, is as follows:—"Cranborne Curia Chaceæ ibidem tent die mercurii, xij die Octob, anno regni regis Edwardi Quarti, post conquestum Anglie octavo." And on those held in the reign of Charles II.

"The Court of the Chase of Cranborne, for the noble William, Earl of Salisbury, Lord of the Chase aforesaid then held at the mansion-house of the said Earl at Cranborne, according to ancient custom." In warrants under the seal of the Steward, the Bailiff is ordered to summon the Chase Court of Cranborne, to be holden at the place accustomed.

Presentments from the Chase Rolls relating to Places beyond the small or in-bounds.

NORRINGTON.—9 Charles II. *April* 15*th*. The Bailiff of the Chase returned that he had distrained Thomas Gowring, Esq., by a white cow value £10, to appear according to the precept, therefore because he had not appeared, he had forfeited the cow, or the value thereof, and he was ordered to be further distrained. At the same Court, Hugh Mansfield was ordered to be distrained, but the Bailiff returned "no effects," therefore it was ordered, that the Bailiff should attach his body.

13 Charles II. *October* 17*th*. The Bailiff of the Chase returned upon his oath, that he had distrained upon David Long, of Norrington, Wilts, by a bull and oxen, but because he was ill, it was adjourned to the next Court, and he was ordered to be attached.

14 Charles II. *April* 3*rd*. That David Long had driven away his black bull, so that the same could not be seized, therefore he was attached, *de novo*, by a brown cow, but not appearing, he was ordered to be further attached.

15 Charles II. *April* 22*nd*. David Long on his distress appeared, submitted and paid 5*s*., to the Bailiff, and promises &c., and had his beast returned.

ALVEDISTON.—Edward IV. John Turvil, of Up-woodyates, submits to the Court, for permitting the hedges of his coppices at Manwood to stand longer than the Assize, contrary to the custom of the Chase, and was fined 12*d*.

17 Henry VI. William, the servant of the Rector of Berwick, submits by his pledge William White, that on Monday, after the Feast of Epiphany, in the fifteenth year of Henry VI., he entered the Chase at Manwood and killed two Deer, and his fine is less, because he told the Foresters of his offence aforesaid, of him and his companions. John Lambert and others were attached, for killing two Deer with nets and cords at night, within the Chase at Manwood.

21 Henry VI. Lawrence Pinnocke presented for making a hedge of his coppice of Manwood, higher than by custom of the Chase he ought. Distress continued against the same, for cutting down his coppices at Manwood, and suffering the same to be open of Vert.

10 Edward IV. Henry Jennings submitted for killing a prickett at Manwood, and was fined 2*s*.

26 Henry VI. William Bithychurch, of Knighton, submits to the mercy of the Court, that he broke the hedges of the coppices at Manwood, and entered with his cart without license, and his fine was assessed at 12*d*.

44 Elizabeth, *April* 15*th*. Presented that Thomas Hemming killed a sore in Manwood within the Chase, with a greyhound, on the 22*nd* of *March*, he was ordered to be attached.

— James I. John Young, for the same in Manwood.

15 Edward IV. Nicholas Newporte, of Alvediston, was presented for pasturing three hundred sheep at Manwood, contrary to the custom of the Chase. John Salisbury, of Alvediston, for the same. Stephen Newporte aud Thomas Lynce, on the 20*th* of *December*, entered the Chase at Alvediston and killed a sore, ordered to be attached.

9 Charles I. *April* 15*th*. The Bailiff of the Chase returned that he had distrained William Gould, of Aston, gent. by a white mare value £4. and because he did not appear, the same was forfeited, and he was ordered to be further distrained upon.

13 Charles II. *October* 17*th*. The Bailiff returned that he had summoned and distrained George Saunders, of Alvediston, by two pigs, he not appearing, the same were forfeited, and he ordered to be further attached.

14 Charles II. *April* 3*rd*. The Bailiff returned that George Saunders had drove away the pigs, so that the same could not be seized, that he had attached him by a black cow, and he not appearing, was ordered to be seized.

15 Charles II. *April* 22*nd*. George Saunders appeared and denied driving away the two pigs, and on his humble admission was excused for that time.

Ashcombe.—5 Henry VI. Edward Prentis, of New Sarum, Wilts, in the day before the Feast of the Nativity of St. John the Baptist, entered the Chase at Ashcombe without license, and took and killed there one buck with a bow and arrows, to the damage of the Lord.

20 Henry VI. At this day came Octobonus Thorne, of Berwyke, Wilts, husbandman, and put himself on the mercy of the Court, for that he on the Monday after the Feast of the Purification of the blessed Virgin Mary, entered the Chase of the Lord at Ayshcombe without license, and there took and killed one fawn with his dogs, to the damage of the Lord, and his fine was taxed as appears upon his head.

21 Henry VI. The Foresters being sworn, present that Henry Moreyew, of Donhead St. Andrew, Wilts, husbandman; William Pope, of Donhead, husbandman; Robert Pope, Jun., of Tollard, shepherd; and Robert Pope, of Donhead, husbandman; and John Stacy, servant to Walter Gaye, of Donhead; entered the Chase at Ashecombe without license, and there took and killed with nets and cords nine sores, and otherwise broke the Chase of the Lord, to the damage &c. Henry Moreyew, Robert Pope, Jun., and Robert Pope of Donhead, came and confessed themselves guilty and put themselves on the mercy of the Lord, and their fines are taxed as appears upon their heads. William Pope, and John Stacey, are not yet attached, therefore they are ordered to be attached by their bodies, to answer &c. The Foresters came and presented that John Moreyew, of Donhead, Wilts, husbandman, entered the Lord's Chase, without license at Ashcombe, and took and killed there one buck, with his dogs, to the damage &c., and as he has not been attached, he is ordered to be attached by this body &c.

3 James I. *April 3rd.* Presented that John Cliffton, of Ashcombe, on the 26*th* day of *October*, forestalled at Ashcombe, within the Chase, and killed two pricketts, with dogs called greyhounds, therefore let him be attached.

1755. *Oct.* 10*th.* At a Chase Court, William Parnell, returned on oath two brace of blooding Deer found by Chase hounds at Ashcombe.

Rotherley, in the Parish of Berwick, Edward IV. William Webb, of Eston, appeared and submitted to the mercy of the Court, for that he killed one tag at Rotherley, with his dogs, without license, and his fine was assessed at 6*d*.

15 Edward IV. Presented that William Bark, farmer of Eston, destroyed the feed of the Deer, at Rotherley, and ordered to be distrained &c. As yet to be distrained, William Bark, to answer to the Lord, why he cut the underwood in Rotherley, and ordered to be distrained against the next Court.

3 James I. *April 3rd.* Presented that Christopher Short, of Burchalke, in Wilts, husbandman; and John Laws, of the same place, husbandman, with many others unknown, on the 25*th* of *Sept.* last at Rotherley, within the Chase, coursed a sore, with greyhounds, from thence by the Salisbury way to Topps, and killed it, therefore ordered to be attached &c.

9 James I. *July* 19*th.* Presented that John Shilly Esq., — Moore, gent., had cut down a coppice called Rotherley, lying within Donhead, in Wilts, therefore &c.

Presented that Robert Moore, gent., kept sixteen sheep, and seven calves, in Rotherley coppice, within the parish of Berwick, within the Chase, when only one year old, to the destruction of the coppice.

Rushmore, Parish of Berwick, 26 Henry IV. *August* 26*th.* Presented that William Oakley, of Berwick, in Wilts, husbandman, on Monday next before the Feast of All-souls, in the twenty sixth year of Henry VI. entered the Chase of the Lord without license, at Ruysshemers, and with nets and other engines, took and killed two Deer to the damage &c. And the said William being present in Court, says he is not guilty and puts himself to his law, and a day is given him to do his law at the next Court that he is not guilty by the pledges of William Wademanton, and Robert Budden.

16 Henry VII. *April* 11*th.* Presented that William Butler, of Wodecotts, permits his pigs to go unwrung within the Chase, at Rushmoreland in destruction of the herbage of the Deer against the custom of the Chase.

26 Henry VIII. *April 27th.* Presented that John Butler, permits his pigs to go unwrung within the Chase at Rushmoreland, in destruction of the herbage, ordered to be distrained.

27 Henry VIII. At the Court appeared John Butler, of Wodecotes, and submitted to the mercy of the Court, for his trespass done and presented at the last Court, and his fine was assessed by the affeerors so that he did not more offend and was dismissed.

PARISH OF BERWICK.—21 Henry VI. *August 26th.*—Roger Blake, in mercy because he has not Lawrence Gawayne, of Norrington, in Wilts, Esq., for making his fences about his coppices within the Chase, within the Bailiwick Buckdon too high. The same Blake against Thomas Gawayn Jun., of Northington, in Wilts, Esq., to answer to the Lord why he has cut and carried away certain trees and underwood, in Grolesgore, in destruction of the vert of the Deer, and ordered to be distrained.

— Henry VIII. *Oct. 26th.* Peter Trenssham, of Tollard, appeared and put himself upon the mercy of the Court, that he at Tinkly, within the Chase, killed a fawn, and his fine was assessed.

26 Henry VIII. Presented that Edmund Bower, of Bridmore, permitted his sheep to feed on Costhead, and in Whitehazle coppice, contrary to the custom &c., ordered to be distrained.

3 James I. Presented that Robert Topp, of Bridmore, permitted his sheep to feed in Whitehazle coppice, and Costard's coppice within the Chase, to the damage of the woods there, and prejudice of the Deer.

1 Charles I. 31*st of March.* Presented that William Grace, of Berwick St. John, in Wilts, shepherd, had placed a halter in the hedge of his Garden at Berwick, to take the Deer coming there, and he came into Court, confessed, and submitted to the mercy of the Court. Therefore ordered, that he should be committed to the prison of the Chase, to the dungeon of the capital messuage of Cranborne, to the custody of the Bailiff of the Lord for three days, and was in mercy 3*s.* 4*d.*

The Berwick Woodward presented that Grace, the wife of

William Grace, had carried away the hedges of Hewits within the Chase, she acknowledged it, and promising to amend, it was forgiven.

Presented that Thomas Lodge, of Berwick, had carried away the hedges of Hewits Coppice, and had drawn young plants at Shiftway coppice, at Berwick within the Chase, to the prejudice of the Vert.

9 Charles I. *April* 15*th*. At the Court, the Bailiff of the Chase returned "no effects," therefore it was ordered that the Bailiff should attach his body.

7 James I. *September* 19*th*. Presented that — Vincent, of Berwick St. John, keeps his sheep on Tinkly Hill within the Chase, where he ought not to depasture to the injury of the Deer, therefore he was amerced 10*s*.

9 James I. *July* 19*th*. Presented that Henry West, of Berwick St. John, Wilts, yeoman, with his two servants, cut and carried away out of Pond coppice, in Berwick within the Chase, certain young oaks called handals, to the damage of the Lord of the Chase, and against the statute in that case made, and against the orders and customs of the Chase, ordered to be distrained against the next Court.

Presented that Edward West keeps divers horses in Parson's coppice, within the Chase not two years old, and he submitted to the mercy of the Court, and was fined 3*s*. 4*d*.

Presented that John Crowter usually put his beasts in coppices of Berwick, to the destruction of the said coppices, therefore &c.

Bridmore. — Edward IV. John Baker, servant to William Cole, submitted to the mercy of the Court, for destroying and feeding the pasture of the Deer in Parson's wood and Brydmere's leyes, with his sheep, and his fine was assessed.

16 James I. *April* 16*th*. Allen Isaac, of Bridmore, because he had not appeared, being attached by one beast, value 20*s*., to answer the Lord of the Chase for divers trespasses and offences in the Chase, as were presented in that Court, 20*s*.

10 Charles I. Edward Topp, of Bridmore, for the same.

11 Charles I. *April* 19*th*. At a Court, the Bailiff returned that he had distrained the said Edward by twenty sheep, value £5. and because he did not appear, he had forfeited the said goods and was to be farther distrained to appear at the next court.

EBBESBORNE.—8 Edward IV. Stephen Bottom, and John Colin, servants to Jacob Barto, submitted, for that on the Feast of All-souls 6 Edward IV. at Eastcombe within the Chase they killed a Deer, and their fines were assessed.

9 James I. Presented by the keeper, that a Deer was killed out of Eastcombe, and thereupon he drew with his hounds the house of John White, of Ebbesborne, where he found two dogs covered with blood, therefore he was ordered to be attached.

— Henry VI. Henry Wodehouse, of Ebbesborne, submits to by his pledge William Jeffrey, that he on Thursday, before the Feast of the Purification of the blessed Virgin Mary 17 Henry VI. at Mayble Wanlase, within the Chase, killed a fawn.

15 Edward IV. Presented that William Taylor of Alweston, destroyed the pasture of the Deer at Limepitts, and other places within the Chase, and ordered to be distrained.

26 Henry VIII. Presented that William Thomas, farmer, of Ebbesborne, permitted his pigs to go unwrung at Limepitts coppice, within the Chase, and ordered &c.

13 James I. *September* 17*th*. Presented that William Penny and others, hunted in Limepitts coppice, they appeared, submitted, and were fined 25*s*.

— Edward IV. William Hodges, of Ebbesborne, submitted for killing a fawn at Wake's Dean, and was fined 6*d*.

15 Edward IV. William House, *alias* Hodges, of Ebbesborne, and Thomas Thorne, submit themselves to the Court, for that they have destroyed the wood in Limepitts coppice, called Harling.

John Joliff submits for having destroyed the pasture of the Deer with his sheep, and his fine was assessed at 8*d*.

— Henry VI. Presented that William Jeffrey has depastured two horses in Ebbesborne coppices, in destruction of the Vert, and beasts of the Chase, ordered to be distrained.

9 James I. *July 9th.* Presented that Peter Marwin, gent., and others, hunted a Deer out of Lye coppice, *alias* Chadwell's coppice within the Chase, which Deer with others, were kept for the coming of the King, therefore they are ordered to be attached.

CHALK.—15 Edward IV. *October 13th.* Presented that Thomas Saunders, of Broadchalk, on the 10*th* of *August*, 15 Edward IV., entered the Chase at Chalk-field, and there with his greyhounds killed a buck without license, therefore he was ordered &c.

8 Edward IV. *October 14th.* Stephen Marshall, farmer, of Broadchalk, appeared, and submitted to the mercy of the Court, that he had destroyed the underwood called Harlin in Great Ditch, in destruction of the Vert, and that he had cut the borders of one of the coppices there, and his fine was assessed.

— Edward IV. The Foresters for not distraining John Newman, of Broadchalk to answer the Lord, wherefore he permitted the hedges of his coppices at Great Ditch, to lay open for one year after their cutting, and ordered to be better distrained.

15 Henry VIII. *October 31st.* Presented that John Martin, of Burchalk, permitted forty sheep or more, to depasture within the Chase at Great Ditch, to the great prejudice, and against the custom of the Chase.

16 Henry VIII. *April 11th.* John Martin came, and Edward Shergole, and submitted, and their fines were affeered by the affeerors so that they would not further offend, and were dismissed the Court.

25 Henry VIII. *October 7th.* The Woodward of Burchalk came, and presented all things well.

26 Henry VIII. *October 7th.* Presented Thomas Bostone, Jun., of Fifehead, that he killed a buck out of a coppice called Great Ditch.

26 Henry VIII. *April 23rd.* Thomas Boston appeared, submitted, and his fine affeered so that he did not further offend.

8 James I. *September 25th.* The Keepers present that the Free Grain was paid out of the farm at Broadchalk.

9 Charles I. Distrain against Michael Shergole, of Burchalk. At a Court he appeared, was fined, and paid the fine.

ALDERHOLT WALK.—15 Edward IV. Gilbert Moleyns, of Fordingbridge, was attached by his body to answer the Lord, for that he, together with John ———, late of the same, who hath left this country, is a common disturber of the wild beasts of the Lord at Goldencrofte, Ydelake, and La Breche, of Rockborne, to the destruction of the wild beasts, and asserts the above places are not within the Chase, to the great damage of the Lord &c.

15 Henry VIII. *October 30th.* The Forester comes and presents that Thomas Willis, of Eastworth, hath hunted and disturbed the wild beasts of our Lady the Queen from the coppices and wood, to wit, twice this year, on Monday after the Feast of last St. Martin, and on Sunday afterwards, to the great damage &c,. and contrary to the custom of the Chase.

26 Henry VIII, The Foresters came and presented all things well to this day; nevertheless there remain presentments as yet upon Richard Bairn, *alias* Rouff, servant to John Martin, of Edmundesham, as appears at the next preceding Court.

26 Henry VIII. *April 26th.* The Foresters then came and present nothing, but that all things are well; and besides present that Richard Wiltshire had forbidden Walter Wythyton, Forester, to go and walk within the limits and bounds of the Chase in execution of his office, contrary to the custom of the Chase, therefore he is distrained.

26 Henry VIII. *October 7th.* The Foresters then come and present that Thomas Macham, hunted at Castlehill, on the Feast of Philip at St. James the Apostles, and chased and disturbed the wild beasts of the Lady the Queen from their resort, to the great damage &c., therefore he is distrained. And that the said Thomas hunted at Hithecross and elsewere within the Chase, to wit, Thursday on the Feast of Pentecost last past, and during the time one wild beast was killed and never found, to

the great damage &c., therefore he is distrained. And that John Garrett, William Burge, and —— Pottle, are common hunters, and especially in one night, to wit, on Thursday in Rogation week last past, at Horethorner within the Chase, to the great destruction &c., therefore &c. As yet there remain presentments upon Richard Baron *alias* Rouff, servant of John Martin, of Edmundesham, because he killed certain Pheasants and Partridges within the Chase without leave, to the prejudice of the liberties of the Lady the Queen, and contrary to the custom of the place aforesaid, therefore &c.

VERNDITCH.—15 Edward IV. *Oct.* 13*th.* As yet to be attached, the bodies of William Davy, of Felston, and John Luxhall, of the same, to answer the Lord why they are common hunters in the Chase, *viz.* at Eastgrove, Vernditch, Cobley, Wakesdene, and Okle, in destruction of the Deer, to appear at the next Court. The like for not attaching John Gartick, of Chalk, and Thomas Alwen, of Broadchalk, for being common hunters in the Chase at Vernditch.

17 Henry VI. *August* 6*th.* Presented that Michael, the servant of the Rector of Chalk, on the Feast of St. Gregory, 17 Henry VI. came into the Chase at Vernditch, with his bow and arrows to kill the Deer, therefore he was ordered to be attached.

1672 *March* 11*th.* By Indenture made between Anthony, Earl of Shaftesbury, of the one part, and William, Earl of Pembroke, on the other part.

Reciting,—that the said Earl of Shaftesbury, was seized to him and his heirs, of and in Cranborne Chase, extending itself into the counties of Dorset and Wilts, and that Lord Pembroke, had then lately built a house upon a certain bushy and waste ground called Lowseplecke, in the parish of Chalk, parcel of the manor of Chalk, in the county of Wilts, which had been erected on purpose to be an habitation for such person or woodward, as Lord Pembroke shall appoint, to look after his and their liberties within the said manor, and likewise his other woods and coppice, lying contiguous to one another round about the said house; all which woods and coppices were subject to the feeding and preservation of the Deer of Cranborne Chase.

"And the said Earl of Shaftesbury doth hereby disclaim to have right to the wood or soil of the said bushy and waste ground, woods, and coppices, within the said manor of Chalk; or to the wood, or soil of a certain walk, a Franchise stored with Deer, commonly called or known by the name of Fernditch; or any right to have liberty of feeding or preservation of Deer within the said Walk or Franchise of Fernditch, or any part thereof.—

"*And Reciting*,—that the Earl of Shaftesbury had had, and then had, and of right ought to have by reason of the Chase aforesaid, the liberty of feeding and preservation of Deer within the said parcel of bushy and waste ground, woods and coppices, lying contiguous to one another round about the said house. Therefore for an amicable compromise of all suits and differences which had or might arise by reason of the building of the said house &c., *It is witnessed*,—and Lord Shaftesbury releases to Lord Pembroke all actions &c., on account of building the said house.—And the Earl of Pembroke covenanted with Lord Shaftesbury that he, Lord Shaftesbury, and the Keepers of his said Chase or any part thereof, should have the sole habitation, use, and dwelling of, and within the said house, which Keeper, should look to the preservation of Lord Pembroke's woods and coppices, *proviso*, that such Keeper should not cut wood for firing without Lord Pembroke's license. And Lord Shaftesbury, in consequence of the aforesaid grant, consented to supply yearly, Lord Pembroke, one Buck and one Doe.

Minutes of Depositions taken in a cause between the Earl of Salisbury, Plaintiff, Lord Arundell, & others, Defendants.

March 13*th*, 15 James I. ***Evidence for Defendants***,—RICHARD HARDING, ÆT. 50, deposed *(inter alia)* that Burseystool and the West Lodge are accounted the ancient Lodges within Cranborne Chase, and the Lodge then called Rushmore Lodge was in ancient time a tenement, and some lands therewith used, and rent paid for the same. There is a new Lodge built in the Chase called West Lodge, upon the lands of Robert Swayne, and thinks, by the appointment of the Earl of Salisbury, and with the lease of Robert Swayne. And another new Lodge built near Burseystool, not far from the next Lodge, in or near Farnham common, and in his passage toward Lay, another Lodge built near about Woodyates. The country about Cranborne Chase depends chiefly on the coppice woods there, for fire-bote, hedge-bote, watling, hurdling, spikes for thatching; and that the coppice woods are much wasted and spoiled.

JOHN SWAYNE, ÆT. 69, deposed *(inter alia)* about thirty years sithence, that he with Mr. Chafin, Lord of the manor of Chettle, and High Sheriff of the County of Dorset, did hunt in Littlewood coppice, parcel of the said manor, and killed a Deer, for which, by process, they appeared before the Justice in Eyre, one Mr. Norath, who demanding if any corn was growing where the Deer was killed, and being answered there was, said, "'twas a pity it should be spoiled by the Deer."—And on Mr. Chafin's acquainting the Justice that he had Free-warren, the Justice said, "he might then kill the Deer there and spare not,"—thereupon they were discharged. Mr. Chafin afterwards killed many Deer in his manor of Chettle without interruption, and hath heard, that the whole manor of Tarrant Hinton lyeth quite out of the bounds of the Chase. Knoweth the Parish of Gunville, having been Incumbent there forty-five years; that the manor of Gunville always reputed to be quite out of the bounds of the Chase, and his father and brother as Lords of the manor and park of Gunville kept a Keeper for twenty years, and by themselves, and keeper, and servants killed above forty Deer, and that at their pleasure, within the park and grounds within the manor.

THOMAS BOWER, ÆT. 92, deposed *(inter alia)* that he had known Tollard seventy years, and dwelt with his brother-in-law Edmund Goddard, farmer, then ten years and above, and with their men and servants, with Mr. Bennett, of Tollard, killed a brace of Deer in a morning out of Tollard Park before sun-rising, and brought them home; and killed divers Deer out the common fields there in the day-time, so often, that they were weary of venison, for they did often eat the same boiled with bacon.

WILLIAM PENNY, ÆT. 45, deposed *(inter alia)* that Fernditch was never accounted part of the Chase, being a particular ground of itself to keep the Deer in; he was underkeeper in Fernditch under his father for four years, for the Earl of Pembroke. The Earl had Freewarren there, and the deponent killed many Deer there. That Mr. Swayne, owner of Gunville Park, about twenty-three years past, used to hunt and kill the Deer of the Chase which came into the park, and carried them away.

WALTER SNELGAR, ÆT. 70, deposed *(inter alia)* that at his first coming to be a Keeper of Rushmore-walk, there was one only ancient Lodge called West Lodge, and a dwelling house called Rushmore Lodge, that stood upon the inheritance of the Earl of Pembroke, and was parcel of his manor of Berwick St. John. And saith, there were three other curries or small cottages for lodging of Keepers within the said Chase, to harbour themselves in Cobley-walk, and the other in Burseystool, which then stood on Mr. Philpot's land. There had been within twenty years past, four new Lodges built within the Chase, whereof one near the old West Lodge; the second in Burseystool-walk, on Lord Arundell's land; the third, in Staplefoot-walk, upon the lands parcel of the manor of Berwick, bought by the Earl of Salisbury of the Earl of Pembroke; aud the fourth Lodge stands in Cobley-walk upon the common of Pentridge. That Thomas

Gawen, Esq., owner of the manor of Norrington, had Freewarren there, and did in the day-time hunt in Manwood and some other grounds adjoining, with his greyhounds, and killed many Deer. Norrington and Manwood are accounted out the bounds of the Chase. Lord Salisbury had but one coppice lying in the Chase, called Lodge coppice. Remembers the place where the Shire oak did stand, which was felled by Mr. Stockman's order in Lord Pembroke's right, as within his manor of Burchalk; it did stand in the way between Shire-oak coppice, and adjoining to the south-east side of Upper Hogdran. There may be conveniently kept within the compass of the lesser bounds, five-hundred Deer. Lord Pembroke kept a Ranger in Fernditch, to walk the ground and look to the Deer in is own right, and not as part of Cranborne Chase. Knew one Style, servant to Mr. Hawles of Monkton, hunt and kill Deer in Oakley wood, without any controul; and that Oakley, and the manor and lands of Monkton Upwimborne, were not accounted to lye within the lesser bounds. The manor, &c., of Chettle, are reputed to be without the compass of Cranborne Chase, and are Freewarren. One Mr. Chafin, owner of Chettle, about forty years before, did bring an action against one Tinker and Morgan, then Keepers of the Chase, for hunting within his woods of Chettle, and recorded against them. Gunville Park, Valleys Wood, Ranston, Iwerne, and Tollard, were reputed to lie without the bounds of the Chase. Sir Mathew Arundell, was about forty years before, deputy Ranger of the Chase under the Earl of Pembroke, and one Tinker, who was Keeper of Burseystool-walk, did then walk in Tollard Park, coppices, and grounds of Tollard, and a difference arising thereupon between the Earl and Sir Mathew, the latter was displaced, and Sir Henry Ashley, put in his place. And after Sir Mathew was displaced he kept a man of his own, Roger Morgan, to walk Tollard Park, and the grounds and coppices thereof, and Morgan forbade Tinker to come there to walk as a keeper, and Tinker forbore; afterwards they quarrelled, and the keepers hounds were killed out of the grounds &c., of Tollard, for hunting there. Bridmore was reputed to be out of the bounds;

Sir Edmund Uvedall, Lord of the Manor, had Freewarren there, and Robert Topp, farmer, made great hedges and ditches, to keep out the Deer.—Knows the two Parks of Red and Fallow Deer, called Wardour Park, and the new grounds inclosed with a wall intended for a Park, called Wilton Park; Breamore Park, Burgate Park, now disparked; Folston, now disparked; Blagden Park, now disparked; Gunville Park, and the grounds called Tollard Park,—Lord Arundell, of Wardour, sued in the Star-chamber, one Clark, Garrett, and Weeks, of Martin, for hunting Deer in the Fallow Deer Park, and they were fined three hundred marks a-peice.—The Freeholders and tenants in Chettle, are freed by the charter of the Abbot of Tewkesbury, from payment of toll at the markets and fairs in Dorset, and from appearing at assizes and sessions, in the same County.

Barnaby Lewis, Æt. 65, deposed *(inter alia)* that the manor of Bridmore is without the bounds of the Chase. He dwelt in Ebbesborne about thirty years ago, during which time, if any Deer of the Chase should happen to come within certain woods in Ebbesborne, adjoining to arable fields there, then such as were of the town of Ebbesborne, or the Lord would kill him if they might, and the woods were accounted no parcel of the Chase, and heard that there was Freewarren belonging unto Ebbesborne. The farm of Bridmore adjoineth to the Chase, and the farmer thereof, doth always pay to the Earl of Pembroke about forty quarters of corn yearly, and £6,—as deponent thinketh for chief rent, and £25 per annum to the Lord of the fee thereof, and if the said farm should be used as Chase for the feeding of Deer, than the farmer would not be able to make the rent and discharge the same; and that since the suit (Topp, *versus* Weare,) surceased, there were no keepers walked the grounds and killed farmers dogs there as they formerly did, until Complainant's father purchased the Chase, for the Ranger and keepers of the Chase, before the Earl of Salisbury, deceased purchased the same, have been often denyed withall for the same.

Robert Dashwood, Æt. 45, deposed *(inter alia)* that he has seen a Charter granted by King Edward I. of the manor of

Bridmore, and that in the late Queen's Majestie's reign, it was pleaded by *quo warranto* brought against Henry Uvedale, Lord of Bridmore farm, with the confession thereunto:—that Shapwick, More Critchell, Blandford, and Pimperne, and Deane farm, were holden of the Dutchy of Lancaster. A purchase was made by Henry Uvedale of More Critchell, of the manor of Tarrant Monkton, in 4 Queen Elizabeth. The coppices of Tarrant Monkton, and a Lodge standing in a common called Manwood Stubbs, which was built for the herdsman of the said manor, and parcel of the manor and inheritance of Edward Uvedale, Knt., and in the sixth year of the King's reign, the Earl of Salisbury purchased the said Lodge of Uvedale, and gave for the same £12, and £1 per annum to the said Sir Edward Uvedale. Henry Uvedale granted Sir Henry Ashley a lease of his Freewarren of Bridmore, with a proviso, that Uvedale, his heirs, and assigns should kill any beasts or fowls within the same.

Roger Morgan, Æt. 64, deposed *(inter alia)* that thirty years since he knew but one Lodge, which was the West Lodge, that it was an ancient Lodge; that about three years past, a new Lodge was set up in West-walk near the old one, upon the land late Mr. Swayne's; that there is another new-built Lodge in Farnham Common, which is Lord Arundell's land, used ever since with Burseystool-walk. The Chase in Dorset will keep seven or eight hundred Deer. That the grounds of Gunville are reputed to be out of the Chase.—After a trial between Mr. Swayne and some others, who pretended his grounds to be Chase, the Keeper did forbear to walk there, and Mr. Swayne placed one Walter Snelgar, who walked the Park and grounds for twelve years, and killed Deer there at their pleasure; before the trial, the Keeper of West-walk walked the Park and grounds of Mr. Swayne, and hunted and fetched home the Deer which fed there; and the Park and grounds were accounted Freewarren. The grounds of Fontmel, Sutton, and Compton, are reputed to be out of the bounds, and the owners and inhabitants have often killed and carried away Deer day and night, which have fed in the corn-fields and grounds there.

John Gatehouse, Æt. 60, deposed that about the 22 Elizabeth, he was Steward to Mr. Chafin; that Mr. Chafin had Freewarren within his manor of Chettle, and did kill the Deer there at his pleasure, and once in the view of Sir Henry Ashley, then deputy Ranger; that Mr. Chafin was subpœnaed before the Justice in Eyre, who, upon shewing forth his Charter, desired Mr. Chafin to use the Queen's game favourably, and allowed his right in Chettle.

Mark Haskall, Æt. 50, deposed that Norrington lands and Manwood, have been reputed out of the bounds of the Chase, and that deponent and other keepers were forbidden to walk in Manwood; that his master desired Mr. Gawen to be favourable to the game that came into Manwood coppice, and deponent with his hounds, should be ready to Mr. Gawen's pleasure to hunt game for him in Manwood coppice, or any other coppices lying near; whilst he was under-keeper, he found a shepherd tearing the coppice hedge of Manwood, wherewith he acquainted Mr. Gawen, who then willed this deponent, if he found this shepherd eftsoons to offend in that kind, he should beat him well.

William Bembury, Æt 75, deposed that William Cifewest, dwelt in the farm of Tollard, and forbad the Keepers to come there, and once the Keepers hunted a Deer out of Rushmore-walk into a pond in the open street of Tollard, and Mr. Cifewest, took away the Deer and cut him in pieces and gave it away and said he would justify it, and he did about the same time beat one of the Keepers for coming on his grounds—forty years past deponent was servant to Topp, farmer of Bridmore, and that Topp, and his servants did kill the Deer that fed in Long Croft and Bridmore Green, but saith that Bridmore coppices lie within the Chase; Topp beat the keepers, and sued them about forty years since; great hedges and ditches, were made at Bridmore, to keep out the Deer.

John Lodge, deposed that he had known the grounds called Blagden Park, for thirty years; and that it was heretofore a Park replenished with the game of Deer, and hath heard that Mr. Hanam, now owner thereof hath Freewarren within the same,—

he had heard old men of Burchalk say fifty years ago, demanding of him where he had been, and he answering them he had been in the Chase, meaning the Earl of Pembroke's woods, in Burchalk, they have told him, you must say you have been at the wood and not in the Chase, for there is no Chase in Wiltshire,—if the Deer of the Chase should feed out into the corn-fields, meadows, and pastures of Burchalk, without restraint, the inhabitants and tenants there would be undone.—He knew Blagden Park, about fifty years since, a Park stocked with Deer, and it was then accounted an ancient Park, and the same was about the same time disparked.

JOSEPH COMPTON, ÆT 72, deposed that forty years ago, there were four odges within the Chase, beside Chitterhead Lodge, *viz.*, West Lodge, Burseystoole, Rushmore, and Cobley, the Keeper of West-walk had then no Lodge, in his walk, but a house of his own at Woodcotes; now there is a new Lodge built in Staplefoot, and three other new Lodges within these eight years by the appointment of the Lord Salisbury, whereof Cobley is one, Burseystoole another, in West-walk a third, and thinketh that Mr. Hooper, was chief Ranger of the Chase, at the building of the same Lodges. Nine years since when deponent was deputy Ranger, there was a difference between the Lord Salisbury, and the Earl of Pembroke, touching the bounds deponent by Lord Salisbury's command accompanied one Norden, to take a map of the pretended in-bounds,—Lord Salisbury, is owner of the Manor of Berwick only, and of Rushmore Lodge, and the ground whereupon the rest of the Lodges stand, but the soil of all the rest of the pretended in-bounds belonged to other men—knows of no Lodge between the large and less bounds—the less bounds will feed two thousand Deer—Oakley wood was reputed to be out of the bounds of the Chase, and Mr. Hollis, then owner was wont to hunt and kill Deer there, but before he did hunt there he used to send word overnight to the Keepers of Cobley, and on the morrow they would blow a horn at Oakley wood, and if the Keepers came they hunted together, but if they came not they hunted alone, but the keepers seldom failed to come,—he hath received 6*s*. 8*d*. of Mr. Henry Leigh, as a fee due to the deponent as deputy Ranger, and twenty loads of coppice wood, as fee wood, due to the Keeper of the walk, wherein the coppice lay that was felled. Dean Hill, was in the life time of Sir Mathew Arundell, a ground well replenished with oaks and timber trees, and the trees have been sometime sold and rooted up, and the bushes and underwood grubbed up, and the grounds converted to tillage, and while the timber trees grew there, Sir Mathew Arundell, had the young Herns which were bred there.

JOHN FRY, ÆT. 80, deposed that three new Lodges have been built within six years, in Cobley, Staplefoot, and Burseystool, by the Earl of Salisbury, that before there was no Lodge there;—does not know whether the owners of lands consented to it.

WALTER DAVIS, ÆT. 87, deposed that Ebbesborne and Alveston, were out of the Chase, that Mr. Boddenham killed Deer there, and cut his coppices without leave of the Ranger, and without paying any fee. He heard Mr. Horsey say, that his warren of Ashcombe was out of the Chase, and if the Deer came there he might kill them.

JOHN MORGAN, ÆT. 72, deposed *(inter alia)* that Robert, Earl of Salisbury, built four new Lodges within the lesser bounds, *viz.*, Cobley, Burseystool, West-walk, and Staplefoot; and that the Earl of Salisbury, hath not any woods or coppices within the pretended lesser bounds of the said Chase in Dorsetshire, unless about his said new Lodges; that the country near adjoining to the coppices and woods within the pretended lesser bounds in Dorsetshire and Wiltshire, are for the provision of fire-bote and hedge-bote, and that they are derayed by the Deer, and if not better preserved than they have been heretofore, it will be a prejudice to the whole country near adjoining.—That twenty-seven years since, he was Keeper of Burseystool-walk for five or six years together, and went into the coppice of Chettle called Littlewood, and hunted Deer out of the said wood into the Chase, and one Watts, the farmer of the grounds, sued him for hunting there, and that he acquainted Mr. Richard Nicolas the deputy Ranger of the Chase with the suit, who told deponent, "he would not justify his hunting in Littlewood," and thereupon paid 6*s*., for the charge of the writ to the farmer; that Mr. Nicolas was deputy Ranger of the Chase, and the deponent was a Keeper under him, and had been often forbid by Goddard, farmer to Sir Mathew Arundell, to walk in the farm, park, and grounds, of Tollard,—and also by Sir Mathew Arundell's servant, who threatened him with law, and deponent acquainted Mr. Nicolas therewith, who told him "he must forbear, for that he could not defend him;" that shortly after Sir Mathew Arundell, placed a Keeper of his own in Tollard Park and grounds; twenty-eight years since, the farmer Goddard killed a Deer in Tollard Park, of which deponent acquainted Sir Henry Ashley, Knt., then deputy Ranger, but saith, that nothing was done against Goddard. That sixteen years ago, deponent heard that defendant Woods killed a Keeper's dog that was hunting in Tollard grounds;—heard that defendant Woods, brought an action against Budden, an under-keeper, the deponent was present at a trial concerning the same, which lasted from nine till three,—the verdict was for Wood,—that while deponent was Keeper, the lands, park, and grounds of Tollard were fenced with great quick set hedges and ditches against the lesser bounds for keeping out the Deer, that the lands and grounds of Charlton and Melbury, are reputed without the bounds of the Chase, and Ashgrove Farm.

Richard Benbury, Æt 63, deposed *(inter alia)* that forty years ago, deponent was underkeeper of Rushmore, under Sir Mathew Arundell, then deputy Ranger, about four years, and did then hunt in a ground called Ashcombe, the lands of Mr. Horsey, for which, deponent was served with a subpœna to answer the same in the Star-chamber, which was heard by the Justice of Assize; that afterwards Mr. Morgan nor his Keepers hunted there no more, only throwed off their hounds to fetch in the Deer; and that Dunhead farm, and Ashcombe, were reputed out of the Chase, and Mr. Horsey did kill Deer at Ashcombe; and that no Deer did come to Dunhead and Ferne, being at a distance.

Thomas Wilson deposed, that Lord Arundell had several people fined about three years since for killing Deer in Wardour Park, others at Quarter Sessions, and others forgiven upon submission.

Richard Combe, Æt. 60, deposed that the fields, grounds, and sheep downs of Fontmel and Sutton, on the west side of the ridgeway between Blandford and Shaston, are reputed to be out of the Chase, and the inhabitants killed the Deer there; that there was a Freewarren at Melbury; that the fields, grounds, and downs of Ashgrove are out of the Chase, and that the inhabitants killed Deer there.

John Kerley, Æt. 80, deposed that sixty years past William Ciferwest lived in Tollard farm, in which defendant Wood now dwells, that he then forbid the Keepers when Sir John Rogers was deputy Ranger, and beat one Cock a Keeper for so doing, who afterwards desisted; and deponent heard Sir John Rogers acknowledge the said farm to be out of the Chase.

Giles Hussey, Æt 60, says that the book now exhibited, he found in his father's study at Edmonsham, one page whereof subscribed by the Commissioners, sets forth the bounds of Cranborne Chase, *viz.*, "the bounds of Cranborne Chase, tempore Edwardi primi";—and concludeth this is a record in the Kings.

William Penny, Æt 45, deposed that about fifteen years since, he being underkeeper at Vernditch, under his Father in the right of the Earl of Pembroke, they with one youth about seventeen years of age, happened to meet with five hunters by night, who had set up buckstalls for the taking of Deer and so they endeavoured to take them, and did fight with them, and one of the five ran away, and they took the other four, and had them down to Mr. Saynt Lo, and it appeared that one of the hunters had received a wound in his head, of which hurt shortly after he died, for which, he, deponent, was called in question at the assize in Sarum, and upon shewing forth of a charter for the grounds called Fernditch, by which it appeared that the grounds were freewarren, he was acquitted and discharged.

Minutes of Evidence taken in the Cause in Chancery, between George Pitt, Esq., Plaintiff. Henry Bower, Thomas Fownes, Richard Andrews, John Wells, and Thomas Bower, Esqrs. Defendants'.

A. D. 1731. *Evidence for Plaintiff.*—That the defendant Fowne's lands are within the bounds of the Chase; there were Deer leaps and creeps in the hedges, and the hedges were the same as in other parts of the Chase; that the Deer at the fall of the leaf straggle from the covert two or three miles, into the open plains of the parishes of Sutton, Iwerne Minster, and other places, and the Keepers, as often as they thought fit, killed or re-chased them back to the coverts; that there have been always racks or ridings in the defendants' woods, cut and shred by the Keepers for the convenience of hunting; that there are several ancient stands, *viz.*, steps cut in the trees for the Keepers getting up into them, to stand on to shoot the Deer in the winter, which are driven by men and dogs towards them; that there were anciently leaps and creeps for the Deer made throughout the defendants' coppice hedges when the coppices were about three years old, till about five or six years since the defendants made ditches, threw up banks, and planted quick-set hedges thereon; that Robert Burbidge, servant and relation of the defendant Bower's father, about twenty years since, was convicted for killing a Deer in Iwerne free downs, (without the pretended short bounds,) was sent to gaol, stayed there a year, and then stood in the pillory at Blandford; that about six years since, the defendant Thomas Bower was taken and sent to gaol for setting toils for killing Deer in Boyne's coppice, but there being some defect in the mittimus, a certiorari was brought, and Mr. Chafin, who committed him, consented for that reason to his discharge. Several witnesses proved the convictions of persons for killing Deer on the defendants' lands, by the Keepers of the Chase.—Mr. Wyche deposed, that about fifty-five years ago he was clerk to Samuel Eyre, the steward of the Chase to the Earl of Shaftesbury, and then Mr. Fownes and Mr. Ryves, in respect of their lands in Stepleton and Ranston, set up a pretence that these lands were out of the Chase and disturbed the game thereof, on which, by appointment, Samuel Eyre met Mr. Fownes, at West Lodge, to reason with him concerning the same, and then he offered Mr. Fownes to try the right at law, which Mr. Fownes declined, and they have ever since been quiet till now; and although he attended many years at the Chase Courts, never then or since heard of any such pretence for the lands in Iwerne Minster.

From the Court Rolls the following Presentments were proved.

---

33 Henry VI. Robert Clare, was ordered to be distrained, because that he with others killed four wild pigs, on Iwerne-hill, within the Chase without leave.

34 Henry VI. The keepers accuse William Swayne, with others unknown, for killing of a Teg, with his hounds, and greyhounds in Iwerne Freedowns, without leave, being within Cranborne Chase, and he is therefore to be attached by the body to answer the fact.

Thomas Robe, Vicar of Iwerne, attached for killing four wild pigs in Iwerne wood, with his bow and arrows without leave.

William Swayne, and others, do put themselves to the grace of the Court, for killing of a Teg, &c.

9 Charles I. *February* 15*th*, by Indenture between William, Earl of Salisbury on the one part, John Freke, Esq., John Fry, of Iwerne Minster, and John Squib, of the same, on the other part—*Reciting*, that there was payable yearly to the Earl as owner of the Cranborne Chase, and to his Rangers, Foresters, and Keepers, out of the manor farm, and demesne lands of Iwerne Minster, or out of some of them four bushels of wheat and one stack of hay,—*Reciting* also, Freke, Fry, and Squib,

did challenge and pretend to have a right of Common, in a parcel of the said Chase, called the Rails, near the West Lodge, in Iwerne Minster, the said Earl in consideration of £30. by them paid, and the release to him by them made, releases to them the said wheat and hay, and they to him the said Common of pasture.

Evidence for Defendants.—That the keepers never came on the out-grounds, till Mr. Freke. purchased the Chase, and were then connived at on account of the intimacy between him and the owners of some of the out-grounds; that the woodmen of the out-grounds never attended the Chase Courts; that the fences and the land measure were different within the Chase and in the out-grounds; that the Keepers never presented Deer killed in the outgrounds, and re-chased the Deer from them; that the browze was left for the Deer within the Chase, and not without; that the country people killed Deer in the parishes of Melbury, Compton, and Fontmel, without interruption; and that Mr. Freke had been heard to acknowledge, he did not claim the out-grounds as part of the Chase; that there had been a difference between Mr. Freke, when owner of the Chase, and Mr. Fownes and other owners of out-grounds, which continued several years, during which time Deer were killed publicly in the out-grounds, and orders were given to forbid the Keepers hunting or shooting on Preston, Ranston, Stepleton, or Gunville, but at last they were reconciled, on the understanding that Mr. Freke was to supply those gentlemen with what venison they wanted, and that the Keepers were to take care to keep the out-grounds as free of Deer as possible, by re-chasing them frequently, and not to shoot on those grounds, and the gentlemen promised not to kill the Deer themselves, or encourage others; that one Elgar Brownsey, had been caught killing Deer on Collier's heath, and taken before Justice Seymour, but was not convicted, because they could not swear the spot to be within the Chase; that Lord Shaftesbury sent venison to the owners of the out-grounds, without the Keepers receiving any fee, and he did not claim right of Chase in the out-grounds; that the ridings in Preston woods were cut by Mr. Fownes for hunting, and that if ever they were cut, or leaps and creeps made by the Keepers in them, it was done in a private manner in order to give in evidence; that cattle feeding in the woods in the out-grounds, were ordered not to be impounded.

Draft of a Petition to the King,

17 JAMES I.

To the King's most excellent Majestye.—Humbly sheweth, Your most faithfull and obedient subjects, John C. and A. T. inhabitants of * * * as well for themselves as the rest of the inhabitants there,—That William, Erle of Salisbury, being seized in fee of the Chase of Cranborne, which lyeth in certaine knowne bounds in the County of Dorsett, which sufficeth for keeping two thousand heads of Deer. The said Erle hath often endeavoured, by strong hand and encroachement, to enlarge the said Chase,—claiming the same to extend into other bounds, in the County of Dorsett, Wilts, and Southampton, which contains about one hundred miles in compass, and includes about seventy parishes, wherein are dwelling at least * * * people; and does also include divers ancient Parks stored with Deer, whereupon divers suits have growne in your Highness's Court of Star-chamber, Chancerye, Exchequer, and Court of Common Pleas, at Westminster, between the said Erle and others. And in Michaelmas Terme, in the fourteenth year of your Majestye's reigne, a tryall was had at the barr of your Highness's Court of Common Pleas, at Westminster, before the Judges of the said Court, touching certaine lands in Tollard Royale, in the County of Wilts, lyeing nigh unto, and without the usuall and knowne bounds, allowed and within the pretended bounds claymed by the said Erle, where the issue was,—whether Tollard was within the Chase or not; and it was then on a full hearing, in the presence of the said Erle, by a verdict found by twelve men, that the Chase did not extend into the lands in Tollard Royale, and judgement was thereupon given accordingly. After which judgement, the said Erle distrusting his pretended interest and clayme to the said usurped bounds, and hopeing to gaine countenance in his feigned title under your Majestye's name and protection, to the great trouble and vexation of many thousand of your loving subjects, did make some conveyance of the Chase onely, but not of any lands to your Majestye in fee, for therewith did take back again an estate to himselfe and the heires of his body of the said Chase, rendering to your Majestye yearly 20*s*. And the said Erle did then presently exhibit a bill in the Exchequer chamber, before the Lord Treasurer and Barons, professing there to have had some orders for establishing of his pretended bounds, contrary to the Judgement so given in Michaelmas term in the fourteenth year of your reigne, and contrarye to another Judgement given also about the twenty-second yeare of the late Queen Elizabeth, and contrarye to several Acts of Parliament. And for that the said conveyance made unto your Majestye by the said Erle, was not made with purpose to advance your Majestye's profitt, but onely to abuse your Majestye's justice, and sett a colourable title to sue in the Exchequer Chamber, and sue to vex many thousands of your loveing subjects. And for that such indirect courses have been unusuall, and suites thereupon have not been allowed, because they tend to the abuse of your Majestye's Justice, and to the greate damage and utter overthrow of all your subjects, and the laws of this realme. And for that the said Erle endeavours also to encroche upon your Majestyes owne lands, and divers other lands, whereof the Reversion is truely belonging to your Majestye.

May it therefore please your Majestye, his permission considered to signifye unto your Court of Exchequer, that your Royall pleasure is not to suffer your name to be used to the hinderance or prejudice of Justice, and that your pleasure is that the bounds of the said Chase shall be tryed in some of the Courts of Justice at the Common Law, where bounderyes ought of right to be determined, and not in the Exchequer Chamber, which is a Court proper for matters of equitye onely. And your subjects shall for ever praye.

The earliest Record concerning the Chase,

ANNO 17 REGIS JOHANNIS.

Johannes Dei gratia &c. Hugoni de Nevill salutem.—Mandamus vobis quod sine dilatione Perambulationem fieri faciatis per probos homines de Visneto de Romesham et de Brustelton* de Brulliis (Bruillis) earundem villarum ad sciendum quæ sit Chacea nostra ibidem et quœ sit Chacea G. de Maundevill, videlicet Chacea quam Willmus quondam Comes Glouc pater Isabellæ uxoris ejusdem Galfridi tenuit, similem autem perambulationem fieri faciatis de Foresta de Craneburn et de Chetreden inter Chaceam nostram et Chaciam quam idem Willmus Com Glouc tenuit et secundum quod perambulationes illæ factæ fuerint faciatis eidem G. de Maundevill, sine dilatione habere Chaceas illas quas prefatus W Comes Gloucestr habuit.

Teste Rege apud Runyngmed xxiii die
Junii anno &c. decimo septimo.

Quo Warranto.

EDWARD I.

Placita de Juratis et Assis coram Salomone de Ross et sociis suis Justiciis Itinerantibus apud Wynton in Comitatu Southton in Octavo Sci Martini. Anno R. R. E. octavo incipiente nono.

Adhuc de fforinsecis placitis Regis.

Dorset, Gilbertus de Clare Comes Glouces et Hertford, alias Coram Justicios Itinerantes apud Schyreburn in Comitatu Dorset summonitus fuit ad ostendendum quo warranto appropriavit sibi liberam Chaciam a via regali quæ ducit inter

* May not these places be Rushmore and Burseystool ?

Schaston et Blaneford, sŭper montem ex parte occidentali ejusdem viæ usque ad aquam de Stures a ponte de Blaneford ascendendo per aquam de Stures usque ad aquam de Sturkel et ab aqua de Sturkel ascendendo per aquam de Sturkel usque ad Schaston infra precinctum cujus appropriationis continentur villatæ de Melleber, Compton, Ffuntemel, Iwerne Menestre, Hamford, Chyldehamford, Iwerne Curteney, Randulneston, Stupelton, Laterton, Assch, Sturepayne, Natford Lok, et Blaneford, et unde Willmus de Gylesham qui sequitur pro Domino Rege dicit, quod cum predictus Comes habuisset Chaciam suam per metas certas et divisas, scilicet, a Chetteslehened usque Grymesdych et de Grymesdytch usque ad Henlegh, et de Henlegh usque la Denne et de la Denne usque Gyssich Sci Andreæ usque Brandon et de Brandon usque Stubhampton et per medium villæ de Stubhampton usque ad capud de Rytheresdenne, de Rytheresdenne usque regalem viam quæ ducit de Blaneford usque Schaston et a via illa usque Thenersdenne et de Thenersdenne usque ad capud de Westewode per viam quæ dicitur Rugwyk quæ ducit versus Salesberye et de Salesbyrye* usque bundas Wyltes quæ se extendunt inter Asmere et Esgrove et sic usque Staunton et de Staunton usque Mortegresmore et de Mortegresmore usque Singhok et de Singhok usque Sondeputte, de Sondeputte usque ad capud de la Lunge Crofte et sic usque Wermere de Wermere usque Bukedon de Bukedon per metas et bundas quæ dividunt Dorset et Wyltes, usque Cheteleshened; Predictus Comes usque metas et bundas illas appropriavit ad Chaciam suam predictam predictas villas de Melleber &c., quæ sunt extra Chaciam suam in eisdem faciendo attachiamenta de viridi et venatione in prejudicium Domini Regis et dignitatis suæ &c. Et Comes venit et dicit quod aliquando facta fuit perambulatio de metis et divisis Chaciæ ipsius Comitis de Craneburn tempore quo Johannes fuit Comes Glouces et dicit quod postea tempore Regis Henrici patris Domini Regis nunc, facta fuit quædam Inquisitio per Galfridum de Langeleye et Ricardo de Wrotham Justicios assignatos de metis et divisis et perambulatione predicta quiquidem Galfridus et Ricardus per

* *read,* "et de *via quæ ducit ad* Salesbyrye."

preceptum predicti Regis Henrici quandem Inquisitionem ceperunt apud novam Sarum anno regni Regis ejusdem xxix per sacramentum subscriptorum, videlicet, Thomœ de Hynton, Henrici de Werleye, Henrici de Melebern, Henrici de Leweston, Rogeri filii Rogeri, Rogeri filii Andreæ, Reginaldi filii Willmi, Andreæ Shirard, Roberti Pilecok, Ricardi de Bello bosco, Rogeri de Stures, et Willmi le Franceys de comitatu Dorset; et Ricardi de Derneford, Ricardi de Esselden, Odonis de Grenestede, Galfridi de Bridemere, Henrici de Den, Nicolai de Doun, Nocolai de Cumbe, Henrici filii Hamonis, Thomœ de Babbington, Nicolai de Wyke, Galfridi Hoese, Andreæ Gerard, Roberti le Bor et Hamonis de Hacche de Comitatu Wyltes, qui omnes unanimiter dixerunt quod hæ sunt metæ et divisæ per quas perambulatio facta fuit de Chaciæ Ricardi Comitis Glocestr et Hertford scilicet, de Bolebrigg in Wylton usque ad Herdecote per aquam de Nodre usque ad molendinum de Dyninton de molendino de Dyninton usque ad molendinum de Tyssebyr et de molendino de Tyssebyr usque Wycham de Wycham per aquam de Noddre usque ubi Semene cadit in Noddre et sic per aquam de Semene usque Semenehened et de Semenehened usque Kingesethe juxta Schaston, de Kingesethe usque Schaston scilicet usque Sleybrondesgate de Sleybrondesgate usque ecclesiam Sancti Rombaldi de Ecclesia Sancti Rombaldi usque la Guldeneoke, de la Guldeneoke usque ad aquam de Sturkell, et per aquam de Sturkel usque ad ripariam de Stures et per ripariam de Stures usque ad pontem de Hayford et de ponte de Hayford usque ad pontem de Blaneford et de ponte de Blaneford usque ad pontem de Crauford et de ponte de Crauford usque Alwynesbrigg subtus Wymborn, de Alwynesbrigg per aquam de Wymborn usque Waldeford usque Wychampton, de Wychampton usque pontem Petræ, de ponte Petræ usque ad longam Hayam quæ ducit ad le Muledich, de Muledich usque Kynges de Kynges usque viam quæ ducit ad Lestesford per medium Estewode, de Lestesforde per aquam de Craneburn usque la Horewyethe et de la Horewyethe usque Albeslake et de Albelake usque le Horeston, de Horeston per chiminum usque ad magnum pontem de Ringeswode, de magno ponte de Ringeswode usque ad pontem de fforde de ponte de fforde usque ad pontem de Dunton, de ponte de Dunton usque Aylwardsbrigg, de Aylwardsbrigg usque ad predictum pontem de Bolebrigg in Wylton. Et dicit quod infra metas et divisas istas predictæ villæ quas appropriasse debuit ad Chaciam suam predictum continentur, unde dicit quod nihil appropriavit ad Chaciam suam predictum de Craneburn ultra metas et divisas perambulationis dudum inde factæ et Inquisitionis dudum super hoc captœ per predictos Galfridum et Ricardum Justicios per preceptum Domini Regis ad hoc assignatos ut predictum est et quod perambulatio facta fuit per metas, et divisas predictas et similiter quod predicta Inquisitio super hoc capta in forma predicta; et Inquisitio illa per prefatos Justicios returnata in Cancellarium Domini Regis vocatur inde ad warrandam Inquisitionem predictam quæ est in Thesaurario Domini Regis, Idcirco mandatum fuit Thesaurario et Baronis de Saccario quod certificarent Justicios ultimo Itinerantes in Comitatu Somerset in Crastino sanctœ Trinitatis super inquisitione predicta et metis bundis et divisis in eadem inquisitione contentis, postea ad diem illum Thesaurarius et Baroni de Saccario mandaverunt sub sigillo Saccarii Domini Regis Transcriptum Inquisitionis predictæ in hœc verba, hœc est Inquisitio facta per preceptum domini Henrici Regis filii Domini Regis Johannis die Jovis Proxima post festum sancti Dionisii Hen. xxix per Sacramentum Thomœ de Hynton &c. qui dicunt quod hæ sunt metæ et divisæ per quas perambulatio facta fuit de Chacia Ricardi Comitis Gloucestr et Hertford de Craneburn tempore quo Dominus Johannes Rex fuit Comes Gloucestriæ, scilicet, de Bolebrigg &c., postea dies datus est ei a die Sancti Michaelis in tres septimanas apud Westminster ad parliamentum &c. Et deinde datus est dies apud Wynton in octavo Sancti Martini, ad quam diem predictus Comes comparuit et petiit recordum et judicium suum &c. Et quia per predictam Inquisitionem compertum est quod predicta perambulatio facta fuit de Chacia predicta tempore quo Johannes fuit Comes Gloucestriæ per metas et divisas per quas predictus Comes de modo tenet, et similiter predicta Inquisitio capta per prefatos Galfridum et Ricardum per preceptum Domini Henrici Regis patris Domini Regis nunc ut predictum est, DOMINUS REX CONCESSIT predicto Comiti quod teneat Chaciam suam predictam per metas bundas et divisas in Inquisitione predicta contentas salvo semper jure Domini Regis et aliorum quorumcumque cum alias inde loqui voluerint, ET MANDATUM EST vice Comiti Dorset quod permittat predictum Comitem tenere Chaciam suam de Craneburn predictam per metas bundas et divisas in Inquisitione predicta contentas.

Grant of the Manor with the Chase of Cranborne &c., to Richard Lovell.

8 EDWARD II. ANNO 1315.

Rex commisit Ricardo Lovell Manerium de Craneburn, cum Chacea, et aliis pertinentibus suis in Comitatu Dorset et Maneria de Pymperne Tarente Gundeville, Stupel cum Hundredis ibidem, Portlond et Wyk et Burgos de Warham, et Weymuth cum pertinentibus in eadem Comitatu quæ fuerunt, prefati Comitis et quæ per mortem ejusdem in manu Regis existunt, quæ etiam ad centum sexaginta et quindecimo libras tres solidos, et septem denarios extenduntur per annum, Habendum, a Festo Pasche proximo futuro quamdiu Rex placuit, reddendo inde Regi per annum ad Saccarium suum quadragintas Marcas, unam videlicet mediam ad Saccarium Regis Sancti Michaelis, et aliam mediam ad Saccarium Regis Pasche.

In cujus &c. Teste Rege apud Westminster xij die Febrii.

Grant of the Office of Ranger of the Chase to Walter Harding.

1 EDWARD IV.

Rex omnibus ad quos &c. salutem.—Sciatis quod, Nos de gratia nostra speciali consideratione boni servitii quod fidelis Ligeus et Serviens noster Walterus Hardyng, Patri nostro defuncto impendit et nobis in posterum pro termino vitæ suæ impendet, dedimus et concessimus eidem Waltero Officium Rangeatoris Chaceæ nostræ de Craneburne in Comitatu nostro Dorset, habendum et occupandum pro termino vitæ suæ, ades largo et amplio modo prout idem Walterus Officium predictum, antea per Litteras Patentes predicti Patris nostri habuit.

In cujus &c. Teste Rege apud Westminster, vj die Novembris. Per Breve et Privato Sigillo et de Dat &c.

Grant of the same to Thomas Dakham, 22 EDWARD IV.

Rex omnibus ad quos &c. salutem. Sciatis quod nos in consideracione veri et fidelis servitii quod dilectus serviens noster Thomas Dakham valettus Cameræ nostræ nobis impendit et durante vita sua impendere intendit, Dedimus et Concessimus eidem officium Rangeatoris Chaceæ nostræ de Cram-bourne ac officium custodis Logeæ nostræ vocatæ Russhemer quæ jam vacata existunt ratione mortis Walteri Hardyng, nuper valletti Coronæ nostræ, habenda et occupanda dicta officia eidem Thomœ per se vel per sufficientem Deputatum suum cum vadiis et Feodis eisdem debitis et consuetis pro termino vitæ suæ habenda et percipienda ad terminos Sancti Michaelis et Pasche per equales portiones una cum omnimodo proficuis commoditatibus et advantagiis eisdem officiis pertinentibus sive spectantibus in eodem modo et forma prout predictus Walterus Hardyng pro executione dictorum officiorum habuit et percepit.

In cujus &c. Teste Rege apud Westminster xviii die Junii Per Breve de privato Sigillo et de Dat &c.

Abstract of the "Bill for Disfranchising Cranborne Chase, in the Counties of Dorset and Wilts."

9 GEORGE IV.

Whereas,—the Right Hon. George Lord Rivers, is the owner of a certain Franchise or Chase called Cranborne Chase, extending over divers manors, and a large tract of land and ground situate and being in the several counties of Dorset and Wilts, and as such owner is possessed of divers valuable and extensive rights and privileges over the same, which, if strictly used may lead to great litigation and dispute; and whereas, the said Lord Rivers, in right of the said Chase, hath constantly exercised, and still exercises the privilege of feeding and preserving Deer within the said Chase, and the number of Deer fed and presented therein, it is computed, amounts to upwards of twelve thousand, but does not exceed twenty thousand, and the Deer range over the property of the different proprietors of lands within the limits of the said Chase, without interruption and are very detrimental to the crops of the lands within the said Chase, which Deer range cannot, consistently with the rights of the said Lord Rivers, be legally and effectually prevented; and whereas, the exercise of such privileges, and of feeding and preserving Deer in right of the said Chase, is extremely injurious to the owners of lands within the limits of the said Chase, and is a great hindrance to the cultivation of such lands, and tends greatly to interrupt the industrious and moral habits of the labouring classes of the inhabitants residing in and near the said Chase; and whereas, the said Lord Rivers, and several of the proprietors of lands within the limits of the said Chase have entered into a treaty for the disfranchisement of the said Chase, and the said Lord Rivers has agreed to accept the clear yearly sum of £1800. to be apportioned, and made payable, in the manner hereafter directed or provided in that behalf, as a compensation and satisfaction for the extinguishment of his said franchise upon the said Chase, which extinguishment will be highly beneficial to the owners of lands within the limits of the said Chase, and will also be of public utility; but such beneficial purposes cannot be carried into execution without the aid and authority of Parliament.

May it please your Majesty,—That it may be enacted; and be it enacted by the kings most excellent Majesty &c., that Philip Williams, Barrister at Law, shall be, and he is hereby appointed Commissioner for appointing the said yearly rent or sum of £ 1800 with power to make surveys, admeasurements, plans, and valuations, of the lands within the limits of the Chase to deposit a map or plan at some convenient place for the inspection of all persons interested in the said lands, and the disfranchisement, and to hear objections &c. And be it further enacted, that such several annual rents, or sums as shall amount in the whole to £ 1800 shall be for ever issuing and payable to the said George Lord Rivers, his heirs, and assigns, from and out of the lands within the limits of the said Chase, (except the lands of Lord Rivers, which are to be exempt therefrom) rateably and in proportion to the values of the respective estates, such proportions to be ascertained by the Commissioner, and set forth in his award; to be paid in two equal half yearly payments, on the 10*th. Oct.* and the 10*th April*, free and clear of all taxes, rates, dues, and assessments whatsoever: the first payment to be made on the 10*th Oct.* 1829 Recovery of arrears by distress. And be it further enacted, that the said Lord Rivers, his heirs and assigns, shall be allowed to retain the same right of feed and range for the Deer, within the limits of the said Chase, and all other rights and privileges until 10*th Oct.* 1830, from and after which day, all his rights and privileges in respect of the said Chase, shall cease, determine, and be for ever extinguished, and the said Chase shall be disfranchised to all intents and purposes whatsoever. And be it further enacted, that the said Commissioner make an award of the quantity and contents of every estate which shall be charged with any proportion of the said annual rent, with the names of the owners, and sums payable by each &c., such award to be executed by the Commissioners, in the presence of such owners as shall attend at a meeting to be called for that purpose, due notice being given; and the execution shall be proclaimed on the next or some following Sunday, in the parish Churches of Tarrant Gunville, and Tollard Royal, from which time it shall be considered as complete, and shall be afterwards deposited with the Clerk of the Peace, for the county of Dorset, for inspection, on payment of a certain fee, and two copies shall be made, one of which shall be delivered to Lord Rivers, and the other shall be deposited in the parish Church, of Blandford-Forum, and kept in a box in the Vestry, under the care of the Churchwardens, for inspection (on payment of a certain fee).—The award to be completed before the 10*th Oct*. 1829.

The expences of the act for making surveys, award, &c., to be defrayed, one moiety by Lord Rivers, the other, by the owners and proprietors of the lands.

Any person aggrieved by any thing done by the Commissioners in pursuance of this Act, may appeal to the general Quarter Sessions of Dorset and Wilts; the decision of the Justices to be final.

Notes.

Note *a* page 10.

The Crane, (grus cinerea) though at the present time an occasional and very rare visitant to this country, was formerly much more frequent. Dr. Turner states that he often saw young birds in our marshes. Sir Thomas Browne, of Norwich, who wrote in the time of Charles II. says in his works, "Cranes are often seen here, in hard winters, especially about the champaign and fieldy parts. It seems they have been more plentiful, for in a bill of fare when the mayor entertained the Duke of Norfolk, I met with Cranes in a dish." In the Norfolk Household book they are noticed, and in Dugdale's Origines Juridiciales, the price of a Crane in London is 10*s*. Leland in his "Collectanea" says in the bills of fare at the feast of Archbishop Neville, two-hundred and four Cranes are mentioned, and according to Sir David Lindsay, they formed a part of the bill of fare at the grand hunting entertainment given by the Earl of Athol to James V. of Scotland, and to the Queen's mother on the banks of the Loghaine, in Glen Tilt. At a Sergeants' dinner given at Ely House, A.D. 1555 *Oct.* 16*th* before the King, Queen, Judges &c., there were seven dishes of Cranes and three of Bustards. There are only five or six instances on record of its having been killed in this country during the last fifty years. With regard to the Bustard, which was formerly so abundant that a flight of twenty-five was seen by Mr. Chafin, on Salisbury Plain in 1751, it is now exceedingly rare. A female Bustard was shot on Colden Common near Winchester, in January 1839. *Yarrell's Birds &c.*

Note *b* page 10.

There are two tradesmen's tokens one of "Nicolas Barnes in Cranborne 1659"—the other of "Robert Alner in Cranborne 1669." There were formerly seven Inns, four of which, *viz.*, the Swan, Red Lion, Black Horse, and Chequers, have disappeared and "left not a rack behind." With respect to another of them, still existing, and called "the Sheaf of Arrows," the learned author of "the Halle of John Halle" remarks, "the ancient but principal Inn in the Town of Cranborne (bordering on the neighbouring Woodland Chase) bears this cognomen and probably derived its appellative from its being the place whereunto the sportsman resorted in the olden time to fill his quiver." Truth compels us to demolish this ingenious hypothesis, by simply stating that the "Sheaf" or Bundle "of Arrows" is the crest of the Cecil family, whose arms are displayed over the Inn Door. The eldest son of the Marquess of Salisbury bears the title of Viscount Cranborne—*see page* 70.

Note *c* page 11.

The term Borough, (Burgh) was originally applied to such places as had some kind of defence around them, and was afterwards appropriated to such Towns as sent Burgesses or representatives to Parliament. Though Cranborne itself was never fortified, it had probably some of the privileges belonging to Borough Towns, attached to it by charter at an early period of its connexion with the Honor of Gloucester.

Note *d* page 19.

"The Monastery of Tewkesbury was founded, A.D. 715, by Odo and Dodo, two brothers, being almost ruined by age and the fury of wars, it was repaired by Robert Fitz-Haman, a Norman, (translating Monks from Cranborne in Dorsetshire hither) previously designing to make what satisfaction he was able for the loss of the church of Bayeux in Normandy sustained, which Henry I. consumed with fire, to free him from prison, but afterwards repenting of the fact, re-built it. "It cannot" saith William of Malmesbury, "be easily conceived how much Robert Fitz-Hamon, adorned and beautified this Monastery, where the stateliness of the building ravished the eyes, and the pious charity of the monks the affection of all persons that came thither.—*Camden.*

Note *e* page 19.

In this County belonged to this Abbey the Manors of Tarrant-Monkton, Cranborne Priory, Monkton Upwimborne, Chettle and Boveridge; lands in Knoll in Purbeck, Hampreston, Fifehead, Quintin, Orchard in Purbeck, Eastworth and Horsythe; tithes in Milborne, Divelish and Thorncomb; the advowsons of Ashmore, Frome, Saint Quintin, Pentridge, Chettle, Cranborne, and portions out of the Rectories of Langton Matravers, Ockford Fitz-payne, Tarrant Gunville and Bellchalwell. A. D. 1100, Henry I. confirms the Grants of Fitz-Hamon, and others to this Abbey. A. D. 1109, Roger Bishop of Sarum, confirms the same.—*Hutchins.*

Note *f* ibid.

This Gerald had been originally a Monk of Winchester, and A. D. 1109, on refusing to gratify the covetous disposition of Henry I. was compelled to leave his Abbey, and returned to Winchester.

In a M.S. of Sir William Dugdale's, in the Ashmolean Museum, it is stated, that in the antient times of the Britons, there was a college of six Monks at Cranborne, built in memory of certain Britons who were there slain; the story is probably traditional and unentitled to the smallest credit.

Note *g* page 23.

Domesday Book, is a survey of the property of the kingdom completed A. D. 1086, for the purpose of levying a tax, on land called the Danegeld, in payment of the enormous sums of money exacted by the Danes, and for other purposes. This tax was first collected by king Ethelred in 990, and levied as late as 21 Henry II. It varied from 1*s.* to 6*s.* per hide.

Explanation of Terms.

Hide,—The Saxon term for a portion of land, as much as one plough could till in a year, therefore varied in quantity according to the quality of the soil,—one hundred acres or more.

Carucate,—The Norman term for the same.

Virgate,—Four to a hide.

Acre,—Forty perches long, and four broad; or twenty long and eight broad.

Furlong,—Forty perches, the perch twenty feet.

League,—Doubtful,—supposed to be two miles.

Serf,—A servant maintained by the Lord, doing his work,—slave.

Villains,—Small renters, who were required to perform certain services to the lord, and were usually sold with the land.

Borderer,—A cottager,—occupier of land on condition of supplying the lord's table with small provisions, doing his domestic work &c.

Demesne,—Crown land,—of course exempt from this tax.

Note *h* page 24.

The Saxon pound which was in use for some centuries after the conquest, was three times heavier than the present money; there were forty eight shillings in the pound, and five-pence in the shilling. It is not easy to determine the value of money in those times, compared with the present, but we may be justified in calculating every sum of money mentioned by historians of that period, as if it were multiplied more than a hundredfold above a sum of the same denomination at present.—

Hume, Hist. England.

Note *i* page 25.

The Saxon style of architecture, which is characterised by the circular arch variously ornamented with zig-zag, lozenge, diamond, festoon, and other kinds of moulding, began in the reign of Edward the Confessor, and terminated about the middle of the twelfth century. It was succeeded by the Gothic, whose peculiarity chiefly consists in the pointed arch, and forms of greater beauty and skill. The characters of this style were greatly modified in successive ages, and we may trace the stages of its progress from the early rude transition forms, to the highly elaborate workmanship of its latest æra, through a long series of years. The first period extends from about A.D. 1150, to about A.D. 1240, the second from A.D. 1240, to about A.D. 1380, and the third from A.D. 1380 to A.D. 1500.

Note *k* page 38.

Charles I. was executed in 1649. "The *confusion* which overspread England after the murder of Charles, proceeded as well from the spirit of refinement and innovation, which agitated the ruling party, as from the dissolution of all that authority, both civil and ecclesiastical, by which the nation had ever been accustomed to be governed."—*Hume, Hist. England.*

Note *l* page 41.

At the Reformation the practice of eating fish on particular days was discontinued, in consequence of which numbers of fishermen were ruined. To remedy this evil, an Act was passed 5 Elizabeth, to make Wednesdays and Saturdays "Fish days," on pain of forfeiting £3, or three months imprisonment "for the increase of fishermen and mariners and repairing of Port Towns and Navigation." But the Bishop of the Diocese, or the vicar, curate, or parson of the Parish might grant a license to eat flesh, to sick persons, and license might be purchased on payment of the following sums per annum to the poor box of the parish, *viz.* Lord of Parliament £1 6*s.* 8*d.* A Knight 13*s.* 4*d.* any other person 6*s.* 8*d.* but not to authorize the eating of beef or veal from Michaelmas to May-day.

Penny Maazine 1834.

Note *m* page 49.

The Honor of Gloucester was one of the principal Baronies in England. A Barony was a large landed estate usually consisting of many manors, possessed by one lord, who was the

Baron. These manors, all perhaps except his own immediate residence, he granted by what was called subinfeudation to inferior lords, who held them of the superior, as the superior held them of his sovereign lord the king. The Barony therefore were actual territories granted by the king and holden of him by homage and military service. When one of these Baronies had been anciently in the hands of the king, it was usual to style it an honor. Some of the greater of these Barons lived in a style of rude magnificence as near to Royalty as their circumstances would permit. They held courts of all kinds, even with the power of life and death; they levied taxes within their Baronies some of them independently of the crown; they granted Charters of Privilege in Royal style, directed to their vassals and subjects; some of them, if not all, coined money. The profits of the Baron arose from fines, reserved rents, mortuaries, licenses to buy and sell, services, customs, tolls &c.

Seyer's Hist. Bristol.

Note *n* page 49.

Inquisitions,—William the Conquerer introduced military services, by which persons held part of their lands on the terms of attending the king in his wars for a certain number of days according to the extent and value of their possessions, and as on the death of these tenants, the heir if of full age, was entitled to enter on the lands, paying what was called the premier seisin, yet if the heir was not of full age, then the king held him and his lands in ward, in other words, was his guardian during nonage; it was obviously therefore necessary that on the death of every tenant under the king, it should be ascertained whether the heir was or was not of age, what too were the services under which the tenant so dying held his lands. For this purpose, on the death of any tenant, a writ was issued to the Escheator of the County in which the lands were situated to summon a Jury of twelve men, who on oath were to inquire into the above particulars. The returns were called "Inquisitiones post mortem," the earliest now extant are of Henry III. reign.

Modern Wilts, C. Bowles.

Note *o* page 50.

Tenure.—All the lands of the kingdom were under the feudal law, held either mediately or immediately of the king, and as he granted them to his nobles, to be holden by certain services, so they parcelled them out to others to be held on similar conditions; hence freeholds were termed Feuda, Feoda, Fees. Services are chiefly classed under two heads, military or Knight service, and Socage, (Soca *a plough*) or rustic service. When a tenant was bound to attend his lord to the wars, in person or by deputy, at his own expense, the days of such service were regulated by the quantity of land so holden; if it extended to a whole knight's fee, then his service was forty days, if to half twenty days &c. There were four hides in a knight's fee, and 60,215, knight's fees in England. This service was sometimes commuted for a payment of money, which was called Escuage or Scutage. Socage tenure was that under which tenants held their lands on condition of ploughing the Lord's land, and of doing other inferior and customary services at their own charge, and this was called Villainage; when a sum of money was annually paid in lieu of these services, it was then called Free Socage. These ancient tenures were abolished by the 12 Charles II.

Note *q* page 55.

Escheat—(From the French Escheoir to fall) the reversion of freehold lands to the king, or other lord of the fee, on the tenant dying intestate and without an heir—also the forfeiture of the lands of a person attainted of High Treason.

Note *r* page 56.

Feodery,—An officer of the Court of Wards whose business it was to be present with the Escheator in every county (an officer appointed to look after the king's Escheats), to give evidence concerning their value and tenure. He also received the Rents of Wards' lands within his district &c. This office was abolished by the 12 Charles II.

Note *s* page 73.

Penbury,—Pen, *a hill top,* burgh, *a fortified place.*—The spot so called is the highest point of Pentridge-hill, and has evidently been occupied as an ancient British Hill-camp. Its elevated and commanding situation caused it to be selected as a beacon for the purpose of alarming the neighbourhood in the event of the anticipated invasion of this country during the last French War. It has been surmised that this was the scene of the memorable battle between Boadicea and the Roman forces A.D. 60; but this is a matter of mere conjecture founded on a fancied resemblance of the features of the country to the description given by the historian of that wherein the battle was fought. There are numerous indicia of an ancient population who were located here, and on the adjacent Downs. At one spot which is undoubtedly the site of a British Village, we found fragments of pottery, and bones, with two coins; Allectus, the Usurper, A.D. 294, and Victorinus, A.D. 265.

Note *t* ibid.

There is a very fine group of tumuli on the Down near the eleventh milestone on the London Road. Their remote antiquity is proved by the circumstance that the Roman road intersects one of the circular enclosures (of which there are several, each containing two small tumuli) as was first observed by Stukely (Itin curiosum). Sir Richard Colt Hoare, investigated most of these ancient graves, and discovered a great variety of interesting relics, such as spear heads, and daggers of bronze, arrow heads of flint; amber, jet, and glass beads; celts, and urns of coarse pottery and rude manufacture, containing burned bones.—*Ancient Wilts, vol.* 1.

Note *v* page 74.

"When we find these works irregular in their form, simple in their construction, and with single and slight banks, and ditches, we may I think pronounce them to be of genuine British origin, and the works of a barbarous and uncivilized people, and when we find the entrenchments multiplied and distinguished by the vastness of their banks, the height of their keeps, and extreme depth of their ditches, we may suppose these to have been the works of people better versed in the art of castrametation. But whenever we meet with works of a square or oblong form, bounded by straight lines, and with rounded angles, we may indubitably pronounce them the works of the Romans."—*Ancient Wilts, vol.* 1.

Camden states this to have been a Roman camp,—were we must not forget that the same places of defence, occupied in succession by people of a different age and nation ; therefore this *may* have been occupied by the Romans, but there is no evidence of it, and we are quite sure it is not of original Roman construction.

Note *w* ibid

Court Leet,—(from the Saxon Lite, *little,* or the German *Laet*, a *Country Judge*) was originally the criminal Tribunal of the Lord, in which the Lord or his Bailiff presided, and consisted of a jury of thirteen persons resident within the manor.

The Court Baron, was the civil tribunal of the Lord, with the Lord's Bailiff as presiding officer, and a jury of Freeholders who held suit and service to the Lord of the manor. If there were not two such Freeholders in the manor, the court was lost.

The functions of these Courts are now exercised by the Assizes and Sessions, but the form of holding the Courts is retained in many manors. The same power that was exercised over a particular manor by these Courts, was also exercised over particular hundreds by the hundred Court, and Leet of the hundred.

Note *x* page 79.

The Itinerary of King John,—from Archœlogia, vol. 22. " A table of the movements of the Court of King John, King of England, from his Coronation May 27th A. D. 1199, to the end of his reign," compiled from Rolls in the Tower of London.

It appears that he was a most restless person, and travelled from place to place with great rapidity; Mathew Paris, who wrote about forty years after his reign, remarks that he travelled "citius quam credi fas est." We will subjoin a few examples of his peregrinations.

December, 1200.

2.	Abbidun, (Abingdon)	...	Berks.
3.	Bedwin ...	...	Wilts.
6.	Lutegareshal (Ludgershall)		Ditto.
8.	Clarendon ...	...	Ditto.
10.	Cranbourn ...	...	Dorset.
12—13.	Canford ...	...	Ditto.
18.	Marlborough ...	...	Wilts.
20—21.	Freitmantle (Freemantle)	...	Hants.
23.	Farnham ...	...	Surrey.
26.	Guilford ...	...	Ditto.
—	Reading ...	...	Berks.
21—31.	Wudstoc (Woodstock)	...	Oxon.

April.

1—3.	Westminster.		
4—6.	Windsor.		
7.	Freitmantle ...	...	Hants.
7—10.	Marlborough ...	...	Wilts.
10—12.	Ludgarshal ...	...	Ditto
15.	Cranbourn ...	...	Dorset.
18—19.	Dorchester ...	...	Ditto.
20.	Bridport ...	...	Ditto
22.	Exon (Exeter)		
30.	Woodstock ...	...	Oxon

January, 1205.

1—2.	Christchurch ...	...	Hants
4—5.	Dorchester ...	...	Dorset
7—8.	Bere-Regis ...	...	Ditto

9.	Cranbourn	Dorset.
12.	Merewell	Hants.
12—14.	Sutton	
15—16.	Windsor	
18—21.	Westminster	
22.	Windsor	
22—24.	Reading	
26—28.	Winton (Winchester)	
29.	Southampton	

August.

13—16.	Tower of London	
17.	Cranbourn	
18—21.	Bere Regis	
22—23.	Corfe	
24—25.	Dorchester	
25.	Poorstock	
26.	Dorchester	
28.	Stoke	Somerset
29.	Ilchester	

April, 1206.

13—16.	Clarendon	Wilts.
16—17.	Cranbourn	Dorset.
17—18.	Clarendon	Wilts.
19—21.	Winchester	

May.

14.	Winchester	
16.	Cranbourn	
19.	Bellus Locus (Beaulieu) ...	Hants.

January, 1207.

14—18.	Clarendon	
20.	Marlborough	
20.	Cranbourne	
20—22.	Dorchester	

25.	Gillingham	
28.	Devizes	Wilts.
30.	Dunton (Downton) ...	Ditto

March.

23—25.	Clarendon	
27—28.	Cranbourn	
28.	Bere Regis	
30.	Poorstock	

April.

1.	Exon (Exeter)	
3.	Sirebourn (Sherborn)	
5.	Gillingham	
6—8.	Cranbourn	
8—9.	Clarendon	

September.

1—3.	Cranbourn	
4—5.	Bere Regis	
6.	Holwell, in Blakemore	
7.	Stanteg (Stanbridge)	
8.	Poorstock	
9—11.	Newton	
11.	Barneton (Barnston, in Purbeck)	
13.	Wells	Somerset.

November, 1208.

3.	Clarendon	
6.	Cranbourn	
11—13.	Christchurch	Hants.
14.	Gillingham	Dorset.
19.	Cranbourn	
24.	Oxford.	

July, 1213.

1.	Stoke	Hants.
4—5.	Bere Regis	Dorset.

6—8. Cranbourn
8—10. Gillingham
23—25. Corfe and Studland
26. Bivendon (Bindon)
27—29. Dorchester
30—31. Poorstock
31. Newton

August.

1. Gillingham
3—9. Corfe
9. Studland
10. Cranbourn
11. Marlborough
12. Clarendon.

Note *y* page 82.

"Assizers of Bread and Tasters of Ale."—The statute 51 Henry III—provided that the price of bread should be regulated by the price of corn; "when a quarter of whete is sold for 12*d*. then the farthynge wastel lofe (fine bread) shall wey £6. 16s. the farthynge cocket lofe (finest) of the same corne shall wey more than the wastel by 2s.; the farthynge lofe of treyt (household bread) shall wey two wastels." Likewise as to Ale; "when the quarter of whete is sold for 3s. or 40d., and barley for 20d. or 2s. and otes for 18d. then the brewers may sell in the cytie two galans of good ale for 1d. and 3 galans for 1d. in borowes, without they ought to sell four galans for a 1d. and they may well do it." The punishment for breaking the assize was a fine for the three first offences, and afterwards the pillory. The penny weighed thirty-two grains of wheat "drye and in the myddes of the eare," and twenty pence made an ounce, and twelve ounces a pound. The oath—"you swear that you will well and truly serve our Lord the King, and the Lord of this Court, in the office of Ale-taster or assize, in this Lordship, for the year to come, and you shall well and truly see that the bread be duly weighed, and that it be of such weight, as is according to the price of corn, as by statue provided, *i.e.* the price of corn in the neighbouring markets. Also you shall diligently look at all Brewers and Tiplers in your office, that they make good and wholesome Ale and Beer for man's body, and that they sell none before it has been assized by you; and all offences committed by Bakers, Brewers and Tiplers, you shall present at this court, that punishment may be administered to them, and in every thing else you shall well and truly behave in your office for the next year, so help you God."

Note *z* page 82.

"Surveyors of Hearths."—The duties of these officers, whose appointments appear to be peculiar to this manor, consisted in a periodical examination of chimnies as to their being properly swept; and in presenting at the court such as were found in a state of neglect, for which the owners were fined. The duties of the office, however, were not strictly attended to, as appears by a presentment made to the Court by the Rev. Mr. Hickman, respecting his neighbours chimney, endorsed "This is probably the only presentation of the kind known and should be preserved as a Precedent."

Note *a a* page 82.

"Searchers, Sealers, and Registrars of Leather."—The laws relating to the tanning of Hides bear the date of 1 James I. The statute enacts that all Lords of Liberties, Mayors, Bailiffs, &c., shall appoint two or more persons, to search and view, and seal such leather as they find sufficiently tanned and curried; and to seize such as was offered for sale, of the contrary description; and they were also required to keep a book or register wherein they should enter all sales of such leather, with the prices, and the names and the dwelling places of the buyer and seller. For selling unregistered leather the offender was fined the amount of its value. By the Act 40 George III. the clause 1 Jac. I. prohibiting the use of horsehides in making boots and shoes, and for better preventing the damaging of raw hides and skins in the flaying thereof, is repealed, and market houses are appointed as the places for examining and inspecting raw hides and skins, for the market, twice a week, on Monday and Friday, between the hours of eleven and one. In pursuance of this Act the Market-house of Cranborne (pulled down a few years ago) was appointed for that purpose, by J. L. D. G. Tregonwell Esq., and the Rev. W. Chafin, two of his Majesty's Justices of the Peace.

Note *b b* page 50.

The Liberties of the Earl of Gloucester,—8 Edward I.—Comes clamat habere in manerio suo de Craneborn liberum Hundredum et liberam Chaceam pertinentem ad predictum manerium secundum perambulationem quondam factam, et warrenam in dominicis terris suis infra predictum Hundredum et Retornam Brevium, cum pertinentibus et mercatum quolibit anno ibidem per duos dies durantem, scilicit in vigilio et in die Sci Nicholai, visum Franci plegii, wayfas, furcas ; Pillorium, tumbrellum, placitum, Sanguinis et Hutesium, Infangenethef, et utfengenethef, emendas Assizæ Panis et cerevisiæ fractæ, et placita vetiti namii, salvis libertatibus quas alii infra predictum Hundredum habere clamant. Clamat etiam ibidem liberam Curiam de Chacea sua predicta et in eadem placitare de viridi et venatione cum attachiamento hominum attachiatorum cum manuopere vel per suspicionem apertam et capere abiis qui super hujusmodi fuerint convicti emendas in eadem Curia. Similar claims in the Hundred of Pimperne, except what belongs there to the Prior of Breamore, and to Robert Kaygnes,—similar claims in Wyke, Portland, Weymouth, and Elwell in Upway besides, wrecks of the sea, the goods of felons, and a market in Weymouth, every week, on Thursday, which liberties formerly belonged to the Priory of St. Swithin at Winchester.

Explanation of Terms.

Return of Writs,—The return made by the Bailiff to the Sheriff of writs requiring certain things to be done in Franchises.

Frankpledge,—It was an ancient custom that every freeman of fourteen years of age should give security for his good behaviour towards the King and his subjects, whereupon a certain number of neighbours became sureties for one another, to see each man of their pledge forthcoming at all times, or to answer for the transgressions of any gone away.

Waifs,—Stolen Goods, *waved* or left by the felon on being pursued, which were forfeited to the Lord of the Manor.

Pillory and Tumbrel,—The Lords of Leet were required to have a pillory and ducking stool, on pain of forfeiture of their Leet.

Pleas of Blood,—The right of judicature in cases where blood is shed.

Infangenethef, Utfangenethef,—The trial of Thieves taken either within or out of the Lord's fee.

Hutesium,—Hue and cry—the pursuit of thieves.

Placita vetiti namii,—When the Bailiff distrains beasts or goods of another, and the Lord forbids the Bailiff to deliver them, when the Sheriff comes to make replevin, the owner may demand satisfaction for the injury, which is called placita vetiti namii.—*Jacob's Dict.*

Note *c c* page 88.

E. Hooper's relationship to the Shaftesbury and Malmesbury families.

Anthony Ashley Cooper, 3rd Earl of Shaftesbury.

1. Anthony Ashley Cooper, 4th Earl. — Edward Hooper, ob. 1750. — James Harris.
2. Dorothy, ob. 1749.
3. Elizabeth, ob. 1744.

Edward Hooper. — James Harris.

James Harris. 1st Earl of Malmesbury.

Note *c c* page 94.

Vindogladia or Ventageladia,—The site of this ancient station on the Via Iceniana, Ikenield Street, Ickling Dike, or Roman Road, set down in the Itineraries of Antonine and

Richard of Cirencester as XII—XIII—XV miles from Sorbiodunum, (Old Sarum) was formerly assigned to the Town of *Win*borne Minster, on no better authority than a monosyllabic etymology; but we may observe that on the same ground the village of *Win*borne St. Giles, or Monkton Up *Win*borne, might claim the like distinction. Dr. Stukely, thus writes in 1786. "It was now my business to look out for the station in Antoninus called Vindogladia, mentioned in the last journey to be twelve miles from Sorbiodunum. By this time I was come to a proper distance, accordingly I found at the end of this heath, *(Thorny Down)* the road which all along is called Icling Dike, descended a valley where a brook crosses it from two villages called Glisset. At All-saints, or Lower Glisset, there was a small alehouse, and the only one hereabouts, (the Rose) my old landlady, after some discourse preparatory, informed me that at Boroston, a mile lower upon the river, had been an old city; and that strangers had come out of their way on purpose to see it; that ruins and foundations were there; that it had seven parish churches, which were beaten down in the war time; that many old coins had been ploughed up when she was a girl, which the children commonly played withal; but the case at present was plainly the same as that of old Troy, described in the ballad upon her wall, where she shewed me these passionate verses.

"Waste lie those walls that were so good
And corn now grows were Troy towers stood."

This account, so natural, satisfied me that Vindogladia must be here fixed, and *Win*born Minster, be robbed of that honor, where the tide of Antiquarians have hitherto carried it, for no other reason but name's sake; the distances and road being repugnant. I suppose the name signifies the white river; *vint*, white; *gladh*, a river; whence our glade or valley where a river runs. This place being not capable of affording me a proper mansion, I left the more particular scrutiny of it for another opportunity."—*Itin. Curiosum.*

The old Lady's traditions referred probably to a spot, a little further on, called Knolton, where there exist some curious Celtic remains, and a church in ruins, but not the least trace of any Romano—British settlement. It was probably a place of Druidical worship. We cannot but smile at the Antiquary's credulity which led him to so hasty a conclusion, and it is recorded as a warning to the brethren of the Antiquarian craft. Much patient, cautious, and laborious investigation are often required for establishing a point of local History ; in this spirit did Sir R. C. Hoare, approach the field of enquiry, and his labors were amply repaid, for he has determined, almost without the shadow of doubt, the site of this ancient station to be these earthworks on Gussage Down. Their proximity to the Roman Road,—their correspondence with the distances laid down in the antient Itineraries, being about XV miles from Old Sarum, the indubitable marks of a numerous and mixed population, of a rude and civilized people, in the mixture of fragments of coarse and fine pottery found here in great abundance; and the extent and importance of the works, are the reasons for placing here the site of this long lost Town. Sir R. C. Hoare, thus writes, "The most careless observer must be struck with surprise at the first view of these earthworks. To us whose eyes had long been accustomed to similar works, *though to none of so great a magnitude or interest*, their history is not mysterious ; they were recognized as the irregular works of a rude nation, living on the produce of their flocks and herds upon the exposed heights of our chalky Downs. In them we see no regular system of fortification, nor any huge ramparts for defence, no well drawn circle, rectilinear square ; irregularity prevails throughout, and we see before us the rude but grand outlines of an original British settlement." And again, "how often have I reviewed with fresh delight this truly interesting ground, which elucidates so strongly the history and manners of the primitive Britons : and with what sincere regret, on revisiting the spot in the Autumn, of 1817, did I notice the encroachments of the plough on this memorable, and till lately, well preserved monument of early antiquity.—*Ancient Wilts, vol.* 2.

How would those regrets have been redoubled, if the *pious* Antiquary had lived to re-visit this darling scene in the year 1840! "Tell it not in Gath."

In Sir Richard Hoare's book (above quoted) may be seen a plan of the works, and we invite all lovers of antiquity to an inspection of this interesting spot, for no verbal description can convey a correct idea of its details. We may however notice, the avenue or cursus,—two slight parallel banks and ditches about one-hundred paces apart, which issuing hence, pursue their undeviating course (*crossed* in one point *by* the Roman Road) across the Down for a distance of nearly three miles, until they are lost in the enclosures at Pentridge.—The situation of these banks and ditches suggested to a Welsh friend of Sir R. Hoare's, an etymology for Vindogladia, *Vin* or *Fin*, end, (Celtic), *dau*, two, and *clawdh*, a ditch; *the end of the two ditches.* But we are now treading on doubtful ground.

The property on which these works are found, belongs to the Marquess of Anglesea, and Lord Portman.

Note page 96.

On Hoar-stones,—From the Archælogia, vol. 25.

The word *Hoar*, Celtic and Welsh *Or*, Latin *Ord*, signifies a landmark or boundary of property, and is combined adjectively with a variety of other words, as descriptive of terminating qualities.

Thus *Hoarwithy*, is a boundary willow tree; at *Horeston*, a boundary stone.

The limits of the new Forest are described in a Forest Roll, 29 Edward I. as going to "Horewythege," and in a perambulation, 22 Car. II. "to Horewithy, in the place (whereof now decayed) a post standeth in the ground."

"Per medium alneti usque ad la Horewythege," in the boundaries of Glaston twelve hides, Somerset.

"Fram Egceanlœa to tham Haranwithie," in a Charter of King Ethelred's to Eynsham Abbey, Oxon.

"On the Haran Withi," boundaries of lands belonging to Wolverhampton.

"On thoune Haran Withig," boundaries of lands belonging to Abingdon Abbey.—The thorn, the hazel, and the apple tree &c., are recited in other ancient records as boundary marks.

"Le Horeston," occurs in the Salop Forest Roll, 26 Edw. I.

"Et sic usque le Horeston," in the Register of Lands belonging to Malmsbury Abbey.

"Descendendo usque Horeston," Monest. Angl. of the possessions of Hilton Abbey.

"On than Haran stan."

Hoarton—Horton—Hoarworth (Worth) signify, enclosure.

Hoarsytch, sike—watercourse.

On a hill in the Parish of Martin, Wilts, three miles from Cranborne, there is a large block of conglomerate, which is called the Wur-stone.

Note *dd* page 103.

Ordæl, Saxon, Ordalium.—The ordalian law, according to Holenshed, was a certain manner of purgation used two waies, whereof the one was by Fier, the other by Water. In the execution of that which was done by Fier, the partie accused should goe a certaine number of paces with an hot peece of iron in his hand, or else barefooted upon certaine ploughshares, red hot, according to the manner. This iron was sometime of one pound weight, and then was it called single ordalium; sometimes of three, and then it was named treble ordalium. And whosoever did beare or tread on the same without hurt of his bodie, he was adjudged guiltlesse otherwise if his skin were scorched, he was forthwith condemned as guiltie of the tresspasse whereof he was accused. There were in like sort two kindes of triall by the Water, that is to say, either hote or cold; and in this triall, the partie thought culpable was either tumbled into some pond or huge vessel of cold water, wherein if he continued for a season without wrestling or strugling for life, he was forthwith acquited as guiltlesse of the fact whereof he was accused; but if he began to plunge and labour once for breath, immediately uppon his falling into that liquor, he was by and by condemned as guilty of the crime ; or else he did thrust his arm up to the shoulder into a lead, copper, or cauldron of seething water, from whence if he withdrew the same without any manner of damage, he was discharged of further molestation ; otherwise he was taken for a tresspasser and punished accordingly. The Fiery manner of purgation belonged only to noblemen and women, and such as were freeborne, but the husbandmen and villaines were tried by water. The ordalian law was abolished by King John.

Manwood's Forest Laws.

Addenda.

Page 12.

The Fire of Cranbourn—In the King's Bench.—Richard Carter, daily agent and servant for, and on behalf of Samuel Stillingfleet, together with John Floyd, the elder, and John Floyd his son, Martha Coker, John Hooper, William Miller, the elder, William Miller, the younger, John Coney, Timothy Coney, Mary the wife of John Clark, the younger, William Read, Edward Bailey, Andrew Coney, the younger, James Read, Henry Elliot, William Compton, Roger Warden, Mary Watts, Mary Paine, do severally and respectively make oath, concerning the damages, and losses that they and the several persons above named sustained, and suffered in and by their respective goods and chattels, for and upon account of the consumption thereof by the sudden and shocking fire that happened to break out in the Town of Cranborne, on the 14*th* day of October, in the year of our Lord one thousand seven hundred and forty eight. Sworn,—The said Richard Carter, for and on the behalf of the said Samuel Stillingfleet, maketh oath that the said Samuel Stillingfleet, suffered by the loss of his goods consumed by the said fire to the value of £54. 18*s*.

	£.	s.	d.
Brought over	54	18	0
The said John Floyd, the elder, and John Floyd the younger, suffered &c. - -	37	15	0
The said Martha Coker, &c. - -	234	12	0
The said John Hooper, &c. - -	140	14	2
The said William Miller, the elder &c. -	27	5	0
The said William Miller, the younger &c. -	21	15	0
The said John Coney &c. - - -	27	7	9
The said Timothy Coney, &c. - -	32	11	0
The said Mary, wife to the said John Clark &c. -	5	7	0
The said William Read &c. - -	39	8	6
The said Edward Bailey &c. - -	21	4	8
The said Andrew Coney, the younger &c. -	8	14	7
The said James Read &c. - -	17	6	0
The said Henry Elliott &c. - -	3	11	6
The said William Compton &c. - -	21	6	6
The said Roger Warden &c. - -	1	6	3
The said Mary Watts &c. - - -	1	4	6
The said Mary Paine &c. - -	2	12	6
The said Jane Paine &c. - - -	7	11	0
	706	10	11

Sworn at Cranborne aforesaid the * * *day of Nov. in the Year of our Lord* 1749, *before me.*

Page 15.

Cranborne is in the Wimborne Division of the County.—Petty Sessions are held every fortnight. Magistrates—The Earl of Shaftesbury; Chairman—H. C. Sturt Esq. M. P. H. B. Monro Esq.; Capt. Markland, R. N.; the Rev. M. King; clerk—Mr. Rowden.

Page 16.

Aid Granted for making the Black Prince a Knight, 20 *Edward III.*
Hundred' de Craneburn.

Dna de Roos et Dna de Clifford; dimid' unius feodi in Tarrant-Vylers q Gilbert de Clare quondam ten' ibm.

De Andrea Turbervill dim' feod' in Acford (Shillingstone) q Brianus de Turbervill ten'.

Bric' de Donyton, Johrs de Fonkere de Bakebere (Bagbur) p quarta parte un' feod' in Bakebere qd Robtus de Bakebere et Gilb' de Castell quondm ten'.

De Johe de Gengnil, Edw' de Gracelyn, et Henr' Wirles pro quarta parte un' feodi in Petrichesham (Petersham) q Will' Franceys, Johes Gengnil, Phus Eleys, quondam ten'

De Edm' Garcelyn pro quarta parte un' feod' ibid', q Will' de Garcelyn quondm ten.'

De Johe Lucy et Alicia quœ fuit uxor' Hug' de Henton pro quarta parte un' feod' in Ham (Hampreston) q Johes de Gouiz et Alicia de Lucy quondm ten.'

De Johe de Cormayles per quarta parte un' feod' in Emelesworth (Emsworth) q Johes de Cormayles quondam ten.'

De Galfro de Bares pro quarta parte un' feod' in Fifhide (Fifehead) q Simon de Sco Quintino quondm ten.'

Page 24.

Particulars in Exeter Domesday, omitted in Exchequer Domesday.

"Cranborna." Of the ten hides "tenuerunt three tegni et adhuc tenent three de Brictrico quæ nor potuerunt separari ab eo, et unusquisque ex eis reddit twenty solidos pr annum excepto servicio. Hœc mansio reddidit twenty-four Libras vivente regina et nunc reddit thirty libras."

Page 26.—*Bells.*

The first Bell has the following inscription in Gothic characters, round the outside of the top "AVE GRACIA PLENA," the salutation of the virgin, to whom it was dedicated. It is probably of the date of the early part of the fourteenth century. The Curfew is rung *every* night, except Sunday, at eight o'Clock. Since the above was written a subscription has been raised, for the purpose of restoring the "merry peal," and from the great weight of metal in the old Bells, the founder has been able to re-cast three of them into four, so that the peal will in future consist of six Bells.

Page 38.

Boveridge Chapel.—From the Register.—Marriage Fees at Boveridge.

"To the Minister seven shillings and sixpence, to the Clerk three shillings and sixpence.	By Licence eleven shillings in all.
To the Minister five shillings, to the Clerk two shillings and sixpence.	By Banns, seven shillings and sixpence in all."

(The Rev. Mr. Hickman's writing.)

Page 120.

View of Deer from a Court Roll.

A. D. 1645.		A. D. 1657.	
West Walk - -	170	West Walk - -	105
Burseystool - -	80	Burseystool - -	20
Rushmore - -	185	Rushmore - -	160
Cobley - -	317	Cobley - -	350
Staplefoot - -	80	Staplefoot - -	55
	832		690

A. D. 1620. - 1170 A. D. 1640. - 1850

Page 121.

The Prince of Wales, afterwards George IV. when he resided at Critchel House about forty years ago, held the deputation of Cobley Walk, and continued it for several years after he left Dorsetshire.

Page 141.

Hic olim mos fuit; custodes Chaceæ adveniente tempore quo damas infæcundas cædere solebant, herbam quæ "Viscum album" vocatur gravidis depascere ponebant, et hæ quidem haud multo post præmature peperunt: dicitur autem, ferinam [illegible] partarum sapore solito caruisse. Idem canibus quod damis accidit.

Plants found in the Chase.

From Dr. Pulteney's "Catalogue of the rarer Plants found in Dorsetshire." Hutchins' 2nd. edit.

Atropa Belladonna—Deadly Nightshade, Churchyard at Chettle.

Campanula Trachelium—Nettle-leaved Bell Flower.

Convallaria Multiflora—Solomon's Seal, Ashcombe.
Cratægus Aria—White Beam Tree.
Daphne Mezereon—Mezereon.
Daphne Laureola—Spurge Laurel.
Hippocrepis Comosa—Tufted Horse-shoe Vetch.
Hypericum Androsæmum—Tutsan.
Hypericum Humifusum—Trailing St. John's-Wort.
Helleborus Viridis—Green Hillebore.
Lichen Plicatus.
Lichen Articulatus.
Lathræa Squamaria—Greater Toothwort, West Lodge & Chettle.
Melica Uniflora—Wood Melic Grass.
Ophrys Nidus Avis—Bird's Nest.
Ophrys Muscifera—Fly Orchis.
Paris Quadrifolia—Herb-Paris.
Prenanthes Muralis—Ive-leaved Lettuce.
Polypodium Cristatum—Crested Shield Fern.
Polypodium Filix Fœmina—Short Fruited Spleenwort.
Polypodium Aculeatum—Soft Prickly Ditto.
Rhamnus Catharticus—Buckthorn.
Ruscus Aculeatus—Butcher's Broom.
Sorbus Aucuparia—Quicken Tree.
Serapias Grandiflora—Large White Helleborine.
Taxus Baccata—Yew Tree.
Veronica Officinalis—Speedwell
Viscum Album—Missletoe, chiefly on the Thorn.
Valeriana Officinalis—Valerian.

The Valerian of Cranborne Chase, has had a preference in Medicine to that of many other parts in England, and is sent in large quantities to the Druggists in London &c.]

FINIS.